Gender, Sexuality and Global Politics

Series Editors: **Ali Bilgic**, Loughborough University, UK, **Synne L. Dyvik**, University of Sussex, UK, **Gunhild Hoogensen Gjørv**, UiT The Arctic University of Norway, Norway, **Thomas Gregory**, The University of Auckland, New Zealand and **Swati Parashar**, University of Gothenburg, Sweden

Expanding the boundaries of International Relations, this series reflects on politics globally with innovative and transdisciplinary perspectives.

With a focus on feminist, lesbian, gay, bisexual, trans and queer activism, the series will examine existing hierarchies, practices and power relations, investigating the often violent effects of these on different peoples, geographies and histories.

Also available

Queer Politics in Contemporary Turkey
By **Paul Gordon Kramer**

Forthcoming

Queering Conflict Research
New Approaches to the Study of Political Violence
Edited by **Jamie J. Hagen**, **Samuel Ritholtz** and **Andrew Delatolla**

Queering Kinship
Non-heterosexual Couples, Parents, and Families in Guangdong, China
By **Han Tao**

The Right Kind of Queer
Race, Sexuality, And Gender in Contemporary Constructions of Swedishness
By **Katharina Kehl**

Black Masculinities and Colonial Legacies
The Global Politics of Jamaican and Diasporic Constructions of Gender
By **Shardia Briscoe-Palmer**

For more information about the series and to
find out how to submit a proposal visit
**bristoluniversitypress.co.uk/
gender-sexuality-and-global-politics**

International Editorial Board

Linda Åhäll, University of Gothenburg, Sweden
Terrell Carver, University of Bristol, UK
Shine Choi, Massey University, New Zealand
Bina D'Costa, Australian National University, Australia
Paula Drumond, O Instituto de Relações Internacionais PUC-Rio, Brazil
Cynthia Enloe, Clark University, US
Des Gasper, Erasmus University, Netherlands
Inanna Hamati-Ataya, University of Cambridge, UK
Catarina Kinnvall, Lund University, Sweden
Rauna Kuokkanen, University of Lapland, Finland
Peace Medie, University of Ghana, Ghana
Annie Paul, University of the West Indies, Jamaica
Manuela Picq, Amherst College, US
Vicki Squire, University of Warwick, UK
Cemal Burak Tansel, University of Sheffield, UK
Maria Tanyag, Australian National University, Australia
Cai Wilkinson, Deakin University, Australia

For more information about the series and to
find out how to submit a proposal visit
**bristoluniversitypress.co.uk/
gender-sexuality-and-global-politics**

DIGITAL FRONTIERS IN GENDER AND SECURITY
Bringing Critical Perspectives Online

Alexis Henshaw

First published in Great Britain in 2024 by

Bristol University Press
University of Bristol
1-9 Old Park Hill
Bristol
BS2 8BB
UK
t: +44 (0)117 374 6645
e: bup-info@bristol.ac.uk

Details of international sales and distribution partners are available at bristoluniversitypress.co.uk

© Bristol University Press 2024

British Library Cataloguing in Publication Data
A catalogue record for this book is available from the British Library

ISBN 978-1-5292-2627-0 hardcover
ISBN 978-1-5292-2628-7 paperback
ISBN 978-1-5292-2629-4 ePub
ISBN 978-1-5292-2630-0 ePdf

The right of Alexis Henshaw to be identified as author of this work has been asserted by her in accordance with the Copyright, Designs and Patents Act 1988.

All rights reserved: no part of this publication may be reproduced, stored in a retrieval system, or transmitted in any form or by any means, electronic, mechanical, photocopying, recording, or otherwise without the prior permission of Bristol University Press.

Every reasonable effort has been made to obtain permission to reproduce copyrighted material. If, however, anyone knows of an oversight, please contact the publisher.

The statements and opinions contained within this publication are solely those of the author and not of the University of Bristol or Bristol University Press. The University of Bristol and Bristol University Press disclaim responsibility for any injury to persons or property resulting from any material published in this publication.

Bristol University Press works to counter discrimination on grounds of gender, race, disability, age and sexuality.

Cover design: blu inc
Front cover image: Stocksy/Laura Stolfi

For Barbara and Leslie

Contents

List of Tables		viii
List of Abbreviations		ix
About the Author		xi
Acknowledgements		xii
1	Introduction	1
PART I	**Conceptualizing Inequality and Insecurity in the Digital Age**	
2	Big Data and the Security of Women: Where We Are and Where We Could Be Going	13
3	Addressing the Digital Gender Gap	42
PART II	**Social Media, Surveillance, and Gender-Based Violence Online**	
4	Extremism and Gender-Based Violence Online	65
5	Technological Surveillance, States, and Gendered Insecurity	87
PART III	**Futures of Technology, Gender, and Security**	
6	Resistance, Resilience, and Innovation	105
7	Cryptocurrency, Decentralized Finance, and Blockchain: Gender Issues in Political Economy and Security	125
8	Conclusion	147
Notes		159
References		167
Index		214

List of Tables

2.1	Comparing gender security and inclusion scales and indices: scores for the United States (2014–2020)	26
2.2	WomanStats Scale 5 versus the author's revised measure	30
3.1	Technology use by gender (2020, as percentage of corresponding population)	46
3.2	Technology use by gender in selected South Asian countries (2020, as percentage of corresponding population)	51

List of Abbreviations

AI	artificial intelligence
APSA	American Political Science Association
BJP	Bharatiya Janata Party
CEDAW	Convention on the Elimination of All Forms of Discrimination Against Women
ERA	Equal Rights Amendment
FARC	Revolutionary Armed Forces of Colombia
FI	financial inclusion
FSS	feminist security studies
GIFCT	Global Internet Forum to Counter Terrorism
GIWPS	Georgetown Institute for Women, Peace and Security
ICSR	International Centre for the Study of Radicalisation
ICT	information and communications technology
IPU	Inter-Parliamentary Union
ITU	International Telecommunication Union
LGBTQI+	lesbian, gay, bisexual, trans, queer, intersex+
MDG	Millennium Development Goals
MGTOW	Men Going Their Own Way
MRA	Men's Rights Activists
NAP	National Action Plan
NGO	non-governmental organization
OECD	Organization for Economic Co-operation and Development
OSESGY	Office of the Special Envoy of the Secretary-General for Yemen
P/CVE	preventing/countering violent extremism
PRIO	Peace Research Institute of Oslo
PUA	Pick-Up Artists
SDG	Sustainable Development Goals
SMS	Short Message Service
SSA	sub-Sarahan Africa
STI	Save the Internet
TRP	The Red Pill
UNDP	United Nations Development Programme

UNESCO	United Nations Educational, Scientific and Cultural Organization
UNICEF	United Nations Children's Fund
WAF	Women's Annex Foundation
WFP	World Food Programme
WPS	Women, Peace, and Security

About the Author

Alexis Henshaw is Assistant Professor in the Department of Political Science at Troy University. Her previous works include *Insurgent Women: Female Combatants in Civil Wars* (with Jessica Trisko Darden and Ora Szekely, published by Georgetown University Press, 2019) and *Why Women Rebel: Understanding Women's Participation in Armed Rebel Groups* (Routledge, 2017). Her work on gender and international security has appeared in peer-reviewed outlets including *International Feminist Journal of Politics*, *Politics & Gender*, and *Journal of Global Security Studies*.

Acknowledgements

The Internet has made content creators of us all, and I am no exception. I never intended to write a book on gender, technology, and security; indeed, I didn't realize this project *was* a book for quite some time. When the COVID-19 pandemic reached the United States in early 2020, I was making plans for archival work in the hopes of developing a different research project. COVID-19 put those plans on hold indefinitely. Fortunately, around the same time I took on a role as an associate fellow with a new research initiative, the Global Network on Extremism and Technology (GNET), a project funded by the Global Internet Forum to Counter Terrorism (GIFCT) and run by the International Centre for the Study of Radicalisation (ICSR) at King's College London. I am grateful to GNET for providing me the outlet and connections to help develop my nascent interest in the gender/technology/security nexus. In particular, ICSR Director Shiraz Maher and (former) Project Manager Ali Bissoondath receive special thanks for the opportunities and encouragement they provided. Erin Saltman of GIFCT likewise offered input and assistance with this project in its developmental stages.

GNET's assistance in allowing me to workshop early research on the topics covered in this book via its blog, conferences, and a report series was instrumental to helping this project come together. I was fortunate enough to participate in a number of other events to share and workshop this research in progress. My thanks to staff at Tech vs. Terrorism, the Jean Monnet Network on EU Counter-Terrorism, the United Nations Office of Counter-Terrorism, and the Executive Directorate of the United Nations Security Council Counter-Terrorism Committee for their invitations to participate in online events held during 2020 and 2021. I similarly thank the organizers of the 2021 *International Feminist Journal of Politics* Conference, the 2021 FemQuant workshop 'Beyond the Binary Variable', the 2022 International Studies Association Convention, and the 2022 workshop 'Telling it Like it Is: Descriptive Work in Social Science Research' for allowing me to present at these events. In particular, the comments offered by chairs and discussants including Sara Rose Taylor, Daniel W. Hill, and S. Laurel Weldon were invaluable to me in developing Chapter 2 of this book.

At Bristol University Press, I thank Stephen Wenham, Zoe Forbes, and the series editors of the Gender, Sexuality and Global Politics series for their support and insight. Gunhild Hoogensen Gjørv spent a significant amount of time working with me on my proposal to make it a good fit for this series. The anonymous reviewers of the manuscript further provided excellent feedback. Portions of Chapter 7 were originally published in the journal *Politics & Gender* as '"Women, Consider Crypto": Gender in the Virtual Economy of Decentralized Finance' (2022). The editorial team led by Susan Franceschet and Christina Wolbrecht oversaw the publication of that version of the work. Their comments and those of the three anonymous reviewers prompted me to think more coherently about my analysis of decentralized finance and cryptocurrency. I likewise gratefully acknowledge the anonymous interviewees consulted for this book, each of whom offered their valuable time during the pandemic in the name of furthering this research.

On a personal level, writing a book during a time of pandemic, social isolation, political unrest, and Zoom fatigue has sometimes been an emotional challenge. To my husband, Ray, I am so thankful for your love and support every day. There is no one I would have rather spent two years house-bound with. My parents, as always, have offered me love and support even when we could not be together. My grandmother, Barbara, has been a supportive force and a model for optimism my entire life – but never more so than during these past two years. This book is dedicated in part to her.

This book also came into being during a time of great loss for our family. In 2022, I lost my most faithful research assistant, Rico. Just as he had during years of graduate school and while I was writing two previous books, he served as my constant companion and made sure to remind me when it was time to eat, to walk, and to put work away. No one will ever take his place in my heart. I also dedicate this book to my late father-in-law, Leslie Charles, who died of COVID-19 in 2020. Leslie, you are loved and missed in our home every day. For the millions of families like ours worldwide who have known pain, anger, and loss during this pandemic: You are not alone. May we all find the inner strength to move forward, the empathy to care for one another, and the will to hold leaders accountable where they have failed so many of us.

1

Introduction

In 2014, a group calling itself the Guardians of Peace – cybercriminals with known connections to North Korea – launched an attack on Sony Pictures Studio in the United States, disabling much of its network and resulting in the leak of confidential data including business plans, emails, and personal information about Sony employees (Stengel 2019). The proximate cause of the attack, as identified in a message from the hackers, was Sony's plan to release a film called *The Interview*, a comedy in which two journalists become reluctant assassins and are enlisted to kill North Korean leader Kim Jong-un. The North Korean government had repeatedly complained about the film prior to the attack, calling it 'an act of terrorism and war', threatening retaliation, and even appealing to the United Nations (UN) to stop its release (Reuters 2014; Stengel 2019).

The resulting hack was considered one of the largest cyberattacks ever launched within the United States, but it turns out it was not unique. Unknown at the time was that North Korean hackers had previously attacked Britain's Channel 4 network, shortly before it planned to broadcast a TV drama that presented the country in an unfavourable light (Sanger et al 2017). Commenting on this latter attack, one British cybersecurity official described the surprise of discovering North Korea's capabilities to mount cyberattacks, calling the country 'weird and absurd and medieval and highly sophisticated' as well as 'isolated' and 'backward'. 'People didn't take it seriously', he summarized (Sanger et al 2017). Such attitudes about the country and its leaders, especially current leader Kim Jong-un and his father Kim Jong-il, are apparently common, if one takes their cues from Western popular culture. During his reign and even after his death, Kim Jong-il had been lampooned on American movies and TV as insane, fat, lonely, effeminate, small, and – generally – someone to inspire mockery rather than fear.[1] During the early years of his reign, Kim Jong-un was likewise caricatured in music videos and other media, reportedly provoking his anger (NBC News 2014).

Media portrayals and viral videos may have been a particularly useful tool for getting under the skin of North Korea's dictators. On the one hand, Kim Jong-il was known to be a film afficionado and likewise claimed in his later years to be an Internet buff (Lankov 2007; Fischer 2015). At the same time, in terms of content, the mocking portrayals struck against a regime that was deeply invested in performative masculinity. While commentators have noted that depictions of North Korean leaders in propaganda (including Kim Jong-un, Kim Jong-il, and Kim Il-sung) co-opt many themes similar to those used in other Cold War-era dictatorships, they also rely on a particularly North Korean brand of masculinity. Baked into this are notions of agency, action, national self-reliance, militancy, and fatherhood (Armstrong 2002; Demick 2009; Myers 2011). The leaders are meant to be seen by their populace as caring providers, with many citizens socialized to regard them as part of an extended family (Demick 2009).[2] Thus, unflattering, un-masculine, and even feminized portrayals of these men are threatening and possibly destabilizing to the country's foundational myths.

If the weaponization of media (including online media) was a uniquely effective way of slighting the regime, North Korea had a uniquely effective form of retribution in cyberattacks. North Korea's cyber capabilities are estimated to include somewhere between 1,400 and 6,000 hackers serving in a 'cyber force' (Haggard and Lindsay 2015; Chanlett-Avery et al 2017). Though Internet access is generally restricted in the country, hackers are believed to have trained in China, Russia, India, and even the United States as well as domestically in North Korean universities (Haggard and Lindsay 2015; Chanlett-Avery et al 2017; Sanger et al 2017; Perlroth 2021a). Some North Korean hackers working on behalf of the government are believed to operate from outside the country (Sanger et al 2017). Whatever the truth about their capabilities, what is relevant to the present analysis is that these attacks were successful – to a point. The Sony attack caused technical and reputational headaches for the company and grabbed headlines worldwide. It deterred many theatres from showing *The Interview*, and was likely a factor in Channel 4's decision to shelve the planned British drama (Sanger et al 2017). Although *The Interview* eventually found a home on streaming media and a smaller number of movie screens, the impact of its intended slight to the North Korean regime was likely blunted by the cyberattack. Kim Jong-un's masculinity was – at least partially – avenged.

Knowing the history of the Sony attack, it is hardly surprising that North Korea–US relations later became the test case for Carol Cohn in her 2018 *New York Times* opinion piece on the importance of feminist security studies (FSS) (Cohn 2018). At a time when geopolitical discourse had sunk to the level of two world leaders comparing the size of their 'nuclear buttons' via the Internet, grasping the role of gender in shaping global security seemed to take on new importance. Cohn's 2018 piece recalled her earlier work in the 1980s, in which she argued that masculinity was interwoven into the work of US nuclear security. She shows – among other things – how women were underrepresented in the establishment, rendered meaningless in the statistics of impact and death tolls, and how the very language of nuclear security was both masculinized and fetishized (Cohn 1987). Decades later, depressingly little appears to have changed in the nuclear security realm, where women continue to report being undervalued and ill-treated (Hurlburt et al 2019). The epidemic further appears to have spread to the growing realms of technology and cybersecurity, where we see an overwhelmingly male workforce, gender stereotyping, ineffectual or non-existent efforts to recruit women, the weaponization of cybersecurity tools against women, and a divorce between clinical discussions of technical impact and the human realities of cyberwar (King-Close 2016; Peacock and Irons 2017; Kshetri 2020; Perlroth 2021a).

The present work looks to move towards closing the gap by offering a discussion of how gender can be mainstreamed into discourse about technology and security. This takes the form of exploring the digital frontiers of current policy frameworks on gender and security (including the Women, Peace, and Security [WPS] Agenda), the relationship between discourse on security and political economy, the lived experience of gendered (in)security in the Information Age, and the intersecting nature of social hierarchies in the digital realm. Exploring these topics involves understanding the need for digital security not just as a discrete, technical issue, but understanding more broadly the interplay between human actions, social forces, and technology that manifest themselves in the social frameworks of Web 2.0 and the emerging visions for Web 3.0, defined as the decentralized Web. A particular focus of this work, therefore, is on the applications of technology for communication, logistics, the provision of information and services, the conduct of political processes, and in crisis response.

As a framework for these discussions, I engage primarily with theories of feminist international relations and FSS, but I also seek to foster dialogue with other critical perspectives – including queer, postcolonial, indigenous, and Black feminist frames – which have arguably outpaced feminist international relations in addressing these issues. As is evident from the Sony/North Korea example and others like it,[3] gendered analysis offers insight into the dynamics of technology and security. As discussed by Tickner (1997), feminist international relations theory is not simply about adding women to existing international relations paradigms. It is, rather, about assessing 'how, all too often, claims of gender neutrality mask deeply embedded masculinist assumptions which can naturalise or hide gender differences and gender inequality'. Feminist international relations addresses the importance of seeing beyond state-focused paradigms of international relations (a point especially apt in the realm of cybersecurity, where a variety of nonstate actors play critical roles), challenging the dominance of positivist and supposedly value-neutral forms of inquiry, and moving outside the disciplinary silos associated with political science (Tickner 1997). Feminist research in international relations generally shares an ethical orientation to highlight the importance of women, improve the lives of marginalized groups, and reflect on the power dynamics of knowledge production (Cohn 2006; Tickner 2006; Weldon 2006). As such, it is pluralistic in its methods of inquiry – though it often casts a critical eye towards purely empirical work, encouraging reflection upon the quality and inclusivity of data sources (Caprioli 2004; Tickner 2006; Sjoberg 2009).

Building on scholarship in feminist international relations theory, FSS emerged as a coherent approach in the early 2000s (Stern and Wibben 2014). Sjoberg (2009), in the introduction to a special issue of the journal *Security Studies*, outlines several unifying themes in FSS work. These include:

- Commitment to a broad understanding of security that encompasses both the private and public sphere, moving beyond defining 'security' as the security of states.
- Agreement that international security is, in practice, defined by a set of values that is gendered.
- A view that the omission of gender from work on international security makes this work not gender-neutral but, rather, gender-biased.
- Reflection upon the diverse roles gender may play in the theory and practice of international security.

Stern and Wibben (2014) further note that FSS has evolved along a trajectory of greater diversity and more intensive engagement. This includes a push towards advocating the mainstreaming of gender perspectives in practice and analysis, rather than accepting the addition of women to existing approaches and institutions. It also includes acknowledging the 'complex, multiple, and context-specific dynamics of gender relations' as they relate to security, incorporating the intersectional impacts associated with racial, postcolonial, and Global South experiences as well as attention to masculinity and issues of the lesbian, gay, bisexual, transgender, queer and intersex (LGBTQI+) community (Stern and Wibben 2014).

As future chapters will explore in greater detail, I believe that in the area of digital politics and digital security especially, feminist international relations/security studies would benefit from interdisciplinary dialogue and intersectional conversations. Issues like data ethics, privacy, surveillance, and digital security have already been a long-standing preoccupation for Black feminist thought, indigenous studies, postcolonial international relations, and queer theory – among others. By comparison, a search of published articles in the *International Feminist Journal of Politics* reveals, as of this writing, no articles specific to cybersecurity, a single mention of 'digital security', and an uptick in discussions about social media only in the past 5–7 years. A core argument of this book is that issues like disinformation, online extremism, and the ramifications of COVID-19 all call for the feminist international relations/ security studies community to become more engaged in discussions about technology and politics. By building bridges – rather than silos – between communities of critical insight, we can begin to navigate a way towards feminist theory and a feminist ethical stance on digital politics and security.

In the following sections, I aim to answer three key questions for the reader. The first, already alluded to in the examples discussed earlier, is why it is worth discussing technology in relation to gender and security. The second asks why a security discourse is appropriate to deploy, and what tradeoffs we should be aware of when we parse these issues as security concerns. The final question, building from that, elaborates in greater detail on the need for intersectional dialogue in exploring the topic. Having addressed each of these issues, I go on to introduce the remainder of the text.

Why technology?

The present text argues that seeing gender and security in the digital realm takes on more urgency as our lives and conflicts come increasingly online. By referring to the 'digital realm', I reference not just the narrow definition of cybersecurity – defined by one US government agency as 'the art of protecting networks, devices, and data from unauthorized access or criminal use and the practice of ensuring confidentiality, integrity, and availability of information' (US CSIA, nd). As discussed in the following chapters, I argue that a feminist approach entails recognizing the interaction of technological tools with social forces and hierarchies. This means asking questions about equitable access to technology, assessing whether users can enjoy the potential benefits of technology with a reasonable expectation of privacy and without undue harassment, and adopting an ethic of responsibility that encourages reflection on the outcomes of technology with an eye towards mitigating harm.

Intertwined with these goals is a recognition that the online environment has taken on a dual form. While online communications remain a concern insofar as they represent a potential conduit for real-world violence or security threats, the digital realm has also become a distinct site for the formation of new ideologies and new forms of violence aimed at creating instability and insecurity. Much of the discussion in this book focuses on technologies closely associated with Web 2.0 – the participatory or social web where users increasingly also function as content creators. This includes social media, messaging services, and technologies that fall broadly into the realm of information and communications technology (ICT). In terms of extremism, discussed in more detail in Chapter 4, we have seen the Internet and ICT platforms used both to spread ideologies developed offline (such as jihadist or White nationalist ideas) and to develop new, digitally native forms of extremism like incel thought or the QAnon conspiracy theory. Though these latter examples draw on long-standing ideas of anti-feminism, misogyny, homophobia, anti-Semitism, and the like, they have arguably combined extremist ideas in new ways through large and geographically diverse online communities. These communities have served to develop and grow these new varieties of extremism while at the same time incubating them in areas resistant to outside critique or content moderation.

Similarly, in the case of acts of violence, we have seen technology deployed not only to facilitate familiar forms of gender-based violence like domestic abuse, verbal harassment, and even sexual assault (as discussed further in Chapters 3 and 4). We have further seen the digital space become a site of new and distinct forms of violence and harassment against women and other marginalized groups. This includes the development of synthetic deepfake or cheapfake pornography – images and videos entered into wide circulation with the purpose of humiliating or silencing the subjects portrayed, the vast majority of whom are women (Hao 2021). Similarly, the problem of revenge porn – the nonconsensual distribution of genuine, sexually explicit photos or videos without the permission of those depicted – disproportionately targets women (Goldstein 2020; CCRI 2021; Hao 2021).[4] More recently, the COVID-19 pandemic brought forth the phenomenon of 'zoombombing', the intentional disruption of online gatherings – usually through the broadcast of profane and/or graphic material. Early research on zoombombing incidents has suggested that it too disproportionately targets events convened by or about women, people of colour, and LGBTQI+ populations (Burton et al 2020; UN Women 2020). All of this reinforces the importance of understanding technology's relationships to gendered forms of violence and insecurity.

There is arguably even more impetus to delve into these issues given developments further on the horizon. Analysts and developers argue that we are already seeing the movement from Web 2.0 to Web 3.0,[5] a new paradigm in which the digital space will become increasingly dominated by open, trustless, and permissionless networks (Mersch and Muirhead 2020; Silver 2020). Chapter 7 explores some of these networks in greater detail, particularly as they relate to decentralized finance, blockchain, and cryptocurrency. But, briefly, while Web 2.0 can be characterized by the decentralization of content *authorship*, Web 3.0 extends the trend to decentralization of content development, data storage and management, and interactions among users – all of which are envisioned to take place without the engagement of a central governing body (Mersch and Muirhead 2020). Champions of Web 3.0 argue it represents a potential revolution for both freedom and privacy on the web – representing a departure from the consolidation of communications, data, and computing power among major technology companies (Silver 2020). However, the discussion in Chapter 7 cautions that we may be headed towards seeing more of the same inequitable outcomes without the engagement of proper ethical and analytical frameworks.

Why security?

From a feminist perspective, it is worth briefly discussing the benefits and limitations of deploying a security discourse to frame the issues explored in this text. Many of the themes identified in the following chapters have an undeniable connection to security and insecurity, among them extremist violence, conflict, human trafficking, sexual violence, domestic violence, and conflict resolution. Other issues, though, including surveillance and privacy, the gendered digital divide in technology access, and inequality in relevant professions, can be understood through other frameworks as well, that is, as economic or human rights issues. Feminist scholarship understands that discourse has power, and that designating something as a security issue carries certain consequences (Weldon 2006; MacKenzie 2009, 2012). MacKenzie (2009, 2012) draws connections between feminist work and the Copenhagen School of international relations theory. Work in the Copenhagen School recognizes the constructed nature of security, where the term refers not necessarily to objective threats, but to subjective 'threats' designated as such through discourse, framing, and political process (MacKenzie 2009; Diskaya 2013). The designation of threats carries power and endows power, as the securitizing act potentially allows agents to justify extraordinary means to combat threats in the interests of survival (Diskaya 2013).

Critical understandings of securitization sit alongside the concept of militarization, another issue of concern for feminist research. Enloe (1999) defines militarization as a state of dependence upon the military or control by the military. Up to this point, a great deal of work in international relations that deals with digital security or cybersecurity has arguably been securitized and militarized, taking the security of states and institutions (and the possibility of militarized response) as a referent. One of many possible contributions that feminism can make to this discussion is to re-centre the unit of analysis. Engaging a 'human-centric' (Mhajne 2021) approach that sees individuals, communities, and minority or minoritized groups as the reference point represents a course-correction. It offers a natural extension of human security as a concept, leads to calls for accountability and transparency in digital/cybersecurity discussions, and calls upon policymakers to avoid the traps of abstraction and dehumanization.

Similarly, as discussed further in Chapter 3, some of the issues I explore are also dealt with via frameworks of international development. This is particularly true of efforts to promote gender equality within the technology sector and to close the gap in gendered access to technology. At the international level, these issues have often been delegated to the work of development agencies and are packaged into frameworks like the UN's Millennium Development Goals (MDGs) and Sustainable Development Goals (SDGs), which emphasize themes of equality, education, and economic empowerment. Feminist work tends to regard these neoliberal logics with suspicion, seeing them as another method of instrumentalization – this time in the service of wealth rather than security. Feminist analysis of microcredit and financial inclusion initiatives, as discussed in Chapter 7, provides one example where such logics are problematized, insofar as they incentivize the valuation of women primarily as a financial asset for their family rather than as people deserving of rights (Keating et al 2010; Rabiul Karim and Kong Law 2013; Paprocki 2016). More broadly, feminist work has challenged the separation of security and development issues as a false dichotomy, with gendered security indivisible from matters of the global political economy (Madhok and Rai 2012; Stern 2017). Thus, in engaging with discourses of security, one must also be conscientious of the degree to which security is inseparable from other goals and ideologies.

Why intersectionality (and interdisciplinarity)?

As alluded to earlier, I see this work as an opportunity to also hold feminist international relations/security studies accountable as it looks to engage with these issues. In spite of claims to inclusivity, feminist international relations has, at different times and for different reasons, been branded a less-than-fully-inclusive space (Caprioli 2004; Parashar 2016).[6] Compared to many of our colleagues across the social sciences and humanities, we are also latecomers to the discussion of security in the digital realm. Black feminist and intersectional work in information studies has already probed the gendered and racialized impacts of algorithms and the intersectional experience of online security (Noble and Tynes 2016b; Noble 2018; Benjamin 2019). Indigenous perspectives have shed light on how power relationships are encoded and enacted via the 'science' of data (Walter and Andersen 2013; Kukutai and Taylor 2016). Indigenous work also centres conversations about resistance and reclaiming power via data, a theme that likewise appears in feminist and queer work in data studies (Walter and Andersen 2013; D'Ignazio and Klein 2020; Guyan 2022). The contributions go on – and though I hope to do justice to these connections in the following chapters, we can and should continue conversations beyond what appears in these pages. It is also worth recalling that, in the academic realm, silos are not created by chance. The disciplinary structures that divide and scatter critical scholarship do so by design and are a form of policing what conversations can be had and where. In both scholarship and practice, we must work to make the information landscape one that dismantles, rather than reproduces, the artificial boundaries that separate feminist international relations/security studies from those who might be our natural partners in co-liberation.

Gendering technology and security: moving forward

This chapter has offered a brief introduction to the topics, scope, and theoretical underpinnings of this work. The remainder of the text proceeds as follows.

Chapter 2 introduces the technology of big data while also providing a methodological foundation for the remainder of the book. Discussing the definition(s) and history of big data, I discuss how it has often been mobilized in support of privileged groups and instrumental motives. I compare this to the development of norms surrounding the production of gender-disaggregated data, promulgated by international actors from the mid-1990s into the early 2000s. I argue that the emphasis on quantification and gender-disaggregation has resulted in outcomes that are more comprehensive than what came before, but which are at the same time elite-focused, closely tied to policy outcomes, and questionable in both validity and reliability. I discuss strategies deployed by feminist researchers to develop more robust outcomes, as well as examining how literature in the realm of critical data studies can point us towards strategies that harness data for meaningful social transformation.

In Chapter 3, I offer a somewhat more extensive assessment of where the world stands in terms of gender mainstreaming of technology. This includes an exploration of gendered patterns of technology access, the representation of women in the technology sector, and some reflection on the social outcomes resulting from patterns of inequality. This chapter combines a critical analysis of data on gender and technology access with a case study of gendered insecurities and resistance in South Asian nations including India, Pakistan, Nepal, and Bangladesh. This chapter ultimately raises ethical questions about the advancement of efforts to bridge the digital gender divide as a normative 'good' in an environment that is largely blind to gendered insecurities. It also demonstrates the potential for understanding these insecurities through a postcolonial lens and developing resistance movements that illuminate the role of global hierarchies in shaping access and experiences.

Chapter 4 looks at how ICT and the Internet have fostered gendered insecurity in the context of extremism and radicalization. Examining cases including the Islamic State and incel or male supremacist communities, I show how the online environment poses new challenges related to the protection of women and the prevention of violence. Through these cases,

I argue that technology has both facilitated gender-based violence and perpetuated gendered logics of radicalization, incentivizing the recruitment of individuals to violent groups based on their gender and using gender roles as leverage. Drawing on original content analysis, I argue that the decentralization of extremist conversations (especially, their movement beyond mainstream social media platforms) requires further study. I also offer support for hypotheses recently advanced by practitioners and researchers in preventing/countering violent extremism (P/CVE), showing a trend of cross-pollination between gender-based extremist communities and other conspiracy- or hate-based groups.

Chapters 5 and 6 pivot to a discussion of surveillance, resistance, and the prospect for feminist innovation in the digital space. Drawing on case studies and interviews with practitioners, Chapter 5 discusses how states can also act as agents of gendered digital insecurity through high-tech policing and the surveillance of feminist activism. This chapter also discusses the relevance of surveillance studies literature to international relations. In Chapter 6, I discuss how social media and communications technology has been used in places including Colombia and Afghanistan to promote peace activism and/or women's rights advocacy in hostile environments. Incorporating interviews with practitioners, the chapter addresses successes and barriers in this area, in particular challenges faced by feminist innovators during the COVID-19 pandemic. Drawing on these interviews, I further reflect upon the roles of various stakeholders – including states and technology companies – in creating more space for feminist advocacy online.

Chapter 7 moves into the realm of exploring how technology and gender interact in the areas of relief and post-conflict recovery. The discussion specifically explores how emerging technologies of blockchain, cryptocurrency, and decentralized finance (those technologies most closely associated with the emergence of the decentralized web) are being applied in fragile and conflict-affected states. I argue that the applications of these technologies by both public and private actors are gendered (and racialized) in problematic ways. Likening them to earlier feminist critiques of microcredit and financial inclusion, I argue that the mere layering of new technologies over existing social frameworks – and in line with neoliberal and neolibertarian priorities – has thus far failed to produce transformative outcomes.

Chapter 8 provides an overall summary for the text, returning to feminist ideas about technology, gender, and security. While reflecting on potential ways forward, the conclusion also represents a call to action for feminist work in international relations and security studies, asking for further engagement with questions about technology. It further calls upon all those involved in the study and practice of technology to see how gender impacts and is impacted by their efforts to create secure online environments.

PART I

Conceptualizing Inequality and Insecurity in the Digital Age

2

Big Data and the Security of Women: Where We Are and Where We Could Be Going

Understanding where we are at and what is at stake with regard to gender, technology, and the security of women involves examining the data. But what happens when the data are part of the problem? The production and dissemination of newer, larger (and, in almost every instance, quantitative) data is in and of itself a technology – one that is inherently gendered. In recent years, a number of authors have raised warnings about how data gaps, misleading interpretations, and algorithms that are both gendered and racialized[1] impact virtually every aspect of women's lives (O'Neil 2016; Noble 2018; Criado-Perez 2019). Work has also interrogated the gendered, racialized, and intersectional power relationships reflected in data collection, which tends to favour elite perspectives and motivations (Walter and Andersen 2013; D'Ignazio and Klein 2020). Discussion of power relationships has further led to reflection on the relationship between data collection, quantification, and surveillance (Walby and Anaïs 2015).[2] This creates a problem, insofar as the call for gender-disaggregated data is deeply embedded in policy initiatives aimed at gender mainstreaming. If this lynchpin of institutional monitoring and evaluation schemes is flawed, what does it mean for efforts to highlight emerging issues in gender and security?

This chapter seeks to present but also critique the data we have on gender equality and gendered experiences of security. This begins with some background, covering the coinciding rise of 'big data' (as a technology and an ethos) and normative frameworks in academic and policy circles that incentivize the collection and dissemination of gender-disaggregated data. From there, I proceed to a discussion of the theoretical, ethical, mathematical, and practical issues involved in the collection and analysis of gender-disaggregated data. Ultimately, I argue that the move towards incorporating big data values into discourse on gender and security has created a problematic environment in which problems including (but not limited to) missing data, subjective coding choices, and the functional erasure of intersectional dynamics abound. Taking these issues into account, I argue that there is a continued need to explore questions about gender and security through a mixed-methods framework. At the same time, recognizing that quantitative interventions in gender mainstreaming are already institutionalized and are unlikely to vanish, I encourage further feminist reflection on how to create richer, more robust futures for the second generation of gender-disaggregated data.

Coinciding trends: big data and gender-disaggregation

The co-development of two trends, the rise in big data and the emergence of norms regarding gender-disaggregated data, shape the current information environment. These trends will be examined in turn. First, what, exactly is 'big data?' The definition differs depending on who is asked. Many responses focus on the 'big' of big data. One report from the US Department of Commerce's National Institute of Standards and Technology offers: '*Big Data* consists of extensive datasets – primarily in the characteristics of volume, variety, velocity, and/or variability – that require a scalable architecture for efficient storage, manipulation, and analysis' (NIST 2015: 5). This definition focuses on the 'Vs' of big data, which refer primarily to size (volume) and change over time (velocity, variability), but also to variety – that is, the inclusion of different indicators with a variety of formats (NIST 2015).[3] Alternative definitions invoke somewhat more specific size parameters, such as the definition used by IBM: '[Big data] can be defined as data sets whose size or type is beyond the ability of traditional relational databases to capture, manage, and process the data' (IBM 2021). Technology company Oracle's definition similarly makes reference to volume, velocity, and variety, but also stresses the need for novelty, noting that big data refers to 'complex' data, 'especially from new data sources' (Oracle nd). Moving further outward from technology professionals, definitions become both less precise and more sceptical. Some commentators view 'big data' more as a cultural term than a technical one, referring to the increasing human reliance on technology for collecting and processing information, while at the same time jettisoning more traditional methods of analysis based on sampling (NIST 2015: 11). Mathematician Cathy O'Neil argues that the cultural shift accompanying big data is primarily rhetorical, engaged with power structures and hierarchies of knowledge (NIST 2015; O'Neil 2016). In some circles, the definition is simply up for grabs: as former Southern Political Science Association president Jeff Gill put it in his presidential address, '[b]asically big data is what anyone wants it to be' (Gill 2021: 3).

Understanding that some functional definition is necessary to carry on a discussion about big data, one can at a minimum glean from these sources that big data is: (a) a concept that purports to be about the use of more comprehensive, voluminous, and high-value data sources; and (b) a concept deeply intertwined with technological developments. Definitions generally agree upon this latter point: Big data is both produced by and, in turn, produces technology. Collecting, storing, and processing this data requires computational power and storage capacity. Meaningfully interpreting this data requires assistive technology, for example the production of data visualizations or the application of machine learning. At the frontiers of technology, the need to process or classify large and complex datasets is presented as a use case for quantum computing (Fisher 2019). Therefore, we can add a third facet to the definition of big data, that it is: (c) either quantitative in nature or expected to be quantified in some form through the analytical process.

Taking this as a starting point, we can begin to reflect on the relationship between big data and policy. Big data and the applications that process it have been held up as something of a panacea, capable of generating new and more effective responses to issues including climate change, cybersecurity threats, public health issues, and social inequality (Fisher 2019; Haleem et al 2020; Katwala 2020). Advocates for big data highlight the COVID-19 pandemic as an ideal use case. Commentators note that, during the pandemic, the collection and processing of vast amounts of patient data allowed policymakers and medical professionals to learn more about the disease, track its spread, create effective lockdown and quarantine policies, and develop better treatments (Haleem et al 2020; Sheng et al 2020; Wu et al 2020; Ma and Lipsitch 2021). Furthermore, the spread of interactive COVID-19 dashboards – providing data and visualization – in many countries brought big data into the homes of millions worldwide.

Yet if the COVID-19 pandemic demonstrates the benefits of big data, it also demonstrates many of its flaws. Perhaps the most glaring among these is that the abundance of data about the pandemic failed to prevent its catastrophic spread. The failure to create effective, data-driven quarantine and lockdown policies in response to the pandemic demonstrates, on one hand, the limitations of data in crafting policy. Absent political will, big data is simply big data. On the other hand, various aspects of the pandemic demonstrated how big data can offer new opportunities to lie with statistics. In the US states of Florida and Georgia – where the government had previously opposed efforts to expand healthcare for the poor – leaders were accused of tampering with or misreporting data in early months to make the pandemic appear less severe (Mariano and Trubey 2020; Wamsley 2020). In Nicaragua, different and contradicting data on COVID-19 was released by the administration of Daniel Ortega and the newly emerged Citizen's Observatory for COVID-19. The truth among the rival data remained elusive. A shortage of adequate testing in the country[4] surely impacted both numbers issued by the government and those issued by anti-government sources. Fine print on the Observatory's website[5] noted that its numbers relied on 'recognized community leaders' who, in turn, reported/verified COVID-19 'cases' that were largely self-diagnosed by those who believed they may have had COVID-19. The Observatory stated that it 'does not perform laboratory testing nor clinical diagnosis' and operated under a 'theory of rumor' which presumed that 'rumors have a high degree of importance given the insufficient official data on the epidemic' (Observatorio Ciudadano 2020). Staffers from established non-governmental organizations (NGOs) in Nicaragua, however, called into question the Citizen's Observatory for COVID-19's status as an independent organization, alleging it in fact had ties to political groups opposing Daniel Ortega (CDCA 2020; Perry 2020). Questions surrounding the origin and independence of the Observatory did not prevent its numbers from being reported as credible in media reports and academic outlets including *Science*, *The Los Angeles Times*, and the *Wall Street Journal*, which variously described the organization as a 'watchdog' group or an independent organization comprised of health experts (Huete-Pérez and Hildebrand 2020; Montes 2020; Linthicum 2021).

The invasive, unreliable, and nonconsensual ways in which COVID-19 data were collected worldwide similarly reflects ethical concerns about big data. A high-profile study in medical journal *The Lancet* on the effects of hydroxychloroquine treatment for COVID-19 was retracted after authors admitted they could not independently verify the veracity of the large-scale dataset used in their analysis, which came from a private health company (*The Lancet* 2020; Mehra et al 2020). In an open letter signed by over 100 medical professionals and researchers, experts questioned not only the veracity but also the ethical and legal procedure by which the data were collected (Watson et al 2020). In some countries, methods including facial recognition technology and mobile phone apps were used to track and control the spread of COVID-19 (Eck and Hatz 2020; Wu et al 2020). Eck and Hatz (2020) report that 34 countries, the majority of them democracies, implemented some surveillance measures in response to the pandemic. Experts have worried that the deployment of these technologies may have long-term consequences for surveillance. In Myanmar, for example, the organization Freedom House notes that oversight and surveillance measures deployed with the stated purpose of stopping the pandemic were deployed to censor websites critical of the government and to limit telecommunications through unregistered devices (Freedom House 2020b).

What does this have to do with gender? Just as big data has become highly valorized in recent decades, the production of gender-disaggregated quantitative data has been embraced as a mechanism for empowerment. Both trends likewise benefit from developments in information technology that facilitate the collection, creation, and rapid dissemination of data. In the WPS Agenda, UN Security Council Resolution 1325 (2000) lays out 'the need to consolidate data on the impact of armed conflict on women and girls'. Subsequent resolutions reinforce the importance of data collection for monitoring and assessment.[6] At the national level, a study of National Action Plans (NAPs) on WPS found that the majority of these NAPs include a monitoring and evaluation plan, most of which incorporate a specification of activities and associated 'specific measurable outcomes' (Hamilton et al 2020: 17–18).

At the time the WPS Agenda was created, the call for gender-disaggregated data was also being institutionalized through international development agencies. The United Nations Development Programme (UNDP) first released its Gender-Related Development Index and the Gender Empowerment Measure in 1995. The MDGs were promulgated by the UN in 2000 and became an important framework for a range of stakeholders. Some of these goals, including Goal 3 (Promote gender equality and empower women) and Goal 5 (Improve maternal health) were specifically tied to gendered outcomes. Others, like Goal 2 (Achieve universal primary education) and Goal 6 (Combatting HIV/AIDS) were implicitly gendered, given significant gender differences in outcomes. Early on in the MDGs period,[7] the UN Secretary General indicated that capacity building efforts to improve global data quality on a number of related indicators – including some specific to the status of women – should be regarded as a priority (UN General Assembly 2001).

More recently, monitoring and evaluation frameworks for the SDGs have harnessed logics of big data in an even more explicit way. The UN Secretary General's Independent Expert Advisory Group on a Data Revolution for Sustainable Development ('Data Revolution Group') has explicitly called for the production of more data, more quickly, and for such data to be disseminated more widely via tools like dashboards and data visualizations (Data Revolution Group 2014). In pursuit of these aims, there has also been advocacy for more public–private partnerships in order to leverage data gathered by private actors (Clausen Nielsen 2014; UN Women 2018b). While the Data Revolution Group noted in one report that 'data' may also include qualitative data, in practice many of the outputs explored in the same report rely on quantitative data (Data Revolution Group 2014). The group's specific emphasis on dashboards, data visualizations, and the like, similarly point towards a positivist/empirical stance on data.

In each of these cases (WPS, the MDGs, and the SDGs), high-level proclamations and recommendations cascade across multi-stakeholder frameworks for implementation. The range of players involved – including state governments, NGOs, regional and international organizations, and civil society groups – becomes accountable for meeting associated standards.

Given that the WPS Agenda and the MDGs were first implemented over two decades ago, it seems appropriate to take stock of the degree to which the vision of data for equality has been realized.

More data, more problems?

An assessment of the advances in the gender-disaggregation of data begins with the question of where gender data fits into the definition of big data. While data collection efforts on the status and security of women certainly purport to share the big data ethos of creating high-value, voluminous, and generally (though not exclusively) quantitative information about the status of women, leveraging available technologies, important gaps remain. First among these is that the data and metrics are often not longitudinal, at least not on the same scale as other conflict-, security-, and development-related indicators. The imperatives for capacity building that accompanied mandates on gender-disaggregated data (especially, in connection with WPS and the MDGs) were generally forward-looking and did not concern themselves with attempts to reconstruct data on earlier periods. Thus, while statistics on matters like interstate conflict or trade volume are frequently available covering several decades (in some cases, extending back to the 19th century or earlier) many indicators relevant to the status of women cover a much shorter time period. Many indicators offer 20–30 years of coverage at most. Even shorter time horizons of 10–15 years (or less) are common.

Additionally, state-level gender-disaggregated data is rarely fully cross-sectional, with a non-random selection of countries (usually authoritarian regimes, fragile and conflict-affected states, and microstates) frequently failing to report information on a variety of indicators. UN Women, in a report on gender issues in the SDGs, notes that the majority of indicators on gender equality (44 out of 54) are not reliably monitored by any agency (UN Women 2018b). Some SDGs lack associated metrics related to gender impact, even where the specific targets associated with the goals call for attention to gender. An example is SDG 6, which deals with clean water and sanitation for all. Though associated target 6.2 calls for 'special attention to the needs of women and girls', there are no associated, gender-related indicators in monitoring and assessment frameworks (UN Women 2018b).

In the case of data specific to matters of WPS, data availability can be further reduced by variability in the unit of analysis and the specified cases of interest. Researchers on WPS have noted that national and international policies on WPS disproportionately envision fragile and conflict-affected states in the Global South as the referent of the Agenda (Shepherd 2016; Parashar 2019; Basu and Kirby 2020; Haastrup and Hagen 2020). With few exceptions,[8] these states have become the focus of related data collection efforts. Considering some of the priority areas for data collection as noted in UN Security Council resolutions – the impact of conflict on women and girls, the makeup of peacekeeping missions, and conflict-related sexual violence – these are not the basis for truly cross-national datasets; the true unit of analysis is not country-year but perhaps conflict-year or mission-year. Missing data therefore plagues many available datasets, and this remains an issue for practitioners or researchers looking to produce robust, cross-national and/or time-series inquiry. These issues described are further compounded by the difficulty in accessing reliable statistics on indicators like sexual violence or domestic violence, topics hindered by variance in national laws and legal definitions – or by the potential risks that subjects themselves may incur for reporting such data.

There is further evidence that the scope of gender-disaggregated and gender-related data that *has* become available on a global level in the past 25–30 years has been sharply defined by the mandates of international policy. Shepherd (2008) discusses, in the context of UN Security Council Resolution 1325, how global policymaking and the attendant bargaining processes serve to frame but also narrow and bound the possibilities associated with new policy frameworks. As noted, in the case of the WPS Agenda, this has largely resulted in a focus on data imperatives that see the need to collect data as closely linked to security emergencies – wars, disasters, and crises. In the case of the MDGs and SDGs, it means that other econometric indicators that could potentially be leveraged to create a broader picture of the lived insecurities of women remain piecemeal, with availability shaped by the relationship between indicators and the mandates of the development goals. Sara Rose Taylor (2020) has written about the 'feminism by indicators' approach deployed in association with the MDG and SDG frameworks. Though ultimately optimistic about the prospects for data-driven change, she notes that there are important distinctions between the MDG and SDG processes. While monitoring and assessment frameworks related to the SDGs were developed through a consultation process that included, inter alia, civil society groups and UN Women, the MDGs were an 'expert-led, closed door' process (Rose Taylor 2020). Because of the lack of gender-informed expertise associated with MDG development and implementation, the resulting data on MDG attainment has been criticized for being too limited in scope and utility (UN Women 2018b; Rose Taylor 2020). Specific examples of such limitations include data on maternal mortality, which was not disaggregated at the subnational level, by race/ethnicity, or according to income level – despite ample evidence on the role each of these factors may play in maternal mortality risk (UN Women 2018b).

A couple of examples from the World Bank's Open Data project further illustrate not only how MDG-related indicators were limited, but also how those limitations will affect compatibility with SDG-related data.[9] MDG 2 (Achieve universal primary education) is a goal with an implicit relationship to gender. Formal, primary education had generally become more accessible worldwide over the course of the 20th century, reaching 83 per cent of all children by the year 2000 (United Nations nd). Yet UN agencies recognized that certain target populations made up the majority of all students out of school. These included children from the world's poorest households, those from conflict-affected areas, and girls – who, due to their lower status in many parts of the world, were often not enrolled in school (UNDP 2015).[10] The United Nations Educational, Scientific and Cultural Organization (UNESCO), from which the World Bank pulls data on primary school completion rates for girls and boys, has some data on these indicators going back to 1970, but there is a clear and drastic change in data availability over time. In the period 1970–1972, less than half of all states (61 total, out of 166 recognized sovereign states at that time) reported gender-disaggregated data on primary school completion rates. By the year 2020, only ten states had failed to report recent data on this indicator (World Bank 2012). This represents a victory for those who champion MDG 2 which, incidentally, failed to meet its goal but did make significant progress, increasing worldwide enrolment from 83 per cent to 91 per cent in 2015 (United Nations nd).

But what about data on educational indicators less specifically tied to MDG 2? Compare the growth in available data on primary school enrolment/completion to data on secondary and tertiary education rates for girls and women. While just ten countries are lacking recent data on primary school completion, 23 countries are missing data on female secondary school enrolment during the 2010–2020 period, and 28 are missing gender-disaggregated data on tertiary enrolment in the same period. After 2015, the MDGs were replaced by the SDGs. SDG 4 replaces MDG 2, shifting from a focus on universal primary education to the broader 'Ensure inclusive and equitable quality education and promote lifelong learning opportunities for all'. UNESCO's Institute for Statistics (one of the feeders for the World Bank's Open Data) makes clear that it, again, sees this as a goal related to gender inequality (UIS/UNESCO 2016). Thus, it may be that we will continue to see more comprehensive data coverage on the educational attainment of women and girls over time. However, these figures will likely have little backward compatibility with the more limited data collected during the MDG period.

What is true of education data is true for many other indicators. Global data related to maternal mortality, including the percentage of women receiving prenatal care and the percentage of births attended by skilled health staff, is unavailable prior to 1984 and grows over time.[11] The UN Population Fund's survey-based data on women's ability to 'mak[e] their own informed decisions regarding sexual relations, contraceptive use and reproductive health care' between the ages of 15 and 49 remains sparse, and is completely unavailable prior to 2006. Overall, it becomes clear that as we move back in time from indicators tied to specific policy mandates at the international level, the quality of data degrades. This poses specific challenges for practitioners and researchers seeking to create meaningful, long-term analysis.

Coping with imperfect data: strategies from feminist and critical research

The issues with data availability will come as no surprise to researchers in FSS, for whom data gaps and biases are a familiar issue. Feminist researchers have long gravitated towards qualitative and interpretive research, viewing the positivist (that is, empirical and quantitative) turn in international relations as influenced by androcentrism – that is, the tendency to view (elite) male experiences and interests as default (Runyan and Peterson 2013). Although some FSS researchers are open to the potential of quantitative work, they also reflect on the limitations and power relations inherent in the data (Caprioli 2004; Tickner 2006). The creation and coding of quantitative data is inherently tied to human biases and power relationships, guided by judgements about who counts and what questions are worth asking (Weldon 2006; Zalewski 2006). As such, a broader range of data sources – including interviews, sites of discourse, fieldwork, case studies, and visual content – are frequently featured in FSS scholarship.

However, the landscape for quantitative research on gender is changing. Coinciding with the new emphasis on capacity building and data collection at the international level, new data sources and corresponding research efforts have emerged. Given that several of these rely on data reported at the global level by international organizations, they are still impacted by the shortcomings of these underlying sources. To mitigate issues with the data, feminist research has adopted various, non-mutually-exclusive strategies to produce stronger findings. These include iterative, indexed or scaled, and mixed-methods approaches (Henshaw 2021). As the remainder of this chapter will show, while growth in the reporting and collection of quantitative data has made iterative or indexed approaches more common and, perhaps, more widely accepted, ongoing gaps (especially, related to intersectional experiences) and elite biases in what we measure call into question the ability of big (or 'soon-to-be-big') gender data to fully encapsulate the lived experience of insecurity. This discussion sets the stage for analyses in later chapters, which generally approach issues of gender and technology using a multi-method approach that is informed by principles of critical work in data studies.

An iterative strategy towards empirical work on gender in international relations can be found in work like that of Caprioli (2000) and Caprioli and Boyer (2001). In her 2000 article, Caprioli drew on some of the few widely available indicators related to the status of women worldwide during the period 1960–1992. Using data on fertility rates, percentage of women in the labour force, percentage of women in national legislatures, and the length of women's suffrage to proxy for gender inequality in various forms, she demonstrated a relationship between the status of women and the bellicosity of states. Her tripartite vision of gender inequality as a concept that can be divided into the sub-dimensions of political, economic, and social inequality continues to be used by others (Karim and Hill 2018).

Indexed or scaled approaches to analysing gender data became more feasible as data sources improved. The foundation of the WomanStats project in 2001 by Hudson et al (2014b) has established new standards in this area. With a team of principal investigators located across institutions worldwide, WomanStats now includes over 350 variables and 170,000 data points (WomanStats nd). Many of these indicators are focused directly on understanding the security of women. The WomanStats data, on the whole, combines the strategies of iterative measures, indexing, and mixed-methods analysis. While the data is well-suited to iterative analysis, it also contains several multivariate scales aimed at producing a comprehensive picture of the status of women. The WomanStats website additionally provides opportunities for mixed-methods research, linking users to relevant primary documents used to code the data. Other major, quantitative data initiatives that rely on scales and indexes to assess gender issues and/or the status of women include the index developed by Karim and Hill (2018) (now part of the WomanStats project) and the global and US-specific indexes on WPS issued by the Georgetown Institute for Women, Peace and Security (GIWPS).[12]

While these data projects represent important and innovative work,[13] they have unsurprisingly failed to eliminate the various sources of data trouble plaguing gender-disaggregated data. Analysis reliant on currently available data sources about gender and the status of women continues to face theoretical, ethical, technical, and mathematical issues that call for serious reflection. From a theoretical and ethical perspective, the embrace of gender as a 'cutting edge' topic in international relations – coinciding with the wider availability of quantitative data on gender – has been regarded with hostility and frustration by feminist and critical scholars, some of whom believe that decades of qualitative research has been overlooked in the quest for novel findings (Reiter 2015; Sjoberg et al 2018; Duriesmith 2020). For those engaged in primarily qualitative international relations research, the underlying suggestion that researchers could only legitimately ask questions about gender once those questions could be answered by quantitative analysis reflects larger biases in the field. Sjoberg et al (2018) argue that mixed-methods analysis and a mindset open to critical perspectives are necessary to advance knowledge in this area. Others argue that even by citing and discussing methodologically flawed work that fails to engage with gender in a critical way, we endow it with a power and legitimacy it does not deserve (Duriesmith 2020).

Beyond academic debates, there are ethical questions that should be addressed. To some extent, the production of gendered data in international relations contravenes best practices adopted by other social science disciplines related to the measurement of hidden concepts and the study of marginalized groups. Some of this literature comes from psychology, a discipline for which the construction of indices and scales representing latent concepts is critically important. In this type of social and behavioural research, the need to engage both a range of experts and members of target populations is considered a best practice when developing indices and scales (Boateng et al 2018). This principle of consultation aligns with guidance in sociology and the emerging field of critical data studies, a genre seeking to incorporate decolonial, anti-racist, and feminist principles in data analysis. Such work argues that researchers must acknowledge and illuminate the power relationships inherent in data collection (and production) and seek results that unsettle these hierarchies. As the process of converting lived experience to data is by nature reductive, critical perspectives demand that we recognize the act of quantification as an act that is capable of harm, thereby calling for an ethic of care and trust (Walter and Andersen 2013; D'Ignazio and Klein 2020).

Authors working in this area point to many historical harms caused by quantification in the service of power. As discussed further in Chapter 5, Black, indigenous, and postcolonial scholars have noted the historical role of data production in upholding systems of surveillance and oppression. Specific examples include the role of data in the slave trade, in colonial systems of identification and monitoring, in the governance and control of indigenous peoples, and in eugenicist medical projects (Browne 2012; Pugliese 2012; L.T. Smith 2012; Walter and Andersen 2013). Queer and transgender scholars further note that the harms caused by quantification may include the use of fixed indicators to categorize fluid characteristics like sexuality and gender identity. The erasure of populations outside of sex/gender binaries is a further concern (Stryker and Currah 2014; Moore and Currah 2015; Guyan 2022). Guyan (2022) notes that corporatized data production tends to erase small minority communities because of the cost and effort involved in reaching or counting them. This impacts small ethnic groups, but also transgender and intersex populations and other groups outside the gender binary. Persons with certain disabilities may also be impacted by the same dynamics. Pugliese (2012), for example, notes that biometric data collection systems can be expected to fail about 1–3 per cent of the time due to disabilities among the general population.

Strategies for resistance and/or reshaping power relations have been advanced in critical data scholarship. Central to many of these discussions is the notion of a paradox of visibility. Though referred to by different names, this concept generally speaks to the awareness that while visibility in data is power, becoming more visible to data systems also exposes minorities and minoritized groups to specific risks (Benjamin 2019; D'Ignazio and Klein 2020; Guyan 2022). Thus, any approach to visibility must also pursue transformation in power relations. Such transformational moves may include capacity building within referent populations, establishing accountability frameworks, taking measures to ensure data sovereignty or data ownership by marginalized groups, and the cultivation of data literacy.

Among indigenous scholar-activists, a movement towards data sovereignty calls for 'a right to identity and meaningful participation in decisions affecting the collection, dissemination, and stewardship of all data that are collected' about referent populations (Kukutai and Taylor 2016: 5). In practice, this means promoting consultation between institutions and communities in the development of data collection efforts, but also investments in capacity building to help referent communities use and maintain outputs (Walter and Andersen 2013; Kukutai and Taylor 2016; Lovett 2016). Such objectives closely align with feminist goals to accurately report upon and, ideally, improve the lives of women through feminist research (Randall 2002; Ackerly et al 2006).

An alternative strategy may be the pursuit of more radical transparency through critical inquiry. Walby and Anaïs (2015) discuss how this could be accomplished through institutional ethnography. Following Smith (1989), they argue this method can be deployed to re-centre the subjective human decision-making processes behind data production, surveillance, and quantification. Institutional ethnographies highlight the voices and perspectives of referent populations *and* labourers involved in data collection and coding, the latter being a group whose labour and choices are often rendered invisible in knowledge production (Walby and Anaïs 2015). These labour issues further raise points of dialogue with postcolonial thought, since the 'ghost work' of processing big data and using data to train artificial intelligence is increasingly performed by low-wage, contingent workers in the developing world (Gray and Suri 2019).

While many gender-focused data collection projects include multinational teams of experts, they do not necessarily include direct consultation with referent populations. In the case of the SDGs, UN Women notes that surveys could potentially ground data more firmly in the lived experiences of women, but they have thus far been seldom used (UN Women 2018b; Rose Taylor 2020). Similarly, while some civil society initiatives have sought to build data literacy and capacity in connection with the SDGs, these efforts have been localized in just a few countries (UN Women 2018b). On the academic side, the authors of *Sex and World Peace* (which includes some of the principal investigators of the WomanStats project) fully acknowledge the limitations of their data and discuss their processes in navigating among various institutional definitions and indicators of gendered security. Dissatisfaction with available indicators led them to settle on compiling a broad range of indicators including multivariate scales, some of them developed by the principal investigators and other academics (Hudson et al 2014a). Karim and Hill (2018) also indicate that they rely upon indicators identified and measured by academics and institutional sources, with missing data on some indicators imputed via Bayesian estimation. The GIWPS/PRIO (Peace Research Institute of Oslo) Index notes that it is 'informed by the policy and academic literature on composite indices' (GIWPS/PRIO 2018).

While many academic approaches to gender data look to *treat* the inadequate data gathered by international institutions, they do not fully *transform* the imperfect processes that produced these data. One obvious commonality among indices and datasets produced by institutions and academics is that they are focused on producing data about *women* rather than data about *gender*. Without comparative data on men and boys, data on women and girls arguably serves to highlight disadvantages while rendering privilege invisible. They also arguably contribute to a deficit narrative, highlighting the insecurities that women face as a result of systems of gender while perhaps overlooking risks these systems also pose to men and boys (D'Ignazio and Klein 2020). At the same time, populations outside the gender binary – which are legally and/or culturally recognized in many parts of the world – are largely absent altogether from existing frameworks, rendering their experiences of security invisible.[14]

The lack of direct consultation with target populations in developing gender-related indicators, including and especially women from marginalized groups and populations outside the gender binary, is an ongoing concern. Institutional measures on gender/ethnic equality and development have been critiqued in the past for embedding elite biases in their definitions (Beteta 2006; Klasen 2006; Klasen and Schüler 2011; Davis 2016). For academic work to repeat these conceptualizations (via data scraping or indexing) risks creating an echo chamber. It also contravenes feminist principles regarding the need to reflect the experiences and interests of women without universalizing their experiences (Runyan and Peterson 2013). Queer, postcolonial, and intersectional frameworks would all suggest the need to reflect upon the context-specific meaning of underlying concepts like gender inclusion, equality, and security.

There is compelling evidence that some indices and scales, impacted by the these institutional concerns and biases yield results of questionable validity and reliability. As an example, I take a cohort approach to comparing a variety of scales and indices that purport to measure outcomes related to the security and empowerment of women. If measures of the same underlying concepts are valid and reliable, they should group countries along similar ranks and/or into similar cohorts. Table 2.1 presents data related to the United States as assessed by seven of these indicators, drawn from institutional sources and academic data projects. These data are presented alongside information about the rank of the United States compared to other countries (where applicable)[15] and some of the country's near peers as identified by these measures.

The data in Table 2.1 make clear that there are vastly different outcomes among different scales and indices purporting to measure the same or similar phenomena. Only one of these measures, the GIWPS/PRIO Index, ranks the United States highly, alongside other consolidated Western liberal

Table 2.1: Comparing gender security and inclusion scales and indices: scores for the United States (2014–2020)

	Indicator	Year reported	Score (including rank/scale)	Comparable countries
Indicators of inclusion	WomanStats Multivariate Scale 5 (Government Framework for Gender Equality)	2015	5 (scaled 0–7)	16 states, including: Israel, North Korea, Oman, Saudi Arabia, Singapore
	Hill-Karim Scale 1 (Inclusion)	2014	0.833	Croatia, Oman, Poland, Tunisia, Uruguay
Combined indicators (inclusion and security)	Gender Inequality Index	2019	0.204 (46 of 162)	Bulgaria, Bahrain, Moldova, Kazakhstan, Slovakia
	Global Gender Gap Index	2020	0.724 (53 of 153)	Luxembourg, Cape Verde, Mozambique, Singapore, Romania
	GIWPS/PRIO Index (Aggregate)	2017	0.810 (27 of 176)	Croatia, Estonia, France, Ireland, Portugal
Indicators of gendered security	WomanStats Multivariate Scale 1 (Physical Security of Women)	2019	3 (scaled 0–4)	62 states, including: China, Cuba, Israel, Singapore, Uruguay
	Hill-Karim Scale 2 (Security of Women)	2014	1.039	Cuba, Georgia, Montenegro, Vietnam

Source: Hudson et al (2014b); GIWPS/PRIO (2018); Karim and Hill (2018); UNDP (2020); World Economic Forum (2020)

democracies. Several indicators suggest that the degree of gender inclusion and security in the United States most closely resembles that of Eastern and/or Southern European countries. On still other rankings, the United States is placed in the bottom tier of countries, alongside some of the world's most authoritarian regimes. While deeper explorations of the relationship between gender, democracy, and authoritarianism are beyond the scope of this book, it suffices to say that these are disparate results. Collectively, these outcomes suggest a low degree of consensus and/or reliability.

Two of these measures in particular stand out as aberrant. The first is the GIWPS/PRIO Index, on which the United States performs highly. A closer examination of the methodology behind the creation of this index shows that the aggregate index (which combines sub-indices on Inclusion, Justice, and Security) places a strong emphasis on indicators associated with economic development. The 'Inclusion' sub-index in particular incorporates measures of cell phone use, education, employment, and financial inclusion (defined as the percentage of women over the age of 15 who report having a bank account or using a mobile money service) (GIWPS/PRIO 2018: 13). As discussed in Chapter 3, the equation of mobile phone use with empowerment is problematic in and of itself. Beyond this, only the final measure in the Inclusion category – parliamentary representation – is not to some extent a proxy for a country's level of economic development.

The other notably aberrant score is the WomanStats Multivariate Scale 5 on Government Framework for Gender Equality. This indicator is impacted by a variety of issues, both conceptual and mathematical. The measure is scaled 0–7, but effectively maps onto four potential outcomes, per the WomanStats codebook. These are grouped as follows:

- 0–1: Strong policies across all three dimensions.
- 2–3: Strong policies exist on most, but not all, dimensions.
- 4–5: Gender equality policies may exist but are inadequate on more than one dimension.
- 6–7: No or very weak policies on gender equality across all three dimensions. (WomanStats nd)

Additionally, the codebook indicates that the scale is a composite of three specific indicators: These are: (1) legal definition of gender equality; (2) existence of a gender equality action plan; and (3) commitment to the Convention on the Elimination of All Forms of Discrimination Against Women (CEDAW). While language in the codebook seems to suggest that these indicators are considered co-equal in the resultant scale, in fact the computation of this measure as a simple additive scale means that CEDAW ratification (which is awarded a maximum of three points) counts more heavily than either constitutional guarantees (two points) or national action plans for gender equality (two points). This would seem to be a conceptual mismatch. As the measure purports to be primarily a measurement of the strength of a state's domestic legal framework, one should think factors that correspond to binding national legislation should be weighted as least as heavily (if not more so) as adherence to the international treaty.

The United States thus quickly falls to the lower levels of this indicator for several reasons. First, the country has failed to ratify CEDAW. Although the United States signed the convention in 1980, it was never ratified by the Senate – a legal distinction specific to the US legal process. As such, the United States is considered to rank 'below' other countries that ratified CEDAW – even where those states ratified CEDAW with reservations. Several state parties to CEDAW have been accused of ratifying the document while including reservations that contravene the designated core provisions of the document. In other words, although a number of ratifying countries did so specifying their intent to pick and choose among what provisions of the treaty to follow, by the mere act of ratifying they are considered to have 'committed' to the document and, by extension, to have a stronger framework for gender equality.

Per this measure, the United States also falls short on its legal definition of gender equality[16] insofar as the US Constitution lacks a specific discussion of gender equality. Here, too, the definitions become thorny. While the failure to pass an Equal Rights Amendment (ERA) to the Constitution is a long-standing issue raised by feminist advocates, the application of the Constitution's 14th Amendment as a bar to discrimination based on gender has been recognized by the Supreme Court since the 1970s. It is entirely fair to point out, as advocates for the ERA have, that judicial interpretations are subject to change (ERA Education Project 2013).[17] Still, the fact remains that this complicates the simple dichotomization of whether the United States does or does not have a constitutional guarantee of gender equality.

While this analysis certainly does not argue there are grounds to place the United States at the top of this or any other measure of gender equality, it does show that there are conceptual and context-specific reasons why this measure produces an aberrant outcome compared to other, similar attempts at measuring the underlying concept of gender equality and/or political inclusion. These context-specific issues also impact countries other than the United States. The over-weighting of CEDAW ratification compared to other component indicators on the scale hurts the overall score of some countries, including Taiwan and Kosovo, whose recognition in the international community is contested. It also, as already noted, rewards countries who ratified CEDAW while objecting to core provisions of the treaty. The UN Committee on the Elimination of Discrimination against

Women has noted that CEDAW Articles 2 and 16 should be regarded as core articles of the treaty, and that no country should be allowed to enter reservations to these articles (UN/UN Women 2009). CEDAW Article 2 deals with imperatives related to the implementation of national law and policy related to gender equality, while Article 16 deals with marital issues including the imperative to establish a minimum age for marriage, freedom of choice in marriage partners, family planning access, and communal ownership of property. Again, arguably, a measurement of Government Framework for Gender Equality should not reward governments for ratifying a treaty when they have objected to the specific articles most relevant to guaranteeing that framework. A total of 32 countries have current reservations to one or both of these articles indicating their intent not to comply with these measures in full (UN/UN Women 2009). What if Multivariate Scale 5 of WomanStats was reconceptualized to consider ratification with reservations to one or more core articles of the treaty akin to non-ratification?

Table 2.2 compares the original multivariate scale to a reimagined version that incorporates three changes. First, the three component indicators (constitutional-level guarantees, CEDAW ratification, and existence of a national plan for gender equality) are now treated as co-equal. Scores on each indicator have been weighted to compensate for the fact that they were coded according to different scales. Additionally, scores for CEDAW ratification were re-coded for any state that entered reservations to Article 2 or 16 of CEDAW, in whole or in part. Entering reservations related to these core articles is now considered akin to non-ratification. Finally, because the scores are now weighted rather than simply totalled, I re-scaled the score from zero to one. Effectively, the resulting score now measures the deviance from what the original authors considered an ideal framework, with 0 meaning a country has attained all elements of the ideal framework and 1 indicating a complete failure to meet the standard.

Observers will note that the top of the scale has changed fairly little. The most notable changes impact a few specific countries. This includes Taiwan and Kosovo, each of which now fare better in the overall ranking, as well as Somalia – which incorporated a constitutional guarantee of gender equality in its 2012 constitution but has not ratified CEDAW. The United States remains fairly low ranked, appearing in the second-lowest decile of states, but it is accompanied in this cohort by several states who ratified CEDAW with objectionable reservations. Syria, which ratified CEDAW with objections to Articles 2 and 16, is now coded as having the absence of any meaningful framework for gender equality. This is just one of many possible reimaginings of this concept. However, I do believe this exercise illustrates the power that subjective coding choices can have in shaping indices and, by extension, related discourse on gender and security.

Table 2.2: WomanStats Scale 5 versus the author's revised measure

Country	Multivariate Scale 5	Revised scale
Afghanistan	2.00	0.34
Albania	1.00	0.11
Algeria	5.00	0.84
Angola	4.00	0.62
Argentina	4.00	0.56
Armenia	0.00	0.00
Australia	3.00	0.39
Austria	2.00	0.28
Azerbaijan	1.00	0.17
Bahamas	4.00	0.67
Bahrain	4.00	0.67
Bangladesh	4.00	0.67
Barbados	1.00	0.17
Belarus	0.00	0.00
Belgium	1.00	0.17
Belize	3.00	0.39
Benin	3.00	0.51
Bhutan	1.00	0.11
Bolivia	0.00	0.00
Bosnia-Herzegovina	0.00	0.00
Botswana	3.00	0.51
Brazil	3.00	0.39
Brunei	4.00	0.56
Bulgaria	2.00	0.34
Burkina Faso	2.00	0.34
Burma/Myanmar	4.00	0.56
Burundi	1.00	0.17
Cambodia	0.00	0.00
Cameroon	1.00	0.17
Canada	1.00	0.17
Cape Verde	0.00	0.00
Central African Rep	3.00	0.45
Chad	3.00	0.51
Chile	3.00	0.39

Table 2.2: WomanStats Scale 5 versus the author's revised measure (continued)

Country	Multivariate Scale 5	Revised scale
China	2.00	0.22
Colombia	2.00	0.22
Comoros	2.00	0.28
Congo	1.00	0.17
Costa Rica	2.00	0.34
Cote D'Ivoire	2.00	0.34
Croatia	0.00	0.00
Cuba	3.00	0.39
Cyprus	2.00	0.22
Czech Republic	3.00	0.39
DR Congo	4.00	0.62
Denmark	0.00	0.00
Djibouti	4.00	0.62
Dominican Republic	2.00	0.22
East Timor	3.00	0.51
Ecuador	1.00	0.17
Egypt	4.00	0.67
El Salvador	3.00	0.39
Equatorial Guinea	1.00	0.17
Eritrea	3.00	0.45
Estonia	2.00	0.28
Ethiopia	5.00	0.73
Fiji	3.00	0.39
Finland	0.00	0.00
France	3.00	0.50
Gabon	1.00	0.17
Gambia	1.00	0.11
Georgia	0.00	0.00
Germany	1.00	0.17
Ghana	2.00	0.34
Greece	1.00	0.17
Guatemala	2.00	0.34
Guinea	2.00	0.28
Guinea-Bissau	1.00	0.17

(continued)

Table 2.2: WomanStats Scale 5 versus the author's revised measure (continued)

Country	Multivariate Scale 5	Revised scale
Guyana	2.00	0.28
Haiti	2.00	0.28
Honduras	2.00	0.28
Hungary	0.00	0.00
Iceland	0.00	0.00
India	5.00	0.73
Indonesia	5.00	0.73
Iran	6.00	0.84
Iraq	5.00	0.84
Ireland	2.00	0.33
Israel	5.00	0.84
Italy	4.00	0.56
Jamaica	3.00	0.39
Japan	1.00	0.11
Jordan	4.00	0.67
Kazakhstan	2.00	0.34
Kenya	4.00	0.62
Kosovo	4.00	0.50
Kuwait	5.00	0.84
Kyrgyzstan	0.00	0.00
Laos	3.00	0.45
Latvia	2.00	0.28
Lebanon	4.00	0.67
Lesotho	5.00	0.84
Liberia	3.00	0.51
Libya	6.00	1.00
Lithuania	0.00	0.00
Luxembourg	1.00	0.50
Macedonia	0.00	0.00
Madagascar	1.00	0.17
Malawi	2.00	0.34
Malaysia	5.00	0.84
Maldives	4.00	0.67
Mali	2.00	0.34
Malta	3.00	0.50

Table 2.2: WomanStats Scale 5 versus the author's revised measure (continued)

Country	Multivariate Scale 5	Revised scale
Mauritania	5.00	0.73
Mauritius	5.00	0.84
Mexico	0.00	0.00
Moldova	0.00	0.00
Mongolia	0.00	0.00
Montenegro	0.00	0.00
Morocco	4.00	0.67
Mozambique	2.00	0.34
Namibia	3.00	0.51
Nepal	1.00	0.17
Netherlands	0.00	0.00
New Zealand	3.00	0.50
Nicaragua	3.00	0.45
Niger	4.00	0.67
Nigeria	3.00	0.51
North Korea	5.00	0.83
Norway	0.00	0.00
Oman	5.00	0.84
Pakistan	6.00	0.89
Palestine	4.00	0.62
Panama	2.00	0.34
Papua New Guinea	3.00	0.45
Paraguay	0.00	0.00
Peru	1.00	0.17
Philippines	0.00	0.00
Poland	1.00	0.17
Portugal	0.00	0.00
Qatar	5.00	0.73
Romania	0.00	0.00
Russia	3.00	0.50
Rwanda	2.00	0.34
Saudi Arabia	5.00	0.73
Senegal	1.00	0.17
Serbia	0.00	0.00

(continued)

Table 2.2: WomanStats Scale 5 versus the author's revised measure (continued)

Country	Multivariate Scale 5	Revised scale
Sierra Leone	2.00	0.34
Singapore	5.00	0.84
Slovakia	0.00	0.00
Slovenia	1.00	0.17
Solomon Islands	0.00	0.00
Somalia	3.00	0.33
South Africa	3.00	0.51
South Korea	4.00	0.67
South Sudan	4.00	0.67
Spain	2.00	0.22
Sri Lanka	3.00	0.51
Sudan	7.00	1.00
Suriname	3.00	0.45
Swaziland	3.00	0.45
Sweden	0.00	0.00
Switzerland	2.00	0.33
Syria	6.00	1.00
Taiwan	4.00	0.50
Tajikistan	3.00	0.39
Tanzania	3.00	0.51
Thailand	2.00	0.33
Togo	3.00	0.45
Trinidad/Tobago	4.00	0.56
Tunisia	4.00	0.67
Turkey	3.00	0.39
Turkmenistan	1.00	0.17
Uganda	3.00	0.45
Ukraine	0.00	0.00
United Arab Emirates	4.00	0.67
United Kingdom	2.00	0.33
United States	5.00	0.67
Uruguay	1.00	0.17
Uzbekistan	3.00	0.45
Vanuatu	1.00	0.17
Venezuela	3.00	0.39

Table 2.2: WomanStats Scale 5 versus the author's revised measure (continued)

Country	Multivariate Scale 5	Revised scale
Vietnam	2.00	0.22
Yemen	4.00	0.56
Zambia	2.00	0.34
Zimbabwe	3.00	0.45

There are additional mathematical and conceptual issues to consider in measurements related to the status of women. Returning to the best practices adopted by other social and behavioural sciences, guidance generally cautions against the inclusion of binary measures or ordinal/categorical measures with a small number of categories in scales and measurements designed to represent latent variables (Boateng et al 2018; Watkins 2018). This is because low variability on such measures limits reliability. Similar to Multivariate Scale 5, as discussed, several other scales in the WomanStats project include one or more dichotomous or trichotomous measures. The Karim-Hill scales likewise incorporates various dichotomous variables. This question of what underlying indicators to include in an index or scale poses a mathematical issue, but also calls back to the discussion of elite bias. As D'Ignazio and Klein (2020) note, data production is an expensive endeavour. This tends to mean that big data projects often originate with elite institutions, like international organizations and research universities located in the Global North. Measurements produced by international institutions including UN agencies have been subject to the critique that they focus disproportionately on measures relevant to the 'most educated and economically advantaged' segments of the female population (Charmes and Wieringa 2003; Beteta 2006; Klasen 2006; Klasen and Schüler 2011). Feminist scholars and practitioners should be conscious of the danger of reproducing these biases. Whether the completion of a master's- or doctoral-level degree should be considered a necessary indicator of women's inclusion in a society (as it is in some of the indices analysed earlier) can be questioned.[18] Tertiary educational attainment also emerges as a conceptual problem in different parts of the world, for distinct reasons. In developed countries, for example, gender imbalances in higher education enrolment generally favour women. On average, men represent 45 per cent of the tertiary education population across Organization for Economic Co-operation and Development (OECD) countries (Stoet and Geary 2020). While some have argued that this may point to important male deficits, it also highlights how educational opportunity is limited in complex and gendered ways. In a Pew Research survey of adults in the United States, men were more likely than women to say they did not complete a four-year college degree because they didn't want one or because they didn't need one to get the job they wanted (Parker 2021). This largely tracks with what we know about employment trends in the security sector, manufacturing, and vocational fields – areas that potentially lead to stable incomes, do not require a four-year college degree, and heavily favour men. At the same time, figures on women's enrolment in higher education elsewhere in the world mask ongoing inequalities with regard to what they may study and whether their degree will lead to employment. In Saudi Arabia, for example, women may enrol in higher education but are not allowed to study certain fields (including engineering and law) and few who complete a degree will ultimately enter the workforce (Alsuwaida 2016). Such examples again highlight the need to revisit and refine indicators, or at least to consider context carefully when deploying some of these measures.

How data on the status of women reflects the lived experience of women from marginalized groups is likewise a question that demands greater attention. The lack of attention to intersecting sources of discrimination impacting women had been highlighted as a shortcoming of existing cross-national data (UN Women 2018b; Rose Taylor 2020). Of the metrics addressed in Table 2.1, none include measures specifically designed to capture the experiences of women from different racial/ethnic groups, the disabled, or members of the LGBTQI+ community. This, despite the fact that some indicators are clearly shaped by intersectional power dynamics. For example, GIWPS notes in its report on the US Index for Women, Peace, and Security that maternal mortality statistics for US states are closely tied to issues of racial discrimination, disproportionately impacting Black, Hispanic, and indigenous women (GIWPS 2020). Feminist approaches to international relations generally caution against universalism – that is, the practice of envisioning women in a unitary way, subject to the same sources of oppression and likely to be helped by the same policy solutions (Runyan and Peterson 2013). Black feminist thought similarly asks that we see intersecting forms of discrimination as something both distinct from and beyond either race-based or gender-based discrimination (Crenshaw 1989, 1990). Thus, from an ethical standpoint, developing metrics that better acknowledge or capture the operation of intersectionality should be a moral imperative.

This analysis has explored existing quantitative data sources on gender and security in a highly critical way. In workshopping this analysis prior to publication, I received two critiques that are worth addressing.[19] The first is that data on gender and security, in its current state, is similar to data on other social science concepts for which we see a variety of scales and measures. That is to say, the analytical landscape for gender and security is not dissimilar to what we see with, for example, scales purporting to measure democracies or datasets tracking battle deaths. In each case, distinctions in conceptualization and operationalization lead to multiple data projects that can yield varying results. This may to some extent be inevitable given the nature of social science and the incentive structures of a discipline like international relations, where the production of newer and/or bigger data is often rewarded with publication in high-impact journals.[20] That being said, I do believe that the ontological and epistemological orientation of feminist research should encourage us to push beyond conventional approaches to data. Rather than seeking to produce gender data that conforms to the norms of mainstream quantitative international relations and to the ethos of 'big data', should we not leverage the principles of feminist research to push the discipline as a whole towards a higher standard? In particular, as discussed in Chapter 1, should we not consider the feminist obligation to create richer depictions of lived experience and to disrupt the power relationships inherent in existing networks of data production?

Going along with that critique, early reviewers of this chapter encouraged me to more explicitly acknowledge how far we have come in data collection on gender and security. It is certainly my hope that nothing in this chapter will be read as an attack on the principal investigators who collect, code, or maintain the datasets I have examined. To the contrary, I believe this analysis likely speaks to what these researchers already know and/or have experienced regarding the limitations of indices and scales based on available data at the international level. To this point, arguably, many of us[21] who create data that supports quantitative analysis on questions of gender and security have justified our work – despite its limitations – on a 'proof of concept' basis. In other words, these initiatives have to date been regarded as first-generation approaches designed to prove the relevance of gender to our understanding of international security. After much research and 20–30 years of reliance on imperfect data, I suggest it may be time to take stock and to reflect on what a second generation of data might look like.

Transforming data for the next generation?

This chapter has offered an initial discussion about the emergence of big data as a technology that has impacted research, practice, and policy development related to gender and the status of women, including monitoring and assessment work conducted through governmental and intergovernmental institutions.

The discussions in this chapter note several shortcomings with current analytical approaches relevant to the study of gender. First among these is the continued lack of meaningful, cross-national panel data on many gender indicators, which makes it difficult if not impossible to track changes beyond the past few decades. A feminist ethos would further encourage us to explore who is rendered silent in the data, like populations outside the gender binary and women from marginalized communities. The lack of comparative data on the status of men and boys further introduces conceptual questions about the extent to which current data efforts render privilege invisible. It can likewise cause us to ask whether we might be ignoring areas where men and boys are disadvantaged by rigid systems of gender. All of this is to say that we cannot simply regard ever-bigger data collection efforts as a panacea. In the second generation of quantitative gender and politics research, more nuanced and refined approaches to data collection should be adopted.

This may seem like an impossibly high standard. But there are entry points for creating better, more responsible data and/or analysis; in adopting such practices, researchers working on gender issues can seek to introduce a new standard for the field at large. One strategy currently deployed in feminist IR research that may point a way to the future is the reliance on mixed-methods research. Mixed-methods work, incorporating quantitative and qualitative elements, is a mitigation strategy in common use by feminist IR researchers seeking to compensate for the imperfections of existing quantitative data (Henshaw 2021). Some data sources, like WomanStats, have facilitated the use of mixed-methods approaches by providing links to archival sources (that is, texts of laws, reports, or government documents) alongside quantitative measures. This kind of methodological pluralism within datasets may provide an example of how technology might help facilitate the emergence of richer data, not just bigger data. As technologies for data storage, processing, and retrieval have grown over time, the creation of repositories that can store documents, photos, audiovisual content, and the like have become a reality. Arguably, international relations and political science have yet to fully embrace the possibilities of mixed-methods datasets. Feminist research could have a role in changing that.

What other features might an approach to international relations informed by critical data science include? Several existing projects or programmes may offer insight, including examples drawn from partnerships with indigenous, minority racial/ethnic, and/or LGBTQI+ populations. A common theme in such projects has been the involvement of grassroots organizations or community members in data project design (Walter and Andersen 2013; Walter and Suina 2019; Johnson et al 2021; Guyan 2022). Such involvement can range from allowing groups/community members input through a consultation process, to allowing direct participation in survey design, to allowing these actors to shape the direction of entire data projects, mapping them onto the community's needs. In the interests of pursuing inclusive data work, projects have taught data literacy or data analysis skills directly to members of impacted communities (Walter and Suina 2019; Johnson et al 2021). In such cases, paying learners a fair wage or a living wage can be important to retention and to acknowledging their labour (D'Ignazio and Klein 2020; Johnson et al 2021).

Indigenous data projects have also raised the importance of data sovereignty. Historically, the extraction of data from indigenous communities has led to exploitation, harm, and surveillance.[22] The ability to retain some form of ownership over their community's data is considered important, especially when dealing with sensitive matters like health (FNIGC 2016; Lovett 2016; Walter and Suina 2019). These concerns over ownership and control may be at odds with norms in the academic community, especially with regard to transparency and data sharing. This may be a consideration not only for the architects of inclusive data projects related to international relations and/or gender, but also for the editors and publishers of academic work that might publish resulting projects. To address this, some initiatives inspired by critical data science principles have also included educational outreach to academic institutions, government agencies, and/or private actors, seeking to educate them about why data sovereignty and inclusive design matters (Walter and Suina 2019).

Another provocative principle that emerges from critical perspectives on data work is to consider when new data collection efforts are even necessary. Guyan (2022), drawing on the Yogyakarta Principles (a set of human-rights based principles on sexual orientation and gender identity, established by an expert panel in 2006 and updated in 2017), points out that collecting data from vulnerable communities in high-risk situations may sometimes cause more harm than good. In these situations, researchers might consider whether the use of existing data is sufficient and more ethical.

Similarly, major data collection initiatives related to gender or the status of women might consider implementing new accountability measures, like engaging in institutional ethnography (Walby and Anaïs 2015). While it is currently the norm in quantitative political science research to introduce transparency into the coding process – for example, by reporting intercoder reliability or using codebooks to address difficult coding choices – institutional ethnography would go a step further, allowing external parties to observe data work or speak directly with those involved in data production. Given that the rote work of data production in many academic collection efforts (that is, review and coding of texts) is performed disproportionately by graduate or undergraduate students, allowing them an opportunity to discuss their experiences and choices outside of their institutional power relationships may offer richer insights than what we get from a simple intercoder reliability score.

Initiatives designed to collect historical and forensic data are another idea that could offer a more complete picture of where we are at and where we could be going. Such efforts would minimize the impact of left-censored data, which obscures experiences of gendered insecurity prior to the arrival of institutional gender mainstreaming mandates. While collecting these data would undoubtedly be easier for some indicators than others, it is worth pointing out that we have a valuable source for knowledge about the status of women over the past several decades available to us, which is the women themselves who lived through earlier time periods. Here again is an area where responsible consultation and cooperation with civil society could lead to richer and more comprehensive outcomes. UN Women (2018b) has discussed the possibilities for crowdsourcing, managed responsibly, as a means of data collection. Should researchers wish to seriously consider the prospects for such an approach, they may want to think about pairing their work with the type of capacity-building approaches discussed in this chapter in order to ensure that communities are informed and have some ownership over their data. They may also want to think about when/how it is appropriate to compensate those engaged in crowdsourcing for their labour. Scholarship from the digital humanities, where crowdsourcing and participatory methods been deployed in novel ways – including in the creation and curation of multimedia archives, might provide useful insights into how to proceed (Carletti et al 2013; Estermann 2014; Jansson 2020). Though there are certainly challenges involved in such approaches, cross-disciplinary learning or even partnership may help avoid some pitfalls while yielding richer data.

Conclusion

This chapter has sought to engage an understanding of quantification and the production of 'big data' as a gendered technology. It argues that the development of a big data ethos in academia, commerce, and government has combined with institutional gender mainstreaming initiatives to produce an environment that valorizes the quantitative analysis of gender issues without adequately reflecting on ethical, practical, and methodological questions. In addressing the shortcomings associated with the current data climate, the analysis offers some suggestions for strategies to mitigate the biases of imperfect data and to move towards the production of improved, second-generation approaches. From a methodological standpoint, the remainder of this volume explores questions about gender, technology, and security while deploying some of the strategies discussed in this chapter. Readers will note that, while making reference to relevant statistics (particularly in Chapter 3), this is not the only (or the primary) method of analysis I employ. A mixed-methods approach that incorporates case study, content analysis, and interviews is adopted throughout this work. To the extent that quantitative data supports this inquiry, it fits into what data scientists might call the realm of exploration or discovery – that is, it acknowledges quantitative data while positioning it as the beginning and not an end point to knowledge formation. This strategy sees quantitative data as an invitation to further interaction with measures, concepts, and trends, rather than as a declarative statement of truth. Long-term, it is my hope that researchers can continue the conversation about how to create richer frameworks for measurement, monitoring, and evaluation related to gender and security. In the meantime, I believe that mixed-methods inquiry is perhaps the best mitigation strategy in an imperfect data environment.

3

Addressing the Digital Gender Gap

Having discussed the various reasons to be critical of both big data and of the available quantitative data on gender and security, I proceed to an overview of the gender gap in technology access. This section begins by presenting some of the available knowledge on gender gaps in technology development, proceeds to discuss gender gaps in technology use and how these can be contextualized within research on FSS, and applies these insights to a case study of regional issues in gender and technology in selected South Asian countries.

The analysis broadly makes the case that gendered concerns about online security should be taken more seriously in discussions about the digital gender gap, which tend to parse the issue through development-focused frameworks. It further calls for reflection upon the roles that various actors – including developers, multinational corporations, and governments – may play in addressing these issues. Finally, the analysis examines the potential role of civil society, which is already calling attention to problems related to inequality (including gender inequality) and digital rights in some parts of the world. In all, I argue that action on the digital gender gap must take into account the extent to which the issue is a question of security, as well as development. Given the range of security and safety issues that women face online (matters discussed in greater detail in the following section of the book), an ethical approach to bridging the gendered digital divide must work to create a safer and more inclusive digital environment.

Gender inequality in technology development

In terms of technology development and representation in the profession, sources universally agree that women are underrepresented. Additionally, there is compelling evidence that this underrepresentation results in androcentric outcomes, producing technology that at best fails to serve women and, at worst, may actively cause harm.

Drawing on statistics from the US Bureau of Labor Statistics and the American Association of University Women, D'Ignazio and Klein (2020) estimate that women make up 26 per cent of technology professionals[1] working in the United States. This number has actually declined over time, with the number of women receiving degrees in computer science peaking in the mid-1980s at 37 per cent. Within certain sub-categories of the tech industry, the lack of women becomes more pronounced. Women comprise just 10–15 per cent of researchers in the area of artificial intelligence, 15–23 per cent of tech professionals at major social media companies, and 23 per cent of employees at cryptocurrency or blockchain companies[2] (Williams 2014; Hao 2018; Brand 2019; D'Ignazio and Klein 2020). Of technology companies founded between 2012 and 2018, just 17.7 per cent had a female founder (Hao 2018).

Underrepresentation is intersectional, too. Just 12 per cent of women in the field identify as Black or Latina (D'Ignazio and Klein 2020). In terms of age, it is estimated that 50 per cent of women working in the tech sector leave the sector by the age of 35 (Saujani 2021). This is likely due to the various ways in which women experience the workplace as a hostile or unwelcoming environment. Some women simply view their prospects for advancement as unlikely, given the absence of women at higher levels of their organizations. High rates of sexual harassment and discrimination are another issue, with up to 40 per cent of women indicating that they experienced gender-based harassment or discrimination during the hiring process (Saujani 2021).

The lack of family-friendly policies in the sector further damage women's prospects for advancement. Criado-Perez (2019) discusses the example of Google, which failed to offer accommodations like preferred parking for pregnant women until a top female executive became pregnant. Initial data on changes to the labour force during COVID-19 further suggests that women find working in technology incompatible with care work demands. During the pandemic, women were estimated to be leaving the sector at a rate four times that of men (Saujani 2021). Anecdotally, too, there is evidence that women feel disadvantaged by a corporate culture – especially at big technology companies – which expects employees to be constantly available and constantly engaged with tech. Saujani (2021) discussed one example at Microsoft, where male interviewers stated a reluctance to hire a female interviewee because she indicated she did not engage with technology in her free time, instead preferring other hobbies. Commentators argue that the increasing use of artificial intelligence (AI)-assisted hiring methods – which often rely on biased or arbitrary mechanisms – is likely to only compound these issues. Amazon, for example, was pressured to abandon the use of one AI recruiting tool after research revealed that it penalized resumes containing the word 'women's' including women's colleges or women's groups (Benjamin 2019; D'Ignazio and Klein 2020). A review of AI-based interviewing technology has demonstrated that some programs appear to penalize users with long or loose hair, while rewarding those who have a background indicative of a traditional office set-up (Harlan and Schnuck 2021). Each of these issues raise the potential for implicit gender bias; while women (including women of colour) seem quite likely to be disproportionately disadvantaged by penalties for long or 'messy' hair, data collected during the COVID-19 pandemic suggested that men were 60 per cent more likely than women to work from home using a dedicated office space. Women were more likely to work in the living room, a bedroom, or at the kitchen table – rendering them more likely to be penalized based on AI perceptions of their workspaces (Ponder 2020).

The outcomes of this gender imbalance in technology development are clear – they produce technology that fails to serve women, while introducing new sources of insecurity and inequality. As discussed in greater detail in this chapter and in Chapter 4, particular technologies have been weaponized in gender-specific ways by individuals with extremist views (Amnesty International 2018; Burton et al 2020; Krook 2020; Hao 2021; Jankowicz et al 2021). The rising use of technology to enable domestic violence is another concern, with domestic violence programmes reporting that victims are frequently subject to online harassment and stalking via social media (Women's Media Center nd; Freed et al 2017, 2018; Woodlock 2017). The harms are often not only gender-based, but intersectional. Women from ethnic/racial or religious minorities, the disabled, and members of the LGBTQI+ community are disproportionately likely to be the targets of violence *and* may experience specific forms of violence (Women's Media Center nd; Amnesty International 2018; Krook 2020; Jankowicz et al 2021). Abusers rely on the fact that victims, law enforcement, and even technology companies lack the awareness or capacity to respond to such abuse. Studies have shown that content moderators working for technology companies are often unaware of culturally specific or group-specific forms of harassment including language and imagery, which complicates response to user complaints (Sambasivan et al 2019; Jankowicz et al 2021).

Gender patterns in engagement with technology: mobile phone use and the Internet

This being the case, one can argue that there are ample reasons why women may choose not to engage with technology, even where it is available to them. The tendency of women to self-censor or remove themselves from social media platforms entirely as a result of abuse and harassment is well-established (Freed et al 2017, 2018; Amnesty International 2018; Sambasivan et al 2019; Jankowicz et al 2021). Yet, work on gender and international development tends to valorize interaction with technology as a net good for women and a proxy for gender equality, security, or empowerment,[3] at times responding with puzzlement to the persistence of these gaps. The failure to see how specifically gendered insecurities impact adoption, usage, and trust in technology speaks to a failure to see how development and security are interrelated, a critique invoked by feminist researchers in international relations (Madhok and Rai 2012; True 2012; Elias and Rai 2015; Stern 2017).

This tendency to silo questions about the digital gender divide within the work of development agencies has resulted in research and analysis that centres discussions of inequality on factors like affordability, lack of infrastructure, education, 'technophobia', and a lack of free time, with the women's disproportionate tendency to experience online violence and harassment considered a secondary concern (where it is considered at all) (Human Rights Centre nd; OECD 2018; ITU 2019). The messaging behind some reports from development agencies is distinctly neoliberal, insofar as it suggests:

1. More engagement with technology is a normative 'good', contributing to overall societal development and the generation of wealth.
2. Women are at least partially at fault in their own technological marginalization insofar as they fail to see technology as beneficial or to educate themselves sufficiently about emergent technologies.
3. These issues can be overcome by greater investments in affordability, infrastructure, and education.

As a result, policy recommendations place a heavy emphasis on changing women's mindsets and behaviours, without placing corresponding focus on male behaviours, online misogyny, or the ways in which the male-dominated technology landscape actually *has* made technology less relevant for women (Chemaly 2016; Criado-Perez 2019).

We can further understand these issues by examining usage data. Data most relevant to the technologies discussed in this volume includes access to cellular phones, the Internet, and social media. Table 3.1 shows selected data from the 4th edition of the Inclusive Internet Index (3i Index) (Economist Intelligence Unit/Facebook 2020). This data covers technology access in 100 countries, gathering data with the assistance of polling firms and from some international organizations, like the International Telecommunication Union (ITU). These data confirm that there is an ongoing gender gap in technology access, disadvantaging women. However, the story appears somewhat different with relation to mobile phone usage and Internet access. Gender gaps in mobile phone usage on a global level have fallen to about 6.3 per cent. The 3i Index's year-over-year change statistics should be regarded with caution, given that the index sampled a somewhat different set of countries between 2019 and 2020, however, the reported decline in the gender gap seems to align with numbers reported by other sources – though

Table 3.1: Technology use by gender (2020, as percentage of corresponding population)

Indicator	Value	Year-on-year change
Female mobile phone users	80.8	+1.7
Male mobile phone users	85.7	+1
Female Internet users	58.8	+5
Male Internet users	64.7	+4.8
Gender gap: mobile phone usage	6.3	-1
Gender gap: Internet access	12.3	-4.1

Source: Economist Intelligence Unit/Facebook (2020)

some note that efforts to close the gap appear to be slowing (GIWPS/PRIO 2018: 4; GSMA 2020).

The 3i Index further reports that, as of 2020, 28 of the 100 countries it measured had either eliminated the gender gap entirely or had tilted the gender gap slightly in favour of more women having technology access than men. There was no regionally specific pattern among those countries where a gender gap was eliminated. Both developed countries (Denmark, Spain, the UK) and developing countries (Mexico, Nicaragua, South Africa) reported having closed the gap. There are, however, regional patterns among those countries where substantial gaps persist. Most of the bottom ten is comprised of sub-Saharan African (SSA) states (Burkina Faso, Burundi, Ethiopia, Liberia, Madagascar, Rwanda). These are accompanied by Uzbekistan and four South Asian countries: Bangladesh, India, Pakistan, and Sri Lanka. Pakistan has the largest gender gap, at 68.2 per cent.

The story for Internet access is somewhat different. Percentagewise, the gender gap in Internet access remains about twice as large as the gap in mobile phone use. While this too shows a trend towards narrowing the divide, just 20 countries report reversing or closing this gap. Again, at the bottom of the list there is a clustering of SSA states (Burkina Faso, Burundi, Liberia, Malawi, Sudan, Tanzania) and South Asian countries (India, Pakistan, Bangladesh). Myanmar, a country where Freedom House notes that 'gender-based disparities in access are generally ignored by the government', rounds out the bottom nine countries (Freedom House 2020b).

These numbers demonstrate that mobile phone access is not necessarily a proxy for Internet access. Other sources have reported that women – especially in the developing world – are more likely to own so-called 'feature phones', that is, cellular phones that lack access to the Internet (OECD 2018; GSMA 2020). While such phones still have a variety of important applications, including calling, texting, and compatibility with text-based services like mobile payment systems, they do not offer the full benefits associated with smartphone use including Internet access. The Global System for Mobile Communications Association (GSMA) (2020) reports that women are on average about 20 per cent less likely than men to own a smartphone. Interestingly, though, even where women do own a smartphone, they still appear less likely than men to use it for regular Internet access. Although GSMA reports that awareness of mobile Internet is comparable for male and female smartphone users, awareness among women is growing more quickly than adoption (GSMA 2020: 32). Even where women own a smartphone, they are 18 per cent less likely to use it to access the Internet on a regular basis (OECD 2018).

Factors like infrastructure and affordability – already cited – do not necessarily explain why women fail to adopt this technology when the means to do so is already in their hands. We must examine other causes, and here the relationship between security and technology becomes clearer. In countries surveyed by GSMA, 'safety and security' and 'relevance' were cited by both men and women as two of the top four barriers to accessing mobile Internet, alongside skill level and affordability. At the global level, these rankings were similar for both men and women. However, women in African countries were more likely than men to cite safety/security concerns, while in Asian countries women reported disapproval from their family – also a security concern – as the number 4 barrier to access (GSMA 2020: 33).[4] The World Wide Web Foundation's Report Cards for gender and Internet access ranked the ten countries it examined[5] a collective 3/10 for Online Safety. Their assessment noted that privacy laws and laws ensuring the protection of interpersonal communication were lacking in these countries, and that courts and law enforcement agencies showed a generally low likelihood of effective response to reports of gender-based violence online (World Wide Web Foundation 2020b). It is worth noting also that the perceived relevance of mobile Internet impacted the likelihood of women using this service. While GSMA data suggests this is on the decline as a barrier to access, the World Wide Web Foundation rated sampled countries as a 4/10 for providing online services relevant to women (GSMA 2020; World Wide Web Foundation 2020b). They suggested that easier access to mobile financial services and health information (especially sexual and reproductive health) could be of importance to female users (World Wide Web Foundation 2020b).

The Internet according to women: experiencing the continuum of online violence

Feminist scholarship encourages us to contextualize harms perpetrated in the digital space within the larger continuum of violence against women (Feminism and Nonviolence Study Group 1983; Cockburn 2017). A full view of this field encourages us to see online violence not merely as a 'new' form of violence, but as a new mechanism for the delivery of the same misogynistic harms directed at women who entered public debates a century or more ago (Krook 2020). In terms of the escalation of violence, the continuum model asks us to see gendered violence not only during what MacKenzie (2010) calls 'security flashes' – moments of immediate and severe crisis – but also in its everyday forms like domestic violence or sexual harassment. Through a feminist lens, therefore, gender-based violence online can alternately be read as extremist and as so deeply normalized as to be overlooked in many situations.

Studies of women active online have found that harassment has become routine for many. Furthermore, gendered harassment is a global phenomenon. In surveys, about one-third of US women and one in five British and Canadian women say they have experienced online harassment (Amnesty International 2018; UN Women 2020). In South Asia, one study found that 72 per cent of women had experienced online abuse (Sambasivan et al 2019). A UN report estimates that overall, nearly one-quarter of all women have been abused online while 10 per cent of girls had experienced some form of online or technology-facilitated abuse before the age of 15 (Šimonovic 2018). Women who are public figures – a category that includes women office-holders, activists, and journalists – experience high rates of online abuse worldwide (Krook 2020). The Women's Media Center argues that not only the experience but the *nature* of online abuse is gendered, stating: 'When men face online harassment and abuse, it is first and foremost designed to embarrass or shame them. When women are targeted, the abuse is more likely to be gendered, sustained, sexualized and linked to off-line violence' (Women's Media Center nd).

Examples of gendered online abuse include cyberstalking – a crime where 70 per cent of reported victims are women – and revenge porn (the nonconsensual sharing of sexual images online) – where women are at least 90 per cent of reported victims (Women's Media Center nd; Šimonovic 2018). During the COVID-19 pandemic, the rise of 'zoombombing' (the nonconsensual disruption of online meetings) has led some observers to argue that we are witnessing the emergence of a new form of online harassment that is gendered and racialized, with up to 87 per cent of reported zoombombing events including racist, sexist, or homophobic content (Burton et al 2020; UN Women 2020).

The emergence of new forms of online harassment speaks broadly to two issues in controlling online violence against women. The first is the gap between technology and enforcement capacity. Law enforcement, justice systems, and advocates are slow to adapt to emerging forms of technology-enabled abuse. One example of this is the fight against revenge porn. As of this writing, only 22 US states have developed laws criminalizing the unauthorized sharing of sexual images (Women's Media Center nd). Abuse victims and their advocates in the United States have complained that procedures for responding to abuse or obtaining orders of protection have not been adequately adapted to take new technologies into account (Freed et al 2017). A similar reaction can be observed in domestic violence response where, despite the frequent use of mobile phones, social media, and other technological tools to facilitate domestic violence, countries often lack a parallel online infrastructure to report or combat such abuse (Women's Media Center nd; Janetsky 2020). Advocates themselves say they feel ill-equipped to handle such cases, at times simply telling victims to delete their accounts or get rid of their devices in response to domestic abuse (Freed et al 2018).

A second issue is the intersectional nature of online abuse. Amnesty International's 2018 report on gender and online harassment on Twitter found that the leading risk factors for online abuse among female users were: sharing feminist content, being a public figure, and being a member of a marginalized group (Amnesty International 2018). Women of colour, disabled women, members of the LGBTQI+ community, and religious minorities are particular targets of online abuse, experiencing higher rates of abuse and, sometimes, specific forms of abuse (Šimonovic 2018). A UK-based survey found that 10 per cent of LGBTQI+ individuals surveyed reported experiencing online harassment in the past month, but with rates particularly higher for transgender or nonbinary individuals (Amnesty International 2018). Here, too, unique forms of harassment like 'deadnaming' (making reference to persons using their birth name rather than their preferred or legal name) have emerged to target transgender, nonbinary, or intersex individuals (Women's Media Center nd).

To the extent that online abuse is linked to real-world harms, countering online violence against women is imperative. While subsequent chapters will explore how extremist organizations have mobilized online threats, conversations, and ideologies, it is relevant to keep in mind how extremist violence fits in to the larger continuum of violence against women. Online abuse in general can lead to mental and emotional health issues, problems reported by the majority of female victims in some studies (Amnesty International 2018; Šimonovic 2018; Sambasivan et al 2019; UN Women 2020). The issue of domestic violence further draws attention to the ways that online harms and physical violence are related. Stalking enabled by surveillance technologies is one of the primary ways that technology is leveraged by domestic abusers (Burke et al 2011; Freed et al 2017, 2018; Matthews et al 2017; Woodlock 2017). In addition to causing psychological harm, surveillance technologies enable abusers to easily find their victims in the real world. In some cases, advocates and victims have pointed to a potential escalation from electronic abuse to physical abuse, creating a catch-22 situation. Making a break from online abuse, for example by getting rid of a corrupted device, can sometimes accelerate this escalation (Freed et al 2017).

The cumulative effect of widespread online harassment has been to limit women's participation in online conversations or to squeeze them out of the online space altogether (Amnesty International 2018; Šimonovic 2018; Sambasivan et al 2019; UN Women 2020). This carries important ramifications because not only do many women *want* to be online, they also find it important for professional reasons like networking, advocacy, and mobilization (Freed et al 2017, 2018; Amnesty International 2018; Šimonovic 2018; Di Meco 2019).[6] During the COVID-19 pandemic, the exclusion or withdrawal of women from online spaces further threatened to limit their access to information and services (UN Women 2020).

The pervasive nature of online abuse may feed gender gaps in trust of technology. Data from the World Values Survey (2017–2020)[7] shows that in 40 out of 49 countries and territories it measured, women were less likely than men to agree that: 'Science and technology are making our lives healthier, easier, and more comfortable' (Q158). In 36 of 49 countries, women were less likely than men to rate the world as 'better off' because of science and technology (Q163).

Though these questions deal with attitudes towards science and technology broadly, data from the 3i Index suggests these sentiments carry over to attitudes regarding social media and the Internet. Among the strongest negative correlates for a country's proportion of female Internet users were trust in non-government websites ($r=-0.43$), trust in social media ($r=-0.36$), and trust in online privacy ($r=-0.32$). In other words, having more women online tends to result in lower overall scores for trust in each of these areas.[8] This, again, suggests that gender differences in technology adoption speak to concerns about security and trust, not just levels of economic development. A closer look at the relationship between gendered insecurity and technology use is undertaken in the following section, drawing on a regional case study.

Technology and the security of women in South Asia

To further understand the interconnection between gendered security, technology, and development, it is worth examining trends in South Asian countries. As noted, this is one of two areas of the world where countries with the largest gender gaps in both Internet access and mobile phone access tend to cluster. Moreover, these gaps continue (and by some indicators are growing) despite significant investments in infrastructure, affordability, industry commitments to close the gender gap, and policy commitments to inclusion. I argue that the resilience of gender gaps in spite of these efforts reflects pervasive problems of online (and offline) gender-based violence that are not adequately addressed via current strategies. High-level efforts to create more technological inclusivity in the region are undercut by an increasing effort to control and surveil technology use in the name of national security, along with a blindness to the role played by masculinity in perpetuating online violence. Multinational technology companies' lack of contextual knowledge about local cultures, languages, and so on, also creates friction. At the same time, this region is not only worth studying for its deficits. South Asian countries are also offering a portrait of how civil society and citizen engagement can push back on invasive and/or de-securitizing technologies. In particular, a digital rights movement in the region is generating knowledge about intersectional inequalities and neocolonial pressures in ways that are relevant for critical scholarship.

In terms of the overall landscape and policy, Table 3.2 shows relevant statistics related to Internet access and mobile phone access in Bangladesh, India, and Pakistan. These numbers reveal significant and persistent gender gaps.

These gaps persist and, in some cases, may be growing even despite the expansion of service in the region. Bangladesh, for example, has made significant investment in technology education, with the majority of secondary and tertiary students now having access to computers (World Wide Web Foundation 2020a). India has made significant investments in improving affordability, creating opportunities for free Internet access, and offering more material in local languages (World Wide Web Foundation 2016; Freedom House 2020a; GSMA 2020). All three countries in Table 3.2 show general trends towards improved service, with both mobile phone and broadband networks showing faster download speeds over time (Economist Intelligence Unit/Facebook 2020). Policies specifically designed to promote a more inclusive Internet have been adopted in all three countries, to

Table 3.2: Technology use by gender in selected South Asian countries (2020, as percentage of corresponding population)

Indicator	Bangladesh (%)	India (%)	Pakistan (%)
Female mobile phone subscribers	70	74	27
Male mobile phone subscribers	87	89	85
Female Internet users	16	15	10
Male Internet users	36	35	34
Gender gap: mobile phone access	17	15	58
Gender gap: Internet access	20	20	24

Source: Economist Intelligence Unit/Facebook (2020)

varying degrees. All countries have some inclusion plan for underserved groups,[9] with each having an inclusion plan specifically aimed at women. They have likewise each created digital skills training programmes targeted at women (Economist Intelligence Unit/Facebook 2020). Major telecom providers in Bangladesh, India, and Pakistan have also been part of an industry commitment to close the gender gap (GSMA 2020). India has a national plan aimed at fostering more education for women in science, technology, engineering, and mathematics (Economist Intelligence Unit/Facebook 2020). Bangladesh – which played an important role in the development of UN Security Council Resolution 1325 – is the only country with a current NAP on WPS, although that framework does not engage directly with technology, cybersecurity, or cybercrime.

Some exceptions to the trend of improved access should be noted. In Bangladesh, the World Wide Web Foundation notes that while most secondary and tertiary education students have access to technology in the classroom, girls continue to be less likely to have similar access at home (World Wide Web Foundation 2020a). It is unclear whether this is the result of family disapproval, or a result of socioeconomic status and competing demands on family resources. There are also significant regional differences in coverage in India and Pakistan, which tend to map onto racial/ethnic, religious, and urban–rural divides. In Pakistan, the Federally Administered Tribal Areas and border areas disputed with India are significantly less likely to have connectivity, and often only have access to mobile Internet (Freedom House 2020c). In India, urban–rural divides shape access patterns. Linguistic differences are also a reflection of how socioeconomic status may affect availability and relevance. The dominance of English-language content online tends to favour those from more affluent and educated backgrounds (Goswami et al 2009). Since 2014, efforts have been made to encourage more content development in local languages. By 2017, Google India estimated that over 90 per cent of new Internet users were consuming material in local languages including audio and video content (Doval 2017; Freedom House 2020a). Elsewhere in India, work suggests that other social hierarchies shape access to the Internet. The country lacks an accessibility mandate for the disabled, while poor and lower-caste individuals face sources of algorithmic bias (Sambasivan et al 2021). These examples ask that we be mindful of restrictions on access that are intersectional in nature, where gender differences in access may vary according to geographic location, socioeconomic status, and ethnic or religious identity.

The importance of regional Internet shutdowns in India should also be noted. India leads the world in shutdowns of the Internet, with state-level shutdowns often justified on national security grounds (Rydzak 2019). The Jammu and Kashmir region, which has a Muslim-majority population, was subject to a complete blackout on service between August 2019 and January

2020, following a move to eliminate article 370 of the Indian Constitution, which established a 'special' autonomous status for the region (Kronstadt 2020). The shutdown, which included cellphone and Internet service, disconnected families from their relatives in other parts of the world. It also allowed the government to suppress coverage of protests and human rights abuses, like large-scale arbitrary detentions (Jammu and Kashmir Coalition of Civil Society 2020; Zia 2020).[10] Unwittingly, technology companies deepened this isolation by booting users in the region from social media services for inactivity while the shutdown was ongoing. In particular, the messaging service WhatsApp (owned by Facebook) had a policy of deactivating user accounts after 120 days of inactivity, a policy it failed to alter despite the political situation in the region (Kronstadt 2020). The result was further emotional distress for those in the Kashmiri diaspora, who – after months of inaccessibility – now saw their friends and family members disappearing from their contact lists one by one (Zia 2020). The prolonged shutdown impacted local businesses, students, researchers, and healthcare centres; effects that disproportionately impacted those who could not leave the region or afford technological solutions (like virtual private networks) to circumvent the shutdown (Imran and Ganie 2020; Jammu and Kashmir Coalition of Civil Society 2020; Rydzak 2020). A report from the Jammu and Kashmir Coalition of Civil Society (2020) estimated over 500,000 jobs were lost in the region as a result of the shutdown. By early 2020, Internet access continued to be restricted despite the onset of the COVID-19 pandemic, rendering many unable to access accurate or independent information about the emerging crisis (Zia 2020).

This incident proved an important legal case for regulation in India. At the time the Supreme Court weighed in on the case in early 2020, it noted that indefinite bans on Internet service are contrary to Indian law and suggested that governments consider the proportionality of bans that fail to exempt essential services like medical, government, and financial functions (Freedom House 2020a; Perrigo 2020).[11] While the decision seemed like a step in the right direction, the initial restoration of Internet access in Jammu and Kashmir came in the form of slow, text-based 2G service that only allowed access to certain sites (Zia 2020). It took until August 2020 for just two of 20 districts to see faster 4G service restored, and until early 2021 for 4G access to be fully restored (AP 2021). Digital rights advocates argue that the blackout in Jammu and Kashmir was a sign of more worrying trends in discriminatory and unlawful government surveillance, with India possibly setting an example for other states on how to suppress dissent via communication blackouts (Rydzak 2020).

Generally, there is a trend towards decreasing the salience of affordability, lack of infrastructure, lack of education, or lack of skills as contributing factors to the digital gender gap in the region. One factor that remains largely unaddressed is the prevalence of online violence directed at women. The lack of meaningful efforts to address or even acknowledge this barrier stands in sharp contrast to the commitments made by governments and telecom companies to address development-related issues. As in many other parts of the world, harassment and threatening behaviours are a part of the daily lived occurrence for women online in the region. The resulting online insecurity further has a strong connection to offline physical violence. Law enforcement and the judiciary system, which often operate in a context of inadequate legal frameworks, disinterest based on gender bias, and a lack of effective cooperation with service providers located in the Global North, are often ineffective in their responses, creating an environment where abusers can weaponize technology with impunity.

Research by Sambasivan et al (2019) found that 72 per cent of women they interviewed had experienced online harassment, most of this taking place via social media platforms. Two-thirds of women indicated experience with cyberstalking (including unwanted contact from another individual online), 15 per cent reported they were impersonated by an abuser, 14 per cent were targeted by someone who exposed or threatened to expose personal information or images about the victim without their consent, and 6 per cent were the target of manufactured pornographic images (Sambasivan et al 2019). Their study found that harms were disproportionately aimed at individuals who were young, had low socioeconomic status, were disabled, or identified as members of the LGBTQI+ community – with 100 per cent of members of these latter two categories reporting some form of abuse (Sambasivan et al 2019). Members of India's LGBTQI+ community have further reported being vulnerable to blackmail and catfishing on dating apps (Malnad et al 2020). While socioeconomic status appears to impact the likelihood of online harassment and violence, women in elite positions are also not immune. In India, women politicians on Twitter were more likely than their peers to report abuse via social media, receiving on average over 100 abusive tweets per day. Muslim women, lower-caste women, and those who were not members of the ruling Bharatiya Janata Party (BJP) saw higher rates of abuse (Amnesty International India 2020).

Findings of these studies broadly correspond to reports from other parts of the region. Reports from Pakistan's Digital Rights Foundation found that non-consensual image sharing and impersonation via fake profiles were top complaints from those who reported abuse. Data from their hotline for victims of online abuse further suggests a spike in online abuse against women and transgender or nonbinary persons during Pakistan's COVID-19 lockdown, with transgender or nonbinary individuals accounting for 1.6 per cent of reported harassment victims (DRF/Hamara Internet 2021). Female journalists in Pakistan have similarly been subject to high rates of abuse (DRF 2020). In Bangladesh, one survey found that 67.3 per cent of women who use the Internet were subjected to online gender-based violence. Among the most frequent forms of abuse were identity theft or someone creating fake profiles in their name, trolling via comments and messages (including threats), and someone sharing private data without their consent. In this survey, 18.6 per cent of respondents said that threats or trolling online had translated into real-world violence, and 15.7 per cent reported having received death threats or threats of sexual violence (including blackmail) (Bytes for All Bangladesh 2022).

While reports from industry agencies indicate that family disapproval is a barrier to technology access for women in the region, they classify this factor separately from concerns about 'safety and security' (GSMA 2020). However, this is a false dichotomy as family members and intimate relations are often involved in issues related to online abuse, either as the source of abuse or as secondary abusers, perpetrating real-life violence in response to online harms. Sambasivan et al (2019) found that 5 per cent of women they surveyed began or resumed a romantic relationship with a partner after being threatened or blackmailed online while 4 per cent of women said they were subjected to domestic abuse by an intimate partner or male relative. These acts of violence were sometimes motivated by concerns about honour or reputation. In Pakistan, research describes husbands and male relatives as playing an important role in technology access, with fathers generally controlling access and brothers taking on an important role where fathers are either absent, ill, or not sufficiently technologically aware (Ibtasam et al 2019). In extreme cases, victims may lose their lives based on abuses in the virtual space. Honour killings, murder, and suicide among women have occurred as a result of interactions with technology, with the mere offence of possessing a phone without a relative's knowledge or permission sufficient to punish by death (Sambasivan et al 2019; Freedom House 2020a, 2020c; Maher 2020; DRF/Hamara Internet 2021).

Women employ a number of coping techniques to manage online abuse, but particularly relevant to this chapter is the rate at which women reduce time on or remove themselves from the digital space based on negative experiences. The majority of women in studies from South Asia report reducing engagement in some way based on their experience of online abuse. This can include deleting social media accounts, moving towards participation only in closed/private forums, posting less, avoiding controversial topics, or not sharing certain types of materials like images (Digital Rights Foundation 2019; Sambasivan et al 2019; DRF 2020). Adopting these kinds of coping mechanisms involves certain tradeoffs, particularly where Internet/mobile phone access is of professional importance to women. The Digital Rights Foundation found that just over 15 per cent of Pakistani women journalists it surveyed deleted their social media accounts entirely due to harassment, a move that impacts their professional profile and access to information

(DRF 2020). In one case, a woman who scrubbed her online presence due to harassment used a relative's identity when she needed to get online for work (Digital Rights Foundation 2019). There is evidence that this kind of technology sharing is more broadly viewed as a means of negotiating online access within families, although this often means restrictions on women's activity as their need for access is prioritized lower than that of spouses, male relatives, and older family members (Ibtasam et al 2019).

These means of, essentially, muddling through the problem of gender-based violence are a broader reflection of the fact that neither authorities nor service providers are viewed as an effective or trustworthy resource in responding to online abuse. Just 2 per cent of individuals surveyed by Sambasivan et al (2019) attempted to report abuses to platforms while only 1 per cent went to law enforcement. In-app blocking functions on social media tend to be ineffective, as users can create new or fake accounts. Blocking a user also does not resolve the issue, where the intent is to share content more broadly that can cause reputational harm. NGOs engaged in responding to online abuse point out that attempts to seek redress from providers are often ineffectual, especially when platforms are located in the Global North. At times, content that is culturally offensive – like photos of women who are fully or mostly clothed – does not violate terms of service and will not be moderated, despite its potentially damaging effects (Devika et al 2019; Sambasivan et al 2019). Others allege that requests for assistance from users in developing countries are less likely to receive a prompt response, due either to bias or to the lack of staff proficient in regional languages (Digital Rights Foundation 2019; Sambasivan et al 2019). In terms of law enforcement, the range of issues contributing to ineffectual response include overtaxed systems, inadequate legal frameworks, bias against women, lack of legal agreement with those countries where service providers are located, and in Pakistan the need to physically present one's self at a Federal Investigation Agency office to register a complaint (World Wide Web Foundation 2016; Digital Rights Foundation 2019; Sambasivan et al 2019; Freedom House 2020a, 2020c; Maher 2020; DRF/Hamara Internet 2021).

In the absence of effective response from authorities, advocates and NGOs have stepped into the gap. Women report being more likely to turn to an NGO for assistance, rather than authorities or platforms (Sambasivan et al 2019; Maher 2020). Yet advocacy for digital rights has progressed along different trajectories in South Asian countries including Bangladesh, India, and Pakistan. While such movements often invoke discourses of anti-colonial resistance, the extent to which they address gendered harms varies. In India, for example, national discourse on digital rights has crystallized around issues of access, surveillance, data privacy, and resisting the exploitation of poor and rural communities.[12]

The Net Neutrality movement that emerged surrounding the planned rollout of Facebook's Free Basics in the country became a focal point for activism in 2014–2015. Free Basics has been marketed as an accessibility solution to connect poor and rural users to the Internet by offering a small menu of services authorized by Facebook including weather, news, health information, job ads, and of course Facebook itself (Facebook 2018, 2021a; Nothias 2020). Although other, similar initiatives had been attempted in India before, Facebook's received specific attention because of its scale, its restrictions, and questions about its relevance (Mukerjee 2016). While Facebook claimed that extending access via such a programme would serve as a poverty reduction measure, evidence did not necessarily support this assertion. English would be the primary language of the service, rendering it of questionable utility towards the populations it claimed to want to reach (Graham 2016). Further, restrictions on the guidelines for 'partner' services meant that Facebook itself would be the only provider allowed to offer access to significant video and image content (Graham 2016; Mukerjee 2016).

The Save the Internet (STI) campaign that emerged around resistance to Free Basics was framed as a struggle for net neutrality and against digital colonialism by a multinational, US-based company that was seen as primarily interested in using India's poor as a resource for experimentation and data extraction (Graham 2016; Mukerjee 2016; Prasad 2018; Nothias 2020). This campaign ultimately prevailed in a court decision in 2016 upholding net neutrality and banning Free Basics. Nothias (2020) compares the contested rollout in India to the much less controversial adoption of Free Basics in many African countries, arguing that successful resistance in India was due to the intervention of a movement that was predominately middle-class, technologically knowledgable, and English speaking. By comparison, much less media attention was devoted to the programme's rollout in African countries.[13] The same could arguably be said for Pakistan, where Free Basics was introduced in 2015, and Bangladesh, where it was rolled out in 2016 through a partnership with telecom operator Grameenphone.[14] In Pakistan, users reported that Free Basics requires demographic data not requested in other countries, offered terms of service only in English,[15] and only offered assistive features for the disabled after its initial launch (Global Voices 2017; Kapadia and Jalil 2017).

Subsequent digital rights campaigning in India built off the architecture developed by the STI movement. The Internet Freedom Foundation, created as part of the STI movement, continues to focus its work on Net Neutrality and privacy, including the need to protect personal data, restrictions on the use of surveillance technology, and the right to be forgotten (IFF 2016). The Centre for Internet and Society (CIS-India) has a mandate that includes accessibility, access to knowledge, transparency, and privacy rights. CIS-India has explicitly engaged on projects related to the status of women and LGBTQI+ communities, including research referenced here. Other organizations – including a variety of digital rights and privacy rights organizations – have addressed the intersection of gender, technology, and security. Yet challenges remain. Concerns about potential exposure to pornography have been used in legal cases to argue for banning content deemed 'obscene' (including LGBTQI+ and educational material) and specific laws to penalize online violence against women are lacking (World Wide Web Foundation 2016; Bhandari 2021). This points to continued issues mainstreaming gender into the conversation.

In Pakistan, a pre-existing digital rights movement addressing violence against women was thrust into the national conversation with the 2016 murder of celebrity Qandeel Baloch. Baloch (her stage name) was known for posting provacative content to social media. She was murdered by her brother in an honour killing after being doxed by a journalist who revealed her birth name online. In her book on the killing, Maher (2020) argues that Baloch's activities were – at least generally – known to her family, and that relatives treated her behaviour with benign neglect for as long as she operated under a false name and shared her income with the family. Because she was doxed, Maher argues that Baloch's brother (assisted by a male cousin) felt compelled to act to restore the family's honour. The murder brought international attention to the risks Pakistani women can face for their social media activity. However, a movement for rights and inclusivity already existed in the country based in part on the work of the Digital Rights Foundation, founded by Nighat Dad in 2012. The foundation initially offered education to women about how to protect themselves online, and has since grown to encompass a hotline service, policy advocacy, and research. In Pakistan as well as in India, discourses of national security, decency, and morality dominate policy discussions, invoked to justify the need for more intensive surveillance and censorship rather than to make online spaces more welcoming for women. Domestic civil society advocacy presents a potentially important avenue for calling such rhetorical moves into question.

Another potential avenue for addressing these issues may be developing synergies between digital rights advocacy and the WPS Agenda. This type of action can be viewed in the context of Bangladesh. As noted earlier, Bangladesh is seen as having the strongest framework for WPS in the region. While its current NAP on WPS does not specifically reference cybercrime or cybersecurity, it does call for capacity building around gender and leadership. It further references the country's national policy on women and development, which in turn includes specific provisions related to technology education, the mainstreaming of gender perspectives in technology development and implementation, and principles of non-harm in the implementation of technology (Government of the Peoples' Republic of Bangladesh 2011). As discussed throughout this chapter, the closer integration of matters of technology into gendered security policy as well as development policy could strengthen frameworks for action.

Seeing masculinities in online abuse

The focus on South Asian nations as a case study should, of course, not be read as a suggestion that online violence against women is an issue unique to South Asia or the Global South more broadly. As noted earlier in this chapter, the data suggest gendered violence in the digital realm is a widespread and global issue. Despite some positive trends in individual countries to create specific responses to issues like cyberbullying and revenge porn, law enforcement agencies and advocates with NGOs still struggle to keep up with technological developments and to fit new forms of abuse into existing legal frameworks (Freed et al 2017). Even in the world's most economically developed countries, the solution is too often for women to disconnect from technologies used to abuse them – an act with concerning impacts for their social and professional activity (Freed et al 2017, 2018; Matthews et al 2017; Woodlock 2017).

But where are the men – or, more specifically, the focus on masculinities – in discussions about online abuse and its effect on women's presence online? To be sure, men and boys can also be the targets of technology-enabled abuse. One can argue that their perspectives as victims are lacking in current research on technology and intimate partner violence.[16] Yet men are often responsible for abusive uses of technology and male biases in development circles can unconsciously (or even consciously) contribute to the problem.

This is an area in which industry players and policymakers are ill-equipped to respond. Industry commitments to close the gender gap have placed an emphasis on making women *feel* safe or empowered, without placing the same emphasis on handling or changing the behaviour of abusers (GSMA 2020). Industry documents have framed the imperative to deal with abusers as an issue for states, not service providers, to handle (GSMA 2020). From the perspective of for-profit companies, it makes simple economic sense that any measure that might result in the removal of content or customers is counterproductive. Social media companies too have taken great pains to avoid large-scale bans on abusive users and content removal, instead resorting to measures like flagging or attaching warnings to harmful content – despite evidence that this strategy does not work (Singer and Brooking 2018; Kreps 2020). The notable exception to this resistance towards aggressive action has been in response to national security threats in developed countries, like the 2016 election and the storming of the US Capitol on 6 January 2020. A spike in hate crimes following the 2016 election resulted in the removal of prominent White nationalist figures from social media platforms, while the attack on the Capitol resulted in a purge of over 70,000 QAnon-affiliated accounts on Twitter alone (Singer and Brooking 2018; Romm and Dwoskin 2021).

Broader concerns about cross-platform extremist activity resulted in collective action from major technology companies[17] via GIFCT, which has leveraged hashing technology[18] and artificial intelligence to facilitate cross-platform identification and removal of terrorist content. A transparency report from 2019 notes that depictions of 'graphic violence against defenseless people' were one category of terrorist content that accounted for 4.8 per cent of catalogued items in the shared database of materials targeted for removal (GIFCT 2019). The mobilization and deployment of this technology to fight extremism will be discussed further in the following chapter, but a salient question is why such technology has been mobilized and deployed in response to issues of national security (and to combat child pornography), while only being used on a much smaller scale to assist victims of revenge porn and online misogyny.[19] The answer unquestionably has implications for whose security is deemed to matter.

Providers of mobile communications services, too, show a tendency to overlook the potential gendered harms of technology they develop or place on offer. Studies have found hundreds of apps in official mobile app stores aimed at surveillance, spoofing, bombarding other users with messages, and creating deepfakes/cheapfakes. A number of these have explicitly marketed themselves as applications for intimate partner surveillance (with female partners generally depicted as the partner to be surveilled) (Chatterjee et al 2018; Roundy et al 2020). Commonly used techniques marketed as measures to enhance user security, like the use of security questions, are cited as another factor that leaves domestic abuse victims vulnerable to hacking or lockouts. Abusers frequently know the answers to these personal questions, providing them a backdoor into a partner's accounts (Freed et al 2017, 2018). To their credit, some technology companies have funded research on these topics and/or implemented changes to address them. Yet these changes are reactive rather than proactive. The fact that they have come only after years of research and complaints from women is problematic.

The more difficult question of addressing and changing the behaviour of men (and boys) is also one that policy solutions, such as the WPS Agenda, are ill-equipped to handle. Research on WPS suggests that attempts to engage men often place elite men at the centre of discussions, looking to engage them as positive role models rather than as agents who themselves need to change (Duriesmith 2017, 2019; Wright 2020). State actors may be particularly reluctant to challenge masculine roles associated with militarization, where they deeply invested in using discourses of masculinity and 'just warriors' to support military activities (Wilcox 2009; Kirby and Shepherd 2016; Shepherd 2016; Wright 2020). The 'bystander' focus highlighted by Duriesmith (2017) sends mixed messages about the position of men with regard to WPS. While highlighting the potential for men to engage in problematic behaviours like online or ICT-facilitated harassment, it also reassures men that they personally are likely not the problem – encouraging them instead to look for problem behaviours in other, troublesome men (Duriesmith 2017). The suggestion that states – especially developed states, who often play a role in framing the WPS Agenda for partners abroad through training and security cooperation – are reluctant to adopt frameworks directly confronting problematic masculine behaviours is a concern (Wright 2020). It has thus far resulted in approaches that fail to truly hold men accountable or transform masculinity.

The online security of women

This chapter has offered an overview of the nature of the gender digital divide, the root causes behind it, and issues with policy narratives surrounding the problem. One of the central arguments of the chapter is that gendered patterns of insecurity must be taken more seriously as a factor contributing to women's limited engagement with technology. Furthermore, in the absence of efforts to address the insecurities faced by women and other marginalized groups, technology access should not, in and of itself, be used as a proxy for empowerment and security. A more comprehensive effort to make technology safe for women would firmly embed discussions of how to improve the safety and security of women as it seeks to expand access to technology. It would address intersectional violence and racialized stereotyping within the 'digital divide' discourse (Benjamin 2019). It would also more directly address the responsibilities of men in addressing and changing toxic behaviours.

The types of civil society advocacy we see in South Asia is important because these organizations fill a gap. Both state actors and industry players have thus far failed to meaningfully address the hostile environment women (especially those from marginalized groups) face online. While state actors have focused on discourses of online security that often are a cover for surveillance, censorship, and algorithmic bias, private companies have denied responsibility and/or presented women as a market to be mobilized, while someone else (states, law enforcement agencies, or even individual users) takes responsibility for their online protection. Without real protections against online abuse, technology is arguably equally if not more likely to disempower women, rather than empowering them.

Ultimately, the narrative from civil society, industry, international organizations, and states alike should not be that women need to come to technology. It should be that technology must come to women – by earning their trust, increasing its relevance, and enhancing its safety. Coincidentally, some efforts towards these goals might have the impact of helping populations more broadly, including the millions of victims of cybercrime worldwide.

Finally, more work can be done to create truly multi-stakeholder frameworks that hold technology companies, international organizations, and states alike publicly accountable for commitments in this area. While the cooperative efforts undertaken to confront violent extremist activities may serve as a template, these initiatives view online security threats narrowly, failing to see the real and daily lived insecurities experience by women and other marginalized groups. Recent research conducted by employees of major technology companies and/or with resources from service providers – like some of the research cited in this chapter – is another positive step. Yet some of this work circulates within narrow disciplinary silos. Greater engagement between work in human–computer interaction, area studies, political science, international relations, and gender studies would likely help move these conversations forward.

PART II

Social Media, Surveillance, and Gender-Based Violence Online

4

Extremism and Gender-Based Violence Online

The previous chapter makes it clear that the Internet and communications technology have become important frontiers in the struggle against gender-based violence. Discussing, in particular, the everyday lived experience of violence against women online, it illustrated the extent to which online gender-based violence has been normalized as well as the direct linkages between online violence, offline harms, and intertwined structures of oppression based on patriarchy, Global North–South divides, and other social hierarchies. While Chapter 3 offered insight primarily into the experiences of domestic and interpersonal violence facilitated through online platforms, it left unaddressed the issue of how gender-based violence can be deployed by extremists using technology to further their own ends. The present chapter explores how online extremist violence both deploys gender discourse and uses gendered labour to further its end. This analysis looks primarily at the role of social media, but also addresses the role of messaging apps, decentralized platforms, and other related technologies.

A necessary first step in this exercise is to define both 'violent extremism' and 'extremist violence', and explore what these terms mean in a gendered context. The definition of extremism is contested and is not always linked explicitly to manifestations of physical violence. While extremism is often associated with radical ideological views, commentators have noted that holding or advocating such views does not necessarily lead to the practice of violence or to a decision to join an extremist group (Griset and Mahan 2002; Horgan 2009; Aly and Striegher 2012; Striegher 2015). Thus, violent extremism is often defined in opposition to terrorism. While 'extremism' denotes adherence to a radical ideology, and 'violent extremism' denotes adherence to an ideology that views violence as a suitable tool in the pursuit of ideological goals, whether extremist violence is also terrorism can be distinguished by whether an individual actually carries out violence and/or whether they are part of an organized group engaged in that practice

(Striegher 2015; UNODC 2018). Extremism, then, is an appropriate conceptual framework for this chapter, which explores how gender-based violence is deployed by a combination of organized armed groups, diffuse extremist movements, and entities that fall somewhere in between.

Applying extremism and extremist violence in a gender-based context can lead to an examination of how extremist groups practice gender-based violence and how they promote an ideology that legitimizes violence as a tool to pursue gendered goals. As seen in this chapter, these goals can include upholding a rigid gender binary, upholding traditional or essentialist gender roles, opposing laws and policies meant to promote the advancement of women, and seeking to disrupt the advancement of women – for example through disinformation or dogpiling[1] tactics. In her book on violence against women in politics, Krook (2020) advances a five-part typology of political violence against women that includes physical and sexual violence, but also psychological, emotional, and semiotic violence. While the majority of these terms will be familiar to readers knowledgeable in this area, semiotic violence is perhaps the least familiar and is defined as violence which deploys words, gestures, and images with the purpose of silencing women or rendering them incompetent (Krook 2020). As a delegitimizing tactic, semiotic violence is not necessarily a new form of gender-based violence, but it may be uniquely enabled by the online environment. Memetic campaigns and information warfare tactics (such as the sowing of disinformation) are useful for enabling semiotic violence. As the examples in this chapter will show, the complex landscape of social media networks, messaging and communications apps, forums, and other means of electronic communication also allow semiotic violence to be coordinated by extremist communities in ways not visible to the public. While Krook (2020) applies these tactics to the study of violence against women in politics – defined as those in political office, candidates, journalists, and activists – definitionally her typology can apply more broadly to gender-based violence as deployed against women and those identifying outside the gender binary. There are additionally connections to race/ethnicity, sexuality, disability, and other axes of difference that call for an intersectional understanding of this violence and its effects. In the case of semiotic violence especially, the concept calls upon us to see acts of violence against women in the collective.

The remainder of this chapter explores the application of gender-based violence by extremists in the online space. Beginning with a brief discussion of the historical and legal context, I proceed to an examination of relevant examples in the context of the typology outlined by Krook (2020) and with reference to recent and currently active extremist groups including the Islamic State, male supremacist and far-right communities, and diffuse but politically relevant communities organized around conspiratorial beliefs.

These examples build on existing work in this area, but I also explore these themes through a content analysis of open-source content from extremist websites. These examples serve to illustrate several points. First, they demonstrate the frequency and ease with which extremists at varying levels of organizational coherence can use technology to further their aims. Second, they demonstrate that both men and women are involved in the practice of extremist gender-based violence in ways that map onto our understanding of violence in other contexts. Third, they demonstrate a trend towards entrepreneurship and the decentralization of online extremism away from the larger social media and communications platforms that have seen the most pressure to respond to this issue. Fourth and relatedly, I argue that these examples point to a need to revisit existing strategies for the regulation of extremism in the online space.

Gender-based extremism: historical context

While much attention has been devoted to extremism in new media and the emergence of groups and ideologies native to the online space, it is important to note the historical continuities that underlie these trends. Not that much is truly new about misogyny, particularly in the context of political and/or extremist violence. Both gender-based violence in conflict and the use of gendered labour to promote violence are long-established phenomena.

The proliferation of communities and sub-groupings under the banner of so-called 'male supremacist' ideologies serves as an illustration of the varied expressions of misogyny and of the migration of these ideas from offline to online spaces. While patriarchy represents an institutionalized form of male supremacy that is centuries old, forms of anti-feminist extremism have existed for as long as there has been a feminist movement. Early feminists in the United States and the United Kingdom were the targets of verbal harassment, harassment in writing (for instance, via mailed letters), physical violence, and sexual assaults. These acts were carried out by security forces and private individuals alike. In the United States, a November 1917 incident (known as the 'Night of Terror') in which suffragettes from the National Women's Party were arrested, tortured, and held in inhumane conditions, became a rallying point by which the National Women's Party sought to sway public opinion (McArdle 2017; Carter Olson 2021). In Britain, feminists of the Women's Social and Political Union experienced their own 'Black Friday' in 1910, when hundreds of women marching on Parliament were physically and sexually assaulted (Raw 2018). Violence against suffragettes – both in contemporary accounts and since – has been justified by claims that it was a response to militance among suffragette groups, but such arguments do not always hold up to scrutiny. In the case of the Night of Terror, women arrested at the White House appear to have been guilty only of civil disobedience. Some had been arrested repeatedly for 'obstructing the sidewalk' in the months prior to November 1917, an offence that had apparently taken on new severity in light of the US entry into the First World War and resultant concerns about domestic dissent (McArdle 2017). In the UK, militant suffragism has been the source of some debate among historians, with accounts diverging on how widespread and how central violence was to women's movements (Kent 1990; Cowman 1996; Mayhall 2003; Bearman 2005; deVries 2013). Generally, feminist historians have argued that militant violence by suffragettes largely consisted of property crimes – like vandalism and arson – and that such tactics were controversial even within the movements of the time (Fowler 1991; Cowman 1996; Mayhall 2003; deVries 2013).

Leaving aside these debates, anti-feminist or anti-women movements continued to coalesce. The emergence of a transnational men's rights movement in the 1970s drew on ideas percolating since the late 19th century, including the idea that men were the truly oppressed sex and that legal and political reforms granted rights to women at the expense of men (Rafail and Freitas 2019; Horta Ribeiro et al 2021). From offline activism in the late 20th century, men's rights activists and advocates have grown into the online space. Grievances expressed within men's rights communities online today include long-standing topics of discussion – inequitable treatment of men in family law and relationships, the victimization of men by the feminist movement, and a perception that men are discriminated against or are unrecognized by domestic violence laws – and newer concerns – like the perceived mistreatment of men in sexual assault policies on college campuses and persistent efforts to discredit statistics and studies showing gender inequality (Rafail and Freitas 2019).

The movement of men's rights discourse into the online space in the early 2000s allowed these communities to extend their reach, but also to subdivide. Today, the term 'manosphere' has come to encompass the range of online entities catering to men's interests, including podcasts, video channels, blogs, websites, and communities. Efforts to map ideological divisions within the manosphere have highlighted several salient groupings. These include:

- Men's Rights Activists (MRA): An extension of the offline movement, with discussions centred in the areas referenced earlier.
- Men Going Their Own Way (MGTOW): A community of men seeking to avoid any interaction with women and to minimize their interaction with society at large, which they believe has become dominated by women.
- Pick-Up Artists (PUA): Men concerned with establishing sexual dominance over women, often advocating the use of deceptive or coercive tactics.

- Red Pill: Communities that combine pro-men and anti-feminist ideas with a broader range of conspiratorial and anti-government views.
- Incels: 'Involuntary celibates' who believe in male entitlement to sex and express resentment towards both women and a hierarchy of men who they perceive as conspiring to deprive them of sex. (Liang Lin 2017; Fitzgerald 2020; Horta Ribeiro et al 2021)

These communities are transnational, diverse in terms of race and ethnicity,[2] easy to find, and – in many cases – closely networked to violent extremist ideologies. Incel communities have arguably received the most popular attention, with incel ideology explicitly linked to the celebration of violence against women and identified as the cause of nearly 50 deaths in incidents across the United States and Canada (Gilmore 2019; Hoffman and Ware 2020; Hoffman et al 2020; O'Malley et al 2020). Incel attacks in the 2010s led Reddit – one of the major platforms where incel communities were based – to ban these groups; however incel forums, communities, and media remain easy to find. This ties in to a larger problem, which is the ease with which individuals navigating the manosphere can be steered from non-violent content to content with extremist, violent undertones. Although friction exists between various manosphere communities (Liang Lin 2017), recent research has argued that boundaries between less-extreme and more-extreme communities are disappearing, with extremist voices increasingly dominating across the manosphere as a whole. In the current environment, purportedly 'moderate' or non-violent groups act as feeders to drive users towards more extreme content – a process facilitated by algorithms on sites like YouTube (Fitzgerald 2020; Papadamou et al 2020; Horta Ribeiro et al 2021). Analysts also point out that there is also cross-pollination between violent male supremacist ideologies like incel thought and other communities built around hate and violence, such as neo-Nazis, Identitarians, White supremacists, and conspiracy-based extremist movements (Clarke and Turner 2020; DiBranco 2020; Henshaw 2021a). This paints an expansive picture of the range of extremist groups capable of perpetrating gender-based violence online.

A look at the historical context of gender-based extremist violence would not be complete without also addressing the role women play in advancing extremist messaging. Recruiting and propagandizing have long been important roles for women in extremist movements and armed groups, with women at times serving as ideological leaders in violent movements (Cragin and Daly 2009; Henshaw et al 2019). Cragin and Daly (2009) discuss examples of women in the 'political vanguard' of insurgencies, including Augusta LaTorre and Elena Iparraguirre of Peru's Shining Path, Susanna Ronconi of Italy's Prima Linea, and Kesire Yildirim of Turkey's Kurdistan Worker's Party (PKK). Latter-day examples could also include women of Colombia's Revolutionary Armed Forces of Colombia (FARC) like Victoria Sandino Palmera (a member of the FARC's peace negotiating team and, subsequently, a Colombian senator), who defined the notion of 'insurgent feminism' as an intersectional, anti-patriarchal, and collective commitment to full gender equality (Sandino Palmera 2016; Phelan 2017). As counterintuitive as it seems, right-wing movements advocating patriarchal structures or male supremacy have similarly been reliant on the work of female ideologues and propagandists. Various authors have explored the roles played by women in American White supremacist movements, including the Ku Klux Klan (Blee 2008; Eager 2008; Darby 2020). Today, much of this messaging has moved online as technology (including social media, podcasts, and video hosting sites) makes it easier for content authors to broadcast to a wider audience. As a result, female propagandists[3] have shown up in corners as diverse as neo-Nazi and ultranationalist militias in Eastern Europe, the Islamic State, and the Pakistani Taliban (Lehane et al 2018; Pearson 2018; Trisko Darden et al 2019; Mehran et al 2020; Ingram 2021).

While extremist violence against women fits within the purview of P/CVE policies and is a threat specifically named in at least one resolution in the WPS Agenda,[4] institutions have struggled to meaningfully respond. Various authors have pointed out the pitfalls and limitations of P/CVE programming that views women in essentialist ways – with women (especially mothers) portrayed as forces for peace and men (especially young men) as the parties at risk of radicalization (Huckerby and Ní Aoláin 2018; Winterbotham 2018; International Crisis Group 2020; Rothermel 2020). The collective failure of the international community to meaningfully deal with female foreign-born supporters of the Islamic State, many of whom have been left effectively stateless and without due process, further highlights the way in which – in spite of over a quarter-century of gender mainstreaming – state and international institutions are perplexed in the face of a phenomenon that upends essentialist understandings of gender.

Case studies in gender-based violent extremism

This section draws on recent examples and the typology discussed earlier – developed by Krook (2020) – to illustrate the various ways in which ICT and social media facilitate gender-based violence. A special emphasis is placed on violence perpetrated by the Islamic State, by far-right groups including male supremacists and incels, and by conspiracy-based movements. These examples illustrate that extremist gender-based violence is both widespread and takes varied forms including those contributing to serious real-world harms. In this way, the types of violence identified by Krook (2020) are not mutually exclusive; to some extent, they are mutually reinforcing. Beyond simple gender binaries, these examples show that violence is intertwined with multiple social hierarchies – disproportionately impacting members of ethnic and religious minority groups, women with disabilities, and members of the LGBTQI+ community. Furthermore, women as well as men take an active role in facilitating these acts, a fact that should motivate a re-thinking of gender approaches to P/CVE.

The Islamic State

The Islamic State has become closely associated with discussions about extremist violence against women. Technology played an essential part in both its transnational recruiting efforts and in its campaign of violence against marginalized groups, including ethnic and religious minorities and the LGBTQI+ community. Scholars have described a complex system of gender relations within the Islamic State. Overall, thousands of women from dozens of countries became affiliated with Islamic State between 2013 and 2018, accounting for approximately 13 per cent of all foreign recruits (Cook and Vale 2018). In addition to these, many women native to Islamic State-held territories either willingly or unwillingly became collaborators with the organization (Moaveni 2015, 2019). This has led some to describe the female population of the Islamic State caliphate as one of in-groups and out-groups (Margolin and Winter 2021). Sunni Muslim women who were 'willing and grateful participants' in the caliphate were generally considered part of the in-group, though their movements and activities remained closely monitored by the organization (Margolin and Winter 2021). Freedom of movement, for example, was restricted; however, women could gain certain access and privileges through participation in a narrow range of occupations deemed acceptable in the caliphate, including as doctors and nurses and as part of the religious police (Moaveni 2015; Margolin and Winter 2021). Even so, escapees from Islamic State territory have alleged that there was differential treatment of women who joined Islamic State from abroad – especially from Western countries – and Syrian and Iraqi women native to the area, with the former being accorded privileges like expanded Internet access or better weapons in the religious police (Moaveni 2015, 2019). Through their participation in the religious police and via their presence online, women affiliated with Islamic State played important roles in the transmission and reinforcement of norms of gender in the Islamic State (Moaveni 2015, 2019; Pearson 2018).

For those in the out-group, including women from Yazidi, Christian, or Druze backgrounds, the LGBTQI+ population, and Muslims who did not ascribe to the extremist interpretation of Islam adopted by the Islamic State, life was considerably more brutal. Many of these communities – including Christians, Jews, and Shia Muslims – could be subject to taxes, seizure of property, or forced conversion (Al-Dayel and Mumford 2020; Margolin and

Winter 2021). The Yazidi minority were the foremost group singled out for the particular subjugation of enslavement. Following the conquest of Yazidi communities, Al-Dayel and Mumford (2020) note that gender was the primary factor in determining the fate of individual community members, with age being a secondary consideration. While adult men were usually executed, women, girls, and boys under the age of eight were more often destined for slavery.[5] Enslaved persons were sold or 'gifted' to Islamic State fighters, with women and girls often sexually enslaved – a practice tolerated and regulated by the Islamic State (Al-Dayel and Mumford 2020; Al-Dayel et al 2020; Margolin and Winter 2021).

ICT including social media directly facilitated slavery and sexual violence against Yazidi women and girls and as well as other 'enemy' populations of the Islamic State. Estimates suggest that up to 9,000 slaves were trafficked within the Islamic State (Al-Dayel et al 2020). Although physical slave auctions were usually held at a few specific sites, slaves were also trafficked via online auctions and through online groups. Platforms including Facebook, WhatsApp, Telegram, and Signal were among those used to sell slaves (Hinnant et al 2016; FIDH/Kinyat 2018; Al-Dayel et al 2020). At least one report suggests that the use of these platforms enabled the expansion of slave markets beyond ISIS territory, pointing to the alleged sale of slaves to buyers elsewhere in the Middle East (Al-Dayel et al 2020). Technology may likewise be extending the life of the slave trade beyond the territorial defeat of the Islamic State. As of 2020, an estimated 3,000 Yazidi women and children were still missing (Barkawi 2020; Hutchinson 2020). Yazidi families have alleged that, in the rush by foreign fighters to abandon Islamic State strongholds, some women held as slaves were sold to criminal gangs and subsequently trafficked out of Syria (Cornish 2019). Based on available data, research estimates that Islamic State-related interests could stand to gain millions of dollars in additional funding through the sale or ransom of those still held captive (Hutchinson 2020).

Technology similarly facilitated and/or amplified violence against sexual minorities and those whose gender identity falls outside the gender binary. Scholars have argued that the Islamic State's publicly circulated ideologies on gender and sexuality served a signalling or outbidding function, both distinguishing the Islamic State from other armed groups in the region and seeking to establish it as the most serious or committed among jihadist players (Tschantret 2018; Szekely 2020). The Islamic State was not alone in targeting the LGBTQI+ community as a form of signalling. Tschantret (2018) identifies 13 non-state armed groups that engaged in targeted homophobic killings between 1985 and 2015. Of these, the majority were in the Middle East and North Africa region and four – including the Islamic State – operated in either Iraq or Syria following the 2003 invasion of Iraq by the United States.[6] As of 2017, human rights advocates had documented more than 60 instances of targeted killings, torture, sexual violence, and other violent acts against members of the LGBTQI+ community in just one area of Islamic State-occupied Iraq (Feder 2017). The Islamic State is also alleged to have carried out targeted homophobic or transphobic violence in parts of North Africa and Pakistan where it is active (Kilbride 2015; Tschantret 2018).[7]

While even an accusation of being gay, lesbian, or transgender may have been enough to provoke targeted violence from the Islamic State, technology was used to support such allegations. Surveillance and searches of mobile phone data were used by the Islamic State to identify members of the LGBTQI+ population (Variyar 2014; HRGJ/MADRE/OWFI 2017). The vulnerability of such data is a particularly important issue, as LGBTQI+ communities in the region often communicate through chat rooms, social media, or messaging apps, given the social stigma associated with homosexuality (Hawley 2015). Executions based on sexuality or gender identity were in turn broadcast on social media as a reinforcement of Islamic State views and punishments (HRGJ/MADRE/OWFI 2017; Tschantret 2018). While most documented instances involve men and boys being executed or tortured, executions of women and children accused of similar offences have also been recorded (HRGJ/MADRE/OWFI 2017).

Taken together, these examples show how a well-resourced extremist group can engage in gender-based (and sexuality-based) violence in ways that cut across the typology of violence against women outlined by Krook (2020). It also shows the roles technology may play in facilitating or amplifying the effects of such violence. In the case of the Islamic State, evidence shows that technology expanded the reach of Islamic State violence, both geographically – as in the case of the expansion of the slave trade – and psychologically – as in the use of broadcasted executions of those accused of homosexuality. Examples like those identified here suggest that technology providers – including social media companies – were often reactive rather than proactive in preventing abuses of technology by extremists.

Male supremacists and the far right

Elsewhere, technology has enabled groups that promote ideologies advocating violence against women. Most notable is the emerging terror threat posed by incels and other male supremacist groups. Incel communities are a subset of the larger ecosystem of online misogynist groups. While the term 'incel' originated as a way to refer to Internet users who were single and seeking community, it has evolved to refer to male extremists – including those who advocate for violence against women. Hoffman and Ware (2020) estimate that approximately 50 people have been killed in incel-motivated attacks in the United States and Canada, with additional plots disrupted elsewhere.

This and other assessments of incel-motivated violence cite highly public incidents like mass killings in Isla Vista, California in 2014, Toronto in 2018, and Tallahassee, Florida in 2018.

Experts argue that incels should be regarded as a salient terrorism threat in the sense that they converge around a defined ideology, coordinate through online communication, and carry out real-world violence with the assistance of opaque networks (Hoffman and Ware 2020; Hoffman et al 2020). The defining elements of incel ideology include: (1) the belief that women are naturally evil; (2) the exaltation of traditional male gender roles; (3) a belief in the oppression of men in modern society; (4) a belief in the existence of a 'sexual market' in which hierarchies of men exist and where more sexually successful men and women act in concert to deprive other men of sex; and (5) the legitimacy of violence as a response to these dynamics (O'Malley et al 2020).

At least some of the ideological points that define incels align with views frequently found in other extremist communities of the far right. Discourse across far-right extremist groups regarding the 'natural' supremacy of men and right to sexual access is pervasive. Furthermore, although academic interest in incels seems to be focused on instances of targeted killings, male supremacist violence may be expressed in ways that are not immediately visible to scholars of political violence, such as intimate partner violence or sexual assault. PUA communities, for example, with their advocacy for the use of deceptive or coercive tactics against intimate partners, challenge the boundaries of what we might call extremist violence.

Male supremacist communities can also have entangled relationships with other, more formal violent groups, including militias and hate groups. Mattheis and Winter (2019), for example, discuss principles of male supremacy in Identitarian discourse in Europe. They find that Identitarianism, defined as 'an ethnopolitical ideology that is committed to ending multiculturalism', incorporates views specifying the belief that feminists are actively working to oppress men, that society should return to traditional gender roles (that is, with women primarily engaged in child-bearing and care-giving), and that modern society has been made possible only through patriarchy – a system in which men perform the labour of social advancement while women passively benefit (Mattheis and Winter 2019: 6, 13). These views overlap with principles of incel ideology. Male supremacist views have additionally become entangled with White supremacist and neo-Nazi ideology. Commentators have noted that Anders Breivik's attack in 2011 was motivated by anti-feminist and homophobic as well as xenophobic views (Moyn 2018; DiBranco 2020). Andrew Anglin, founder of the anti-Semitic and neo-Nazi website *Daily Stormer*, has also sought to cultivate readership through the advancement of male supremacist views (SPLC nd; DiBranco 2020). Women have similarly taken on some important roles in advancing male supremacist views. Somewhat paradoxically – given that the emphasis on traditional gender roles should constrain their involvement in the public sphere – female ideologues on the far-right have played an important role in sanitizing extremist messaging while extending its reach to new communities, such as the 'tradwife' movement, a community of women celebrating traditional homemaker roles (Darby 2020).[8]

As with the Islamic State, violence arising from male supremacist communities cuts across the typology introduced earlier in this chapter. While the deaths of dozens of people across the United States and Canada in incel-motivated attacks demonstrates the potential for deadly physical violence arising from male supremacist communities, less visible are the ways that male supremacist communities perpetrate psychological, economic, and semiotic violence against women. In a broad sense, organized efforts by groups associated with male supremacy have sought to discredit or silence women's voices in strategic ways. These include efforts by far-right extremists to co-opt the #MeToo hashtag and to derail feminist conversations by spamming hashtags like #TakeBacktheTech (a hashtag highlighting gender inequality in the tech industry) with offensive messages and images (Amnesty International 2018; Ebner and Davey 2019). Extremists have become adept at organizing such campaigns in ways that evade content policies enforced by social media companies. For example, groups including neo-Nazis, Identitarians, and White supremacists have used Discord channels and sites like 4chan and 8kun to generate memes and videos for use on more mainstream platforms (Davey and Ebner 2017; Singer and Brooking 2018). Strategies that include the use of coded language, the hijacking of hashtags, and fake accounts have all been used to broadcast extremist messages without necessarily violating terms of service (Davey and Ebner 2017; Ebner and Davey 2019). The use of coded language and symbols in online harassment has been cited as a particular problem for content moderators, as work on gender-based harassment notes that human content moderators are often unfamiliar with niche hate symbols – such as those used to target disabled women (Jankowicz et al 2021).

Beyond these general examples, the targeted harassment of women by extremist groups represents a trend resulting in psychological and emotional violence. An array of women including political office-holders, activists, and journalists have been on the receiving end of gendered abuse. Memetic campaigns and conspiracy theories directed at Hillary Clinton in the lead-up to the 2016 US elections are one example, with authors tracing the origin of some memetic campaigns that employed gendered discourse to extremist communities online (Mitew and Wall 2017). Other well-known targets include German Chancellor Angela Merkel, who was the focus of campaigns organized by groups including neo-Nazis, Identitarians, and other far-right figures in the lead-up to the 2017 German elections. At least some of this critique focused on gender issues, specifically the perceived links between German refugee policy during her term and sexual assaults against German women (Davey and Ebner 2017). US Vice President Kamala Harris was the target of transphobic conspiracies circulated online by QAnon in the lead-up to the 2020 US presidential election (specifically, the rumour that she was a transgender woman) (Jankowicz et al 2021). One study from the Inter-Parliamentary Union (IPU) found that 41.8 per cent of women serving in parliaments worldwide were subject to conspiracies, rumours, or harmful images circulated on social media. A slightly higher percentage of respondents, 44.4 per cent, reported receiving threats of rape, assassination, assault, or abduction – which were most often transmitted via email or social media (IPU 2016).

Targeted harassment goes beyond women at the highest levels of politics. Online harassment campaigns by extremists against women activists, journalists, and professionals – individuals who generally lack the protections that may be associated with holding political office – are particularly insidious and have spilled into real-world acts of violence and intimidation. Campaigns organized by the *Daily Stormer*, for example, have targeted several visible and/or politically active women. Journalist Julia Ioffe was targeted by the *Stormer*'s so-called troll army in 2016 after writing a story critical of soon-to-be First Lady Melania Trump, leading to a campaign of anti-Semitic abuse (O'Brien 2017). Real estate agent Tanya Gersh – who was accused of engaging in a confrontation with the mother of White nationalist Richard Spencer – was the target of a campaign in which she was doxed, enabling far-right sympathizers to harass her and her family by phone and email hundreds of times per day. This incident escalated to threats of an armed protest in her home town before law enforcement and local government took action (O'Brien 2017). Taylor Dumpson, the first Black woman to be elected student body president of American University, was another target of the same organization. Harassment of Dumpson progressed from online threats to racist displays on the campus of American University (Schmidt 2019). In each of these cases, the women affected alleged psychological and economic harm – and the legal system agreed. In 2019, a US court awarded Dumpson damages on the grounds that harassment fomented by the *Stormer* caused a deterioration of her physical and mental health and inhibited her access to an education (Schmidt 2019). Gersh was awarded US$14 million in damages against *Stormer* publisher Andrew Anglin in 2019 on the grounds that he had acted with malicious intent in encouraging harassment against her (Farzan 2019). At the same time, these cases show the limitations of the legal system in responding to online violence against women. More than a year after the judgment in Gersh's case, her attorneys stated in a court filing that Anglin had not paid any part of the judgment and had dropped out of communication, his whereabouts unknown (Kunzelman 2021).

Discussion

The examples in this section demonstrate some common threads in extremist uses of technology to facilitate gender-based violence. First, there is little question that the Internet and communications technology has become an important tool in facilitating both broad-based and targeted violence against women. While the nature of this violence varies between communities, the impacts are often intersectional – disproportionately impacting women of minority ethnic or religious communities as well as members of other marginalized groups. The examples of the Islamic State and far-right or male supremacist communities further show the shortcomings in responses by actors like technology companies and law enforcement. Technology companies have often been reactive, failing to anticipate or immediately perceive how their tools might be used in supporting violence. There is also evidence that there are ongoing gaps in their awareness of varying forms of harassment, in particular the use of niche symbols and language to target specific groups. On the side of law enforcement, the transnational nature of some extremist communities complicated meaningful prosecution of cases involving extremist violence against women. In some cases, women targeted by organized harassment campaigns allege that state governments themselves have been party to the harassment, an issue further explored in Chapter 5 (Jankowicz et al 2021). Taken together, these factors suggest a need to take extremist gender-based violence seriously as a transnational issue that requires a shared recognition of the problem and commitments from a variety of stakeholders to address the issues at hand.

There are, of course, limitations to comparing a well-organized and highly resourced extremist group like the Islamic State to the more diffuse range of communities associated with male supremacism. While the online footprint of the Islamic State was substantial, at one point encompassing tens of thousands of social media accounts on Twitter alone (Berger and Morgan 2015), there is nonetheless evidence that it sought to regulate online communications in the caliphate. In the case of the slave trade, rules regulating the treatment and transfer of slaves were promulgated by the Islamic State (Margolin and Winter 2021). Norms about gender relations were understood to carry over into online spaces, while the control over women's access to the Internet – and, in particular, the differential access accorded to women who joined the Islamic State from abroad – suggested some degree of oversight and consideration as to organizational messaging (Moaveni 2015; Pearson 2018).

The semi-centralized, controlled strategies practised by the Islamic State (at least, during the height of its success) stand in comparison to the more nebulous and decentralized presence of far-right groups. As noted in this chapter, cross-pollination among extremists of varying stripes – including neo-Nazis, Identitarians, White supremacists, incels, conspiracy-minded extremists, and others – is a defining feature of the landscape. Also defining is the broad range of fora through which they operate, including: mainstream social media; small and emerging social media platforms; messaging apps; online message boards; file sharing services like Dropbox; and more. These dual tendencies of cross-pollination and decentralization will likely define the landscape of online extremism in the coming years. While larger social media platforms have sought to become more proactive in policing content, they are supplemented by a growing range of players who either cannot or will not monitor user content. While the organization Tech Against Terrorism (an initiative launched by the UN Counter Terrorism Executive Directorate) offers a mentoring programme for tech startups looking to develop policies to combat terrorist use of their services, participation in this programme requires a good-faith commitment to human rights standards, transparency, and the enforcement of content standards and content moderation policies (Tech Against Terrorism 2020). A subpopulation of tech companies have defined themselves in opposition to these principles, instead promoting themselves as havens of unfettered free speech. This includes social networks like Parler, Gab, Rumble, and MeWe, many of which have capitalized on aggressive content moderation by more established platforms, promising an alternative for right-wing and conspiracy-minded users who view moderation as censorship (Isaac and Browning 2020). Holding these platforms responsible for disinformation or even violent speech has proven difficult, as they are usually backed by web hosting services who further support the mission of free speech (Allyn 2021; Nicas 2021).

Well-intentioned services, too, may find themselves co-opted by extremists where they lack the full capacity to monitor and control content. This was at least partly at issue in the case of the livestreaming platform DLive, which found itself at the centre of debate after the events of 6 January 2021 when it was used by prominent extremists to livestream the storming of the US Capitol. The site, which allows users to livestream and to accept donations via cryptocurrency, was originally created as a rival to the livestream gaming platform Twitch. It relied largely on self-moderation by content authors, a hands-off approach that allowed it to gradually become co-opted by White nationalist and far-right influencers banned by other platforms (D'Anastasio 2021). Communications among DLive executives and employees show that the company was aware of its issues with extremism prior to the 6 January riots, but that it struggled with the potential practical and financial implications of banning extremists. Ultimately, it relied on the hope that its community of users would police itself (Browning and Lorenz 2021).

This diffusion of extremist voices to an array of smaller platforms has contributed to what analysts have called the development of a 'big tent' conspiracy mindset, especially in the wake of the attack on the US Capitol in January 2021 (Argentino et al 2021). Characteristic of this trend is the cross-pollination of ideologies, with some established extremist actors from violent groups actively seeking to reach out to newcomers to platforms like Telegram, looking to steer them towards more extreme channels and content. As a result, Argentino et al (2021) argue that we are witnessing the development of closer ties between militias, conspiracy-based groups like QAnon, and an array of hate groups. These ties often converge around shared narratives, among them misogyny and anti-feminist conspiracy theories, homophobia, and transphobia. The following section explores how these trends play out in one corner of the manosphere, showing both the decentralization and the cross-pollination of extremist discourse.

Into the manosphere: connections between misogyny, conspiracies, and extremism

As noted earlier in the chapter, the 'manosphere' is a collective term applied to a variety of sites catering to men's interests and encompassing several (supposedly) distinct communities. While not all of these communities advocate violence, research suggests that extremist content remains easy to access in the manosphere – even via popular social media platforms like YouTube, Discord, and Reddit. It also suggests that divisions between self-identified manosphere communities like Men's Rights groups, incels, and others are less firm than these groups would like to suggest (Papadamou et al 2020; Sharpe 2020; Horta Ribeiro et al 2021). One factor facilitating the ease of movement between more and less extreme groups has been the diffusion of violent misogyny to purpose-built sites and less-regulated outlets (including 4chan and 8chan/8kun). Researchers attribute this diffusion to actions by social media providers against incels – especially, bans on incel communities, which led to the creation of many alternate sites as free speech havens (Horta Ribeiro et al 2021). This leads to an environment in which allegedly less extreme misogynist communities are allowed to retain a presence on mainstream social media, in turn using this presence to share outlinks to more extreme communities who have been quarantined or deplatformed for violating content policies.

To date, incel communities have been the groups most closely associated with violence in the manosphere, prompting bans on some incel communities – especially on Reddit, where these groups were most active. These bans prompted the growth of purpose-built forums catering to incels. Other manosphere communities – Men's Rights advocates, PUAs, and Red Pill communities – appear to be viewed as conspiracy-based but not as potentially violent; they have correspondingly been allowed to maintain a presence on Reddit, YouTube, and some other major platforms.[9]

The existence of defined subreddits or channels devoted to these groups provides the illusion of barriers, suggesting a distinct population of users and moderators within each group, separated by some ideological firewall. However, researchers have called into question the rigidity of such barriers, offering evidence that users are funnelled from less-extreme to more-extreme groups, with membership overlapping and with more extreme voices gaining purchase across communities (Fitzgerald 2020; Horta Ribeiro et al 2021). At the time of this writing, the most well-known incel and MGTOW communities were banned from Reddit, while larger PUA and MRA subreddits existed as open communities, accessible to any user and publicly viewable without logging in. Subreddits associated with Red Pill ideology existed but were quarantined. 'Quarantines' on a subreddit take the form of a simple content warning when a user enters these communities. Upon acknowledging receipt of the warning and verifying status as a registered Reddit user, the communities are accessible without further restriction.

Subreddits within the manosphere are used to share outlinks to sites and forums that advertise themselves as places where users may speak more freely about gender politics and other matters. In an earlier work, I conducted a content analysis of one dedicated 'Red Pill' forum I accessed through outlinks from Reddit, which hosted (among other topics) an uncensored discussion of conspiracies related to the 2020 US presidential election (Henshaw 2021a). Subsequent to that analysis, I returned to analyse approximately six weeks of posts from that same forum, to further explore how it demonstrates both the decentralization of extremist discourse and the cross-pollination of extremist narratives. The analysis of these posts further demonstrates how entrepreneurial users advocating extremist beliefs can navigate content moderation policies in ways that allow them to retain a foothold on mainstream social media platforms while also steering users towards more extreme communities.

This particular Red Pill forum ('The Red Pill' or TRP) is a standalone site that also maintains what it calls an 'official' presence on YouTube, Twitter, and Reddit,[10] as well as a Discord channel which is occasionally advertised to users. The forum has some nominal content policy that includes the following items:

- no illegal images or images depicting illegal activity;
- no suggestion, incitement, or records of breaking federal or state law;
- no threats;
- no promoting violence or injury;
- no racism or hate speech;
- no doxxing;
- no trolling;
- no profanity in usernames.

While TRP does not specifically disallow women, its terms of service suggest that anyone who does not promote 'masculine interests' or who challenges its users and their 'shared goals' will be advised to leave the site. In both the terms of service and a 'frequently asked questions' document, the founder/moderator makes clear that the site interprets 'Red Pill' as an ideology relevant to 'sexual strategy' and a discussion of 'sexual dynamics' – that is, a foundation specifically relevant to gender. The site appears to sustain itself via referral links on the platforms noted earlier (especially, Reddit), by a system of bitcoin donations, and by use of a crowdfunding model on a Patreon site. Users of Brave – a privacy browser – can also give tips to the site in the form of Basic Attention Token, a cryptocurrency. All material on the forum is publicly viewable, and I did not have to create an account or engage with users to follow this content.

Topics covered on the forum include Red Pill ideology, politics, investments, and general chat. As mentioned, I chose to focus on the subforum discussing the 2020 US election and the presidency of Joe Biden because of the politically relevant nature of the discussion. In a period covering late April to early June 2021, I monitored about six weeks of activity in this forum, totalling 305 posts and replies with unique contributions from 24 users.[11] Though the sub-forum was about US politics, the geographic location of users was unclear. Most appeared to be in the United States, although two identified themselves as being located in Europe. While some analyses of the manosphere have relied on computational text analysis (Papadamou et al 2020; Horta Ribeiro et al 2021), I chose to give a close reading to a smaller number of posts. As noted by Rafail and Freitas (2019), the sharing of information is a substantial part of dynamics in the manosphere. This variously takes the form of the transmission of links, screenshots, embedded videos, and other graphic content that can be difficult to capture in an approach reliant solely on text mining. By reading and coding each post, I hope to better capture the complex nature of the discussion.

Unsurprisingly, given the nature of the board and the site in general, the resulting data show that election and anti-government conspiracies were widespread. Approximately one in every five posts on the board referenced either election-based conspiracies or economic conspiracies. Common among the economic theories was the notion that the government is attempting to devalue citizens' currency by printing more money – a central bank conspiracy with long historical roots which is also common in cryptocurrency communities (Golumbia 2016).

> You're being bled out. They will provide as many excuses as necessary about why your dollars no longer buy things. … Every time that something has been contrived there will be a permanent excuse as to why your pathetic paper dollars no longer are good for anything.

Even more salient than these topics, though, were the expression of anti-vaccination, anti-mask views and the circulation of disinformation about the COVID-19 pandemic, which accounted for 23 per cent of posts. At various times, different users (or, sometimes, the same users) alternately claimed that the pandemic was not real, that it was real but planned by elites and/or China, that masks were ineffective, that vaccines were ineffective, or that vaccines were dangerous for reasons including infertility, the potential to kill recipients (especially children), or because they were used for mind control. Anti-vaccination conspiracies were widespread on social media prior to COVID-19, but during the pandemic researchers found that existing networks for anti-vaccine conversations also became conduits for spreading a variety of conspiratorial views including conservative conspiracy theories (Jamison et al 2020).

> Don't listen to propaganda polls on vaccination numbers. They lied about everything else. … Go out and actually talk to people, I have. Most are afraid of the shots.

Many conspiratorial ideas were supported by similar calls for fellow users to do their own 'research' or consult the 'evidence' provided by others on the forum. Sources cited in the portion of the conversation I followed included programming on Fox News, talk radio shows, podcasts, posts on other social media communities frequented by those with far-right views like Gab, and assorted screenshots of unknown origin. At one point, a user did cite a medical journal article on the supposed ineffectiveness of masks, but this user misrepresented the study's findings. The article in question only argued the ineffectiveness of mask *mandates* and did find mask *usage* effective in slowing the spread of transmission of COVID-19.

While these vignettes show the interplay among conspiracy theories, of greatest interest to this text are discussions of violence and links to misogyny. Considering the nature of the forum, the number of posts on this sub-forum explicitly making misogynist statements was small, only about 6.5 per cent of the total. However, much of that was discourse disparaging or casting suspicion upon female politicians. Female leaders and/or political figures singled out on the forum included: US Vice President Kamala Harris, Congresswomen Nancy Pelosi and Alexandria Ocasio-Cortez, Senator Kirsten Gillibrand, Chicago Mayor Lori Lightfoot, White House spokesperson Jen Psaki, Michigan Governor Gretchen Whitmer, and US Assistant Secretary for Health Rachel Levine. By comparison, the number of male politicians singled out for critique or conspiracies was much smaller. Canadian Prime Minister Justin Trudeau and US President Joe Biden were mentioned multiple times; UK Prime Minister Boris Johnson and US Senator Joe Manchin were also mentioned but only once each.

Previous studies have noted that female politicians are frequently subject to online harassment or conspiracy theories, with women of colour disproportionately targeted for abuse (IPU 2016; Amnesty International 2018; Jankowicz et al 2021). That seemed to be the case on this forum as well. In particular, the focus on Dr Rachel Levine, a transgender women serving at the time as an assistant secretary in the Department of Health and Human Services, also pointed to a virulent trend towards homophobic and transphobic speech. Discourse about Levine specifically has been noted as a common theme across extremist channels and forums, and is seen as a narrative related to preoccupations with threats to the gender binary or masculine gender roles (Argentino et al 2021).[12] On this particular forum, there were more explicitly anti-LGBTQI+ posts (9.5 per cent of all posts) than there were openly misogynistic posts. The existence of an entire other sub-forum for the discussion of gender issues may have impacted this balance, as users specifically discussing gender roles might gravitate to those other discussions; yet concerns over LGBTQI+ rights and transgender rights in general seemed a significant preoccupation among the users. Racial issues were another a significant topic of discussion (8.9 per cent of posts), including condemnation of Black Lives Matter as a violent group and generally anti-racist or anti-immigrant sentiments.

Just over 6 per cent of the posts I coded made reference to political violence, were an incitement to violence, or referenced a coming or ongoing war. This is a small number of the overall posts but is nonetheless concerning. Just four users authored the majority of posts containing violent rhetoric. In previous analysis of this forum, I noted that users referred to a 'Civil War' in the United States and to the country as being 'at war' in the wake of the 2020 presidential elections (Henshaw 2021a). This discourse persisted on the forum months later. There were allusions to civil war in the United States, to a coming world war, and to a need to prepare and defend oneself.

> Lots of people expect the civil war. ... There are already talks of how to cut off the cities the exact moment they try stuff.

> First it was the revolutionary war, then it was the civil war, then it was WW2. Next it will be something of equal scale we haven't seen in 3 generations.

Recourse to violence was justified by this environment of war and by the perceived erosion of traditional security institutions, like the military and law enforcement. Posters repeatedly claimed that the police and military were being purged in advance of some operation to seize property, seize guns, or execute opponents of the government. Some users expressed a fear of being SWATted, that is, harassed or killed by security forces under false pretenses, presumably by government agents looking to silence critics.

User 1:   We will all get swatted one at a time.
User 2:   They don't have to SWAT all of us, just enough to send a signal.

In the face of violent threats, posters justified violent responses, urging one another to arm themselves, stockpile, and be prepared to fight:

> It doesn't matter what Bitcoin is worth or how many millions of dollars you have in the bank if you don't know how to grow food and your hungry socialist neighbors are rounding up anybody who looks like a productive capitalist and shooting him.

To some posters, anyone with opposing political views was a legitimate target:

> No one has any concerns about lining these crazies up against a wall. Even the conservative soccer moms. … If liberals are left in power they will continue to proceed as they have and destroy us until there is nothing left.

Statements like these deploy the discourse of radicalization through dehumanization and the portrayal of existential threat. Again, a small subset of users dominated these discussions, but they expressed these views without visible opposition from others. While I did observe users debating the accuracy of vaccine (mis)information and some economic conspiracies, posts expressing violent rhetoric did not receive a strong rebuke. This points to a systemic failure to moderate the site in any meaningful way. Despite the nominal content policy mentioned earlier, there were clear and repeated instances of hate speech and incitements to violence. This combines with earlier observations of the same forum in which I noted that forum participants were sharing/reproducing images of crimes taking place at the US Capitol on 6 January 2021, another apparent violation of the terms of service. In spite of all this, as noted, this community is allowed to retain a foothold on mainstream social media platforms, with some of the same individuals apparently running those communities and using those sites to advertise links to this offsite location.

These examples serve to illustrate how online misogyny and extremist discourse – even beyond gender-based extremism – are intertwined. They further show how misogynistic communities beyond incels demonstrate violent propensities. Debates over whether to more closely regulate the manosphere, in particular on major social media platforms, are often boiled down to free speech issues. The foregoing examples show the misleading nature of these arguments. On the one hand, social media is not the public square. Platforms are allowed to create and enforce terms of service. There is also an expectation of good faith among platforms and their communities of users. When users access social media sites with the purpose of advertising and recruiting for extremist outlets, that should constitute a clear violation of most platforms' terms of use. Indeed, it seems that a number of manosphere communities in places like Reddit have already been on the receiving end of warnings and/or measures like quarantines. Rather than properly regulating their communities in response to these sanctions, though, rogue actors have continued to find new ways to violate the spirit – if not the letter – of these policies. Where content creators at offsite locations create nominal terms of service, then consistently fail to enforce them, that is clearly a bad faith act. Finally, the very notion of creating sites as 'free speech' havens that promise no censorship, but then *a priori* banning large groups of people – including women, the LGBTQI+ community, and/or anyone who disagrees with the dominant politics – is a contradiction. None of this is to say that men should not have distinct spaces online; indeed, many such communities do exist without devolving into violent discourse. But the experiment in allowing misogynistic groups to thrive in a largely unregulated environment has evidently failed to rein in violent rhetoric and mis- or disinformation. Given the propensity for violence demonstrated by incel communities, there seems to be ample justification for discussions about more closely regulating the manosphere as a whole.

Responding to extremist gender-based violence

How can the problem of gender-based extremism be dealt with? The debate on this subject is also distorted through the fun house mirrors of online discussions. As noted, the call for free speech online has been used as a rallying cry by those wishing to forestall any discussion of content moderation. In a crowded marketplace of forums, messaging apps, social media providers, and file-sharing or media-sharing sites, taking any action that could be branded as censorship becomes both an economic and a moral decision on the part of technology companies. Too often, financial considerations have guided efforts to combat online extremism. A 2021 audit of the GIFCT, a joint initiative established in 2017 by Facebook, Twitter, Microsoft, and YouTube and (as of this writing) consisting of 17 participating member companies, found that the group's efforts too often focused on the low-hanging fruit of targeting high-profile extremist organizations. Islamic communities online, for example, were aggressively policed by platforms for potential extremist content, while right-wing and White supremacist groups were often overlooked. This problem was further complicated by virtue of the number of far-right communities as well as the proliferation of problematic content among individual users rather than easily identifiable groups (BSR 2021). This focus on high-profile activity was also seen as a symptom of Western biases among technology companies, with most GIFCT members concentrated in the United States and/or Europe. The audit concluded that the aim of combating online extremism on a global scale could not be accomplished without buy-in from digital providers outside of the United States and Europe, suggesting that tech companies might also benefit significantly from capacity-building efforts (BSR 2021). The P/CVE community writ large similarly struggles to craft solutions to extremism that avoid stereotypes, with critics noting that efforts lean heavily on Islamic extremism while ignoring other violent ideologies. The role of women in spreading extremist views is another overlooked area, as young men are the primary referent of many initiatives (Winterbotham 2018; Rothermel 2020). Much more remains to be said about this issue, and Chapter 6 explores some spaces where innovators – many of them women – are involved in novel approaches to combat online extremism and harassment. Before that, though, this analysis turns to a related issue: How states also deploy technology for gendered harms.

5

Technological Surveillance, States, and Gendered Insecurity

Examining questions of surveillance and policing in international relations invites us to engage in a conversation with surveillance studies. Lyon (2007) defines surveillance as: 'Focused, systematic and routine attention to personal details for purposes of influence, management, protection, or direction.' Effectively, this can mean any process that monitors behaviour for reasons other than idle curiosity (Lyon 2007). At its most expansive, the definition of surveillance encompasses surveillance for commercial reasons, in a corporate/managerial context, as a security act, or even within the context of the family – that is, surveillance of a spouse or child. Surveillance studies, however, also situates surveillance within the process of modern state-building, drawing on the work of Foucault (2019 [1975]). Beginning with early efforts by the state to collect data and track citizens – often, in the service of taxation or to monitor the spread of disease – surveillance studies sees continuity with the proliferation of surveillance in modern society. As a field, surveillance studies is interested in not only *why* this trajectory has unfolded as it has but also how systems, institutions, bureaucracies, and societies interact to create this landscape (Ball et al 2012). While technology development and computing power (especially, the rise of big data culture as discussed in Chapter 2) are important pieces of the puzzle in understanding the spread of surveillance, surveillance studies also takes an interest in exploring how the rise of corporate cultures, the diffusion of security threats (real or perceived), and permissive attitudes in society and government have facilitated the rise of surveillance (Ball et al 2012; Petersen 2012).

The types of questions asked in surveillance studies invite dialogue with both political science and feminist international relations. While surveillance studies has primarily been viewed as a sociological discipline, its inherent reflections on power dynamics necessarily make these topics political (Lyon 2007). Moreover, the differential impacts of surveillance systems or cultures on marginalized groups invite reflection about how gender, race, class, (dis) ability, sexuality, and other axes of difference play into discussions about surveillance. While gender is in its own right a useful topic of analysis, considering the new forms of insecurity that surveillance introduces for women, authors argue that a feminist approach to surveillance studies must be intersectional (Koskela 2012; Magnet and Dubrofsky 2015). Though surveillance studies broadly has an activist orientation – calling for work that opens up space for resistance, advocacy, and accountability – feminist surveillance studies further calls for attention to the engagement of diverse stakeholders in these discussions (Ball et al 2012; Magnet and Dubrofsky 2015). The goals of feminist surveillance studies, then, align with aims of FSS.

While surveillance as a concept may encompass a range of activities, in this chapter I examine a particular subset of surveillance activities, which is surveillance as a high-tech form of policing. I define 'policing' as activities in support of domestic security forces or the maintenance of domestic political order. This implies, first, an interest in surveillance activities undertaken by a government or those acting on behalf of a government. It additionally implies an interest in the micro- versus macro- level of 'security' interventions – especially, individuals and communities as a referent of security practice. This discussion frames the use of surveillance technologies on marginalized groups as a human security issue.

Though terms like 'security' and 'human security' are more recognized and comfortable within international relations, 'policing' may invite discomfort. Policing as a concept is at once more diffuse and more quotidian than security, traditionally defined. By deploying the concept of policing, I invite reflection upon the messiness of discussions about security, human security, or the security state. Indeed, the emergence of human security as a concept acknowledged that 'security' could no longer be perceived as solely state-centric. Human security speaks to both the proliferation of possible agents of (in)security and the transnational nature of many threats after the Cold War – including crime, ethnic violence, and environmental issues.[1] While human security discussions often envisioned the need for states and international organizations to be accountable for the security of individuals and communities, a discussion centred on policing takes these ideas a step further – introducing systems, corporate actors, developers, and even end users into the discussion.

How does policing enter the realm of international relations? Easily, it turns out. Distinctions between policing entities (broadly defined) and security forces (especially, state militaries) are often rooted in Western concepts of liberal democracy, which see police and military as defined and discrete actors. In many such contexts, militaries are viewed as the agents of external security (with little to no domestic role), while police serve the functions of domestic law enforcement. This does not, of course, map on to systems of government on the global scale. In developing countries, legal systems often fail to articulate (or enforce) a bright-line distinction between domestic and international security forces.

Latin America serves as a prime example of this, with over a dozen countries in the region having constitutional provisions that guarantee a role for the military as agents of internal order. These provisions, often vaguely defined, range from allowing the military to engage in law enforcement, to allowing it a role in 'development', to positioning the military as a kind of check on power akin to a fourth branch of government (Wiarda and Collins 2011). Many of these provisions have historical roots. Smith and Sells (2016) note that, throughout the region, the military plays an important role in national myth, as the prime mover behind independence struggles. Military power is further bolstered by the historical salience of domestic security threats (real or imagined) including insurgencies, organized criminal syndicates, restive populations, etc. In the modern context, militaries in Latin America tend to be viewed as the more professionalized, popular, and trustworthy agents of domestic security, as opposed to police forces – who are frequently associated with dereliction or corruption (Smith and Sells 2016; Pion-Berlin and Carreras 2017). Across the region, police are viewed as the public service most likely to demand and receive bribes – a phenomenon that is gendered. While men are deemed more likely to exchange monetary bribes, sextortion (that is, demands of sex in exchange for services) is a crime that often affects women (Transparency International 2019).

With criminal violence a major security threat in Latin America, the fragmentation of the security state is a critically important issue. The overlapping roles of diverse actors in policing introduces questions about surveillance, the use of force, and accountability. Security cooperation policies further render these issues transnational in nature with financial assistance, training, technology-sharing, and even data-sharing as important elements of regional anti-crime policies.[2] Pion-Berlin and Carreras (2017) point out that, although support for military involvement in policing is greatest in countries with more crime (especially the Northern Triangle of El Salvador, Honduras, and Guatemala), military actors in these countries are often trained to use maximum force in responding to crime – potentially leading to collateral damage or civilian casualties.

The so-called 'false positives' scandal in Colombia demonstrates what can happen when reliance on the military for domestic policing goes wrong. An inquiry by the special court established in Colombia's 2016 peace accord with the FARC concluded that, between 2002 and 2008, military forces killed more than 6,000 civilians, subsequently passing them off as enemy combatants (BBC News 2021). Many of these victims were young men from poor communities. The practice of killing civilians (especially, young men) and subsequently portraying them as members of guerrilla groups has been attributed to a desire to bolster the perceived efficacy of Colombian troops in order to justify continued security aid from the United States, as well as the desire of individual units to receive bonuses promised by the government (Wood 2009; Asmann 2021). The occurrence of false positives thereby shows a clear intent to game a data-driven system of policing and reward. Not only were individuals who committed these atrocities rewarded, but their actions justified the continued policing of the communities where these killings occurred. Thus, in alignment with long-standing institutional biases against poor and rural Colombians, abusive policing became a self-reinforcing system with communities continually subject to surveillance (Gordon 2017).

While the involvement of militaries in policing represents one example of how we can see policing as international relations, the proliferation of private security forces is another dynamic that plays out across multiple levels of analysis. Avant (2004) notes that private security actors have become an important part of war-making, estimating that the ratio of contractors to military personnel was about 1 to 10 during Operation Iraqi Freedom. Domestically, the use (and even deputization of) private security actors has become increasingly common. State governments are the number one employer of private security forces in African countries, with states like Nigeria heavily reliant on private security for counterterrorism operations (Avant and Neu 2019; Suchi 2019). In Latin America, the number of licensed private security firms grew significantly from the mid-1990s into the early 2000s, coinciding with rising concerns about crime in the region (Ungar 2007). In developed countries too we see an increase in private security presence for functions including crowd control, surveillance over high-crime neighbourhoods, and building security (Strom et al 2010).

Relevant to international relations is the extent to which private security is a globalized, transnational industry that impacts domestic and international security. Though states are increasingly reliant on this industry, accountability for these actors is weak (Avant 2004). Avant and Neu (2019) find allegations of misconduct against private security actors spiking in both Latin America and Africa since about 2008. Private security employees were responsible for atrocities during conflicts in Iraq and Afghanistan including the 2007 Nisour Square Massacre, which killed 17 civilians and injured 20 others (Singer 2007). The fact that four employees of Blackwater Security Consulting were convicted of crimes associated with the massacre, only to be pardoned by President Donald Trump in 2020, seems to reinforce accountability concerns. Singer (2007) argues that the US reliance on private security in counterterrorism operations exacerbated the very problems it was trying to resolve. While government agencies were spread so thin as to be unable to properly supervise private security, these actors were increasingly tasked with high-priority work. The results were abuses by private security forces, graft, mission creep, and a growing disconnect from local populations (Singer 2007).

Gender mainstreaming is another area in which accountability for private security is lacking. Ironically, the growing dependence on private security actors coincides with a time in which gender mainstreaming in traditional security forces was gaining traction, in part as a result of UN Security Council Resolution 1325. Security sector reform provisions designed to promote the inclusion of women are one common gender provision in peace accords. Agreements in countries including Afghanistan, Sudan, Nepal, Yemen, and Burundi have addressed the need to build inclusive military and police forces, in connection with the WPS Agenda (Bell et al 2019). Countries including the United States, Liberia, the United Kingdom, and North Macedonia have embedded provisions for security sector reform into their WPS NAPs (Ghittoni et al 2019). Yet private security remains an overwhelmingly male industry. One survey of the profession in the United States found that private security employees were 53 per cent White and 77 per cent male (Strom et al 2010). It is no coincidence that the gender imbalance in private security forces mirrors enduring gender imbalances in police and military forces, as former and even current police and military personnel are given preferential treatment in private security hiring. In the United States, moonlighting by police officers in private security is common (Strom et al 2010). Latin American countries likewise struggle with potential conflicts of interest among police officers looking to supplement low salaries by taking side jobs in private security (Ungar 2007). Feminist scholarship argues that the privatization of security can be parsed both as a neoliberal act and a gendered one, re-masculinizing security in the face of efforts to disrupt traditional sites of masculinity (that is, militaries and police forces) through gender mainstreaming (Stachowitsch 2015).

The addition of surveillance technologies into this milieu further fragments accountability and legitimacy in the security state. Technology companies and developers are unquestionably part of the rise of the surveillance state, meaning that the dynamics of gender imbalance within technology professions (as discussed in Chapter 2) come back into play. Feminist work in surveillance studies has demonstrated how these technologies introduce new forms of gendered insecurity, enabling new expressions of violence against women (like 'upskirt' photography) while also policing the gender binary and conformity with gender norms (Koskela 2012; Petersen 2012). Surveillance systems that flag prosthetics, elaborate hairstyles, or otherwise nonconforming bodies show how surveillance can disproportionately impact women, people of colour, transgender or nonbinary populations, and the disabled (Magnet and Dubrofsky 2015). But who bears responsibility for the abuses of such systems?

As with other cases discussed in this book, the elevation of technology as a force for good and a source of power obscures the human role in creating and using such systems. A surveillance studies approach calls upon us to question the roles of both producers and end users in perpetuating harm. While futurists once predicted that technology would render censorship impossible and serve as an anti-authoritarian force (Kaku 2011), such predictions seem utopian in light of struggles with disinformation and censorship. Technology companies headquartered in developed countries are especially complicit in upholding expansive surveillance systems elsewhere in the world, while paying lip-service to freedom of expression at home. The complicity of companies like Google, Cisco, Microsoft, Apple, and others in upholding China's 'Great Firewall' is one such example that has been widely reported upon (McMahon and Bennett 2011; Simonte 2019). Other recent examples include Facebook's complicity with government surveillance in Vietnam and the role of Twitter and Disney (via its subsidiary Hotstar) in censoring content critical of India's ruling BJP (Rosen 2020; Dwoskin et al 2021; Freedom House 2021). Yet the emergence of new technologies increasingly blurs the boundaries between producers and users, creating fuzzy networks of 'prosumers' (Magnet and Dubrofsky 2015). Especially with systems that leverage AI or machine learning, end users can unwittingly become programmers, feeding data back into the surveillance systems and training them in ways that can perpetuate bias. Many readers of this book have likely taken part in this process without even knowing it. Billions of public user images scraped from Facebook, Venmo, YouTube, and other sites were included in training data for the Clearview AI facial recognition system, a program now used by hundreds of law enforcement agencies, private security companies, retailers, and government agencies who pay thousands of dollars each in licensing fees (Hill 2020; Mac et al 2020).[3] A *New York Times* report showed that law enforcement officers are strongly supportive of Clearview AI and similar facial recognition systems, despite limited understanding of how they work. Some law enforcement agents who used Clearview AI were unaware that images they inputted into the system were being added to the company's database (Hill 2020).

The concept of 'ghost work' or 'fauxtomation' is another source of uncertainty and potential bias in the surveillance workflow. Ghost work leverages large pools of contingent or gig labour to train AI systems with little oversight and for extremely low pay. Increasingly, these tasks include surveillance and/or security-related roles. McCallum (2020) recounts discussions with gig labourers using Amazon's mTurk system who took part in training surveillance systems for unmanned aerial vehicles. Gray and Suri (2019) interview an Indian worker doing content moderation tasks on a similar platform, who admitted she sometimes job shares with her children – relying on them to identify offensive English-language words, presumably for content moderation work. Labour relations play an important role in shaping human-systems interaction, with abusive or rote labour practices contributing to abusive or improper uses of surveillance technology – a finding which should cause us to question the technology industry's widespread reliance on gig labour (Smith 2004). Other studies of how end-users interact with surveillance systems show that human biases can shape how technologies are deployed, with gender, race/ethnicity, and age shaping both who is targeted and who is deemed a security threat (Armstrong and Norris 1999; McCahill 2002; G.J.D. Smith 2012).

Gendering surveillance and policing

Having situated surveillance, technology, and policing as topics that are both interrelated and relevant in the realm of international relations, it is worth looking further at how critical theories have engaged with these concepts. Specifically, we can consider what may be added to feminist international relations theory or security studies by engaging with feminist surveillance studies. Each of these schools of thought shares several common themes: First, there is a concern with the lived experience of gender and with how gender manifests as a power relationship. Second, there is an interest in defining 'security' concerns broadly, especially as they relate to human security and exposure to the continuum of violence. Third, there is a shared interest in how intersectionality shapes experience. Fourth, there is a shared ethical concern surrounding resistance and activism. I will explore each of these points in turn; however, I argue that engagement with feminist surveillance studies also raises the possibility for another connection with FSS, which is the concern over privacy. While privacy as an interest and value is implied throughout FSS, it is not always engaged as directly or as coherently in FSS as it is in feminist surveillance studies work. Additionally, I argue that feminist surveillance studies provokes greater reflection upon the role of technology in shaping gendered security and insecurity – including questions of insecurity by omission.

To begin at a baseline, FSS and feminist surveillance studies each take a clear interest in how gender manifests as a power relationship, shaping both lived experience and ideas about whose experiences matter. In patriarchal societies, institutions, belief systems, and behaviours all serve to dichotomize and police gender binaries, while at the same time creating hierarchies that valorize associations with masculinity (Runyan and Peterson 2013). At times, this androcentric or male-centred focus functions to the complete exclusion of the interests or experiences of women. The result in fields like political science and international relations was a partial knowledge of political phenomena largely based on male knowers, male-dominated power structures, and narrowly defined concepts of security and power that failed to capture the experiences and interests of women (Peterson 1992; Weldon 2006; Zalewski 2006). Women merely haunted the edges of disciplinary knowledge, defined primarily by their absence (Zalewski 2006). In the realm of security, disciplining these boundaries often occurs through a process of coding security threats. 'Hard' security interventions – those associated with technical, quantifiable, and ostensibly more urgent threats – generally take priority over 'soft' interventions – those deemed as social, quotidian, or ongoing, that is, areas in which easy or fast wins are rarely possible (Williams 2002; Cohn 2014). The latter, of course, are often more closely associated with women (including healthcare, safety from domestic violence, and so on) and are feminized and devalued by association (Williams 2002; Cohn 2014). As noted in Chapter 2, though initiatives like the WPS Agenda or the MDG/SDGs were meant to be transformative in this regard, in fact their scope has been narrowed by an overriding concern in showing fast, measurable, and high-impact interventions.

Feminist surveillance studies, too, sees how gendered institutions and social structures have defined our field of vision regarding what it means to be secure. Modern surveillance is seen as reinforcing the 'male gaze', that is, the androcentric perspective that centres male interests and priorities as the default, while distracting from the new manifestations of insecurity that women face from the spread of surveillance technologies (Koskela 2012; Gill 2019). Scholarship in this area suggests that male operators (who, as already noted, often comprise the majority of security actors) frequently deploy surveillance tech in the service of voyeurism, while at the same time overlooking situations, locations, and so on, that represent potential sites of harm for women (Armstrong and Norris 1999; Koskela 2012; Abu-Laban 2015). New forms of insecurity also emerge from new technologies. Upskirt photography, revenge porn, cyberstalking, and even zoombombing are all examples of gendered acts of surveillance which, while possible to some degree without the assistance of modern technology, are facilitated and made more accessible by the spread of surveillance tech (Koskela 2012; Burton et al 2020). Just as FSS calls for attention to the myriad ways in which gendered insecurity is shaped by different agents, feminist surveillance studies calls for attention as well to how wider technology access enables everyone to become the watcher as well as the watched, with peer-to-peer surveillance and even self-surveillance topics of concern, alongside surveillance by governments or private companies (Gill 2019).

The gendered power relationships inherent in surveillance also call for attention to neoliberalism, another shared topic of interest. Insofar as FSS sees security as deeply intertwined with political economy (True 2012; Elias and Rai 2015; Stern 2017), how neoliberalism disciplines gender is interrelated with ideas about security. Neoliberal ideas about masculinity disadvantage women, but also individuals from a variety of minority and/or minoritized groups. Peterson (2003) warned decades ago of the coming virtual economy, in which data would be quantified, analysed, and valorized according to the perceived value of the individual. Following 9/11, Puar

(2007) further cautioned about the construction of militarized data bodies through surveillance, an act encoding the politics of race, gender, sexuality, and so on, in ways that are sanitized by the discourse of security and the processes of technology. Feminist surveillance studies work, too, cautions about the passive construction of 'data doubles'. Increasingly, the average user has little knowledge about or ability to control what these virtual identities say about us (Koskela 2012). Extractive processes of data collection and tracking are particularly pronounced in systems that women are most likely to interact with, including social welfare systems and healthcare systems (Koskela 2012; Mason and Magnet 2012; Abu-Laban 2015).

These interlinkages between race/ethnicity, nationality, sexuality, and class further provoke reflection on the intersectional impact of surveillance. While FSS should take intersectionality as a core value, engagement with non-Western and/or postcolonial perspectives has been a source of tension within FSS (Sylvester 2010; Parashar 2016). These tensions are especially evident in evaluations of the WPS Agenda, where critiques centre around the omission or devaluation of Global South perspectives, the use of WPS as a tool in service of global and racial power hierarchies, and the exclusion of queer populations (Basu 2016; Hagen 2016; Basu and Kirby 2020; Haastrup and Hagen 2020, 2021). Feminist surveillance studies takes intersectionality as a core principle, and indeed analyses reveal how a gendered approach to understanding surveillance cannot exist without attention to other axes of difference (Magnet and Dubrofsky 2015).

Historically, race/ethnicity and gender are seen as co-constituting forces in the development of modern surveillance. In this critical genealogy, surveillance is born not only out of concern with basic institutional functions like public health and taxation, but also from institutionalized practices of slavery and settler colonialism. Biometric data has historically been used against non-White populations including indigenous peoples, slaves, migrants, and colonial subjects in the service of both eugenics and governance (Browne 2012; Walter and Andersen 2013; Smith 2015). The result was systems of surveillance built around institutionalizing racial hierarchies. These include the use of fingerprinting in colonial India as an assistive technology for British government officials as well as the development of analogue forms of facial recognition (via mug books) in the western United States to assist in the policing of Chinese immigrants (Browne 2012; Karimi 2019). Residential schools for indigenous populations like those used in the United States, Canada, and Australia also functioned as a form of surveillance, ensuring students' adoption of 'appropriate' (that is, Western) cultural practices including sexuality and gender norms (Smith 2015).

Today, some of the most important work on surveillance technology as policing comes from anti-racist scholarship. This includes work on AI, predictive policing, facial recognition, and algorithmic bias. Black feminist technology studies and intersectional critical race technology studies see dynamics of race and gender as inseparable in the context of modern technology (Noble and Tynes 2016a). Noble's (2018) work on algorithmic bias demonstrates this, showing how search engine algorithms reinforce the criminalization of men and boys of colour while sexualizing and fetishizing non-White women and girls. Similar biases are baked into facial recognition systems. Buolamwini and Gebru (2018) note that, among the datasets most often used to train facial recognition systems, the overwhelming majority of subjects (over 75 per cent in each dataset) were White. Testing commercially available facial recognition systems, they found that darker skinned women were misidentified up to 34.7 per cent of the time, compared to a 0.8 per cent error rate for lighter skinned men. These findings have obvious implications when these systems are deployed in service of policing and/or security. Errors by facial recognition systems have been responsible for at least two arrests in the United States, but numbers are not widely reported because there is little oversight in how these systems are used. In the United States, authorities are not required to disclose when arrests are made based on the use of this technology (Jones 2021).

In the face of complex inequalities, a call to activism is a final feature that links feminist international relations/security studies work with surveillance studies. Both schools of thought ask researchers to approach study in a way that centres and seeks to improve lived experience for marginalized groups (Tickner 2006; Ball et al 2012; Magnet and Dubrofsky 2015). In the service of this goal, the remainder of this chapter centres experiences of surveillance and abuses of technology by states and state actors in the name of security. This asks us to explore space for feminist and intersectional responses.

Technology and the surveillance of feminist activists

In 2015, discussions about the security of feminist activists entered global discourse following the arrests of China's 'Feminist Five'. The five – Li Maizi, Wu Rongrong, Zheng Churan, Wei Tingting, and Wang Man – were activists arrested in the lead-up to International Women's Day, apparently in response to their plans to highlight the issue of sexual harassment on public transit. At least some of these women had been engaged in feminist activism and protest for years, but at the time of their arrest they were relatively unknown (Hong Fincher 2018). Their arrest and detention, however, captured global consciousness and prompted public protest and calls from world leaders for their release. Though the activists were released after 37 days, they indicated that – in addition to the harassment and abuse they had suffered while incarcerated – they were subjected to ongoing state surveillance and censorship, especially of their online communications (Hong Fincher 2018).

That the women's online discourse was of special interest is hardly surprising. Social media has been credited with playing a large role in the emergence of a new wave of feminism in China. Scholars note that, while women's groups in China had been running hotlines since the 1990s, by 2010 they had developed a substantial presence online including via websites, digital publications, messaging groups, and a presence on the microblogging platform Weibo (Wang and Driscoll 2019; Ling and Liao 2020; Wang and Liu 2020). Of interest to China's feminists were both domestic advocacy – especially, on topics like domestic violence, sexual harassment, and state reproductive policies – and alignment with transnational campaigns like the #MeToo movement (Hong Fincher 2018; Wang and Driscoll 2019; Wang and Liu 2020). Foreign support for feminists in China – including from diaspora groups, NGOs, and foreign governments – may be a factor in shaping state repression (Hong Fincher 2018; Wang 2018). China's version of the #MeToo hashtag, for example, has experienced both state censorship and backlash from prominent figures who have called into question the movement's consistency with Chinese culture and values (Hong Fincher 2018; Ling and Liao 2020). Ironically, though, the arrest of the Feminist Five may have served to strengthen the role of online spaces in feminist discourse (Ling and Liao 2020). Though censorship of feminists online has intensified since the arrest of the Feminist Five, artistic visual (and even meme-able) displays of feminist messaging remain a tool for consciousness raising and a possible means to evade state censorship (Wang and Liu 2020).

As noted, many technology companies located in the Global North have come under scrutiny for their involvement in supporting China's system of state censorship. This complicity has historical parallels. Polaroid's support of the passbook system in apartheid-era South Africa and the involvement of IBM (and its subsidiaries) in supporting Germany's Nazi government during the Holocaust stand out as examples of the historical relation between the IT industry and state systems of surveillance and repression (Black 2012; Benjamin 2019). Furthermore, China is not alone in its deployment of technological surveillance against feminist and other social movements. Authorities in countries including Hungary, Nigeria, Saudi Arabia, the United Arab Emirates, and Russia have been accused of surveilling feminist activists in recent years (Peto and Grzebalska 2016; Lokshina 2017; Onyesoh et al 2020; Walker et al 2021). In addition to these accusations, state interests have been accused of supporting gendered disinformation and ICT-facilitated harassment campaigns against women journalists and public figures in countries including Azerbaijan, Iran, China, Mexico, and Russia (Ahmed and Perlroth 2017; Freedom House 2019; Geybulla 2019, 2020; Jankowicz et al 2021).

These incidents occur amid a wider climate of risk for human rights defenders worldwide. While the threats are diffuse, democratic as well as authoritarian regimes have taken part in the surveillance of social movements involving marginalized groups.[4] The deployment of Pegasus spyware by state security agencies against dissidents and civil rights groups presents a transnational example of this phenomenon. It further shows how the discourse of counterterrorism is manipulated to justify abuses of surveillance that are, at times, gendered.

Pegasus is a tool developed by NSO Group, an Israeli-based cyber-intelligence firm. Its value is that it is capable of breaking encryption on Android and iPhones, allowing the user to access a target's data including contacts, messages and emails, calendar appointments, and the location of the phone via the Global Positioning System. It further allows access to the camera and microphone of targeted devices (Perlroth 2016; Bergman and Mazzetti 2022). NSO identifies its primary interest as developing tools for counterterrorism and law enforcement purposes. Its website notes that it 'only licenses its most well-known software product, Pegasus, to select approved, verified and authorized states and state agencies' including law enforcement entities, militaries, and intelligence agencies (NSO Group 2021a). To date, over a dozen governments are known to have licensed Pegasus. Despite NSO's claims that the tool is incapable of mass surveillance and that it employs a 'human rights due diligence process' to prevent client abuse, a database leaked in 2020 identified tens of thousands of phone numbers targeted by state users of Pegasus, including those of journalists, student organizers, business executives, labour union leaders, human rights activists, and other public figures (NSO Group 2021a, 2021b; Priest et al 2021; Bergman and Mazzetti 2022). Subsequent investigations suggest that political pressure, especially from the US and Israeli governments, may have influenced NSO's decision to license Pegasus to countries that were known human rights abusers (especially, Saudi Arabia) despite the likelihood the exploit would be misused (Bergman and Mazzetti 2021, 2022). Once clients had access to the spyware, there was no oversight of how it was used (Priest et al 2021).

Investigative reporting (including reports by the Pegasus Project, a transnational reporting initiative including reporters from 17 media organizations, working in concert with NGOs Amnesty International and Forbidden Stories), reveal that several governments appear to have weaponized Pegasus to harass or surveil women journalists and women's rights activists. Saudi women's rights activist Loujain al-Hathloul was identified as a possible target just prior to her abduction and arrest in 2018. It is believed that the United Arab Emirates may have added her to a target list (Walker et al 2021). An Emirati human rights activist, Alaa al-Siddiq, was additionally named as a target. Al-Siddiq (who died in 2021) was executive director of the human rights organization Al Qst, whose work included highlighting the persecution of women's rights activists in the Middle East. In interviews after her death, friends and colleagues said al-Siddiq knew she had likely been hacked, and experienced constant anxiety for her safety (Kirchgaessner 2021). Women human rights advocates in Bahrain and Jordan are also among the confirmed targets of hacks using Pegasus (Access Now/ Front Line Defenders 2022). In India, women believed to be targets of surveillance include indigenous and women's rights activist Soni Sori and an unnamed woman who accused the former chief justice of India's Supreme Court of sexual harassment (Chandran and Gebeily 2021; Shantha 2021).

Pegasus also appears to have been weaponized in specific ways against women journalists. In some cases, the hacking was part of a more extensive campaign of disinformation and/or harassment. In Azerbaijan, for example, sustained disinformation campaigns have been waged against women journalists critical of the government. These campaigns have included the use of fake and defamatory social media profiles, the distribution of sex tapes secretly recorded through government surveillance, the distribution of compromising photoshopped images, and disinformation tying the journalists to foreign interests (Freedom House 2019; Geybulla 2019, 2020; Walker et al 2021). While Pegasus was one among many tools used in this campaign, the spyware was used against at least one woman journalist, Fatima Movlamli, who believes the hacking may have been used to obtain compromising photos of her (Walker et al 2021). In Mexico, journalist Carmen Aristegui believes she was targeted for her work exposing corruption during the presidency of Enrique Peña Nieto. After 2014, she details a long history of harassment that she believes included repeated (and aggressive) attempts to trick her and members of her family into downloading Pegasus. By 2015, her teenage son was being targeted with links – including fake, defamatory stories about her – which she believes were sent by state agencies attempting to get him to install Pegasus (Ahmed and Perlroth 2017). Her personal assistant and others close to her were later verified as targets of Pegasus (Priest et al 2021). More recently, the University of Toronto's Citizen Lab and NGO Access Now released a list of verified Pegasus[5] targets in El Salvador that included over a half-dozen women journalists and employees of civil society groups. While many men are also among the identified hacking victims, the organization notes that these revelations come amid a pronounced spike in acts of aggression against female journalists in the country (Scott-Railton et al 2022).

These gendered impacts are important to consider. While women and women's rights defenders by no means account for the majority of state spyware targets, they can experience disproportionate impacts. The susceptibility of women to blackmail in some parts of the world and the likelihood of, for instance, leaked 'indecent' material having career-ending impacts make this type of surveillance a serious concern (Geybulla 2019; Chandran and Gebeily 2021; Shantha 2021). Likewise, for women who have experienced prior sexual assault, torture, or abuse at the hands of state forces, the integrity violations associated with surveillance can have a profound retraumatizing effect (Access Now/Front Line Defenders 2022). For these reasons as well as for the broader ethical concerns, sustained attention should be devoted to the gendered deployment of surveillance technologies.

Conclusion

This chapter has examined how technologies of surveillance and policing are deployed by states in ways that foster gendered insecurity. The finding that states are actively engaged in the surveillance of women's rights activists and other women public figures, and that technology providers are complicit in these abuses, hearken back to foundational arguments in feminist international relations – especially, the argument that the state is not a reliable guarantor of security for women (Tickner 2001). In fact, the examples presented here arguably represent a triple crisis of legitimacy for the state as security provider. First, we have seen how states actively weaponize cyber-arms and -intelligence tools against their own citizens. These weaponized actions, while at times broad in scope, are often tailored to target the most vulnerable groups, like women, ethnic and religious minorities, and LGBTQI+ populations. At the same time, the example of Pegasus shows how even states that present themselves as defenders of free expression (such as the United States) can facilitate other states' access to harmful tools, when it is politically expedient for them to do so. Finally, it is worth noting that even wealthy, liberal democratic states have proven unable to protect their citizens from cybersecurity threats. Several women journalists and public figures targeted by disinformation campaigns originating in Russia, China, and Iran are either based in or are citizens of states in Europe or North America. They have observed little response from either tech platforms or law enforcement in response to the campaigns waged against them (Jankowicz et al 2021). In the case of spyware, too, states who have seen their citizens targeted by other states have struggled to meaningfully respond. In the case of the NSO Group, outcry over the abuses of Pegasus (and related tools) put pressure on the company to release a transparency report, in which it acknowledged some failures of its ethics process (NSO Group 2021b). In 2021, the United States[6] also effectively sanctioned NSO Group, preventing it from engaging in future business with US firms (Bergman and Mazzetti 2022). Yet none of this has prevented the continued abuse of these tools. The Citizen Lab/Access Now investigation of spyware use by El Salvador found that NSO Group tools were still being used to hack journalists and civil society figures as of late 2021, months after the NSO Group had promised to revisit ethics processes (Scott-Railton et al 2022).

Such failures of accountability are emblematic of the broader culture within the cyber-arms market, where states struggle to maintain control and capacity. The lure of greater profit and independence working outside of state cybersecurity agencies makes states highly dependent on private actors for the development and deployment of offensive and defensive tools (Perlroth 2021a). Here again is a callback to feminist international relations, which questions both how technology is gendered in the service of state security narratives and how notions of 'offensive' versus 'defensive' capabilities are constructed in entirely subjective ways (Wilcox 2009). The development of state narratives around cyberwar and cybersecurity, in this sense, likewise resembles an earlier era of nuclear security discourse, in which the human collateral damage of tools developed in the name of state security went largely overlooked (Cohn 1987). State failures to respond to cybersecurity threats against citizens not only damage legitimacy; they also raise the possibility of cyber-vigilantism as a response to state abuses of technology. As noted in the opening chapter of this book, North Korea has been responsible for numerous hacking incidents targeting private entities and even individual citizens. In one arresting example of a hack-back, a single US-based hacker who was attacked by North Korea claims to have retaliated by shutting down the entire country's Internet for at least two weeks in early 2022. While North Korea may have been uniquely vulnerable to such an attack, given its tight state control over Internet access, the hacker indicated that he also intended to send a message to the United States, that is, that the government was not doing enough to protect its own people against foreign cyberattacks (Greenberg 2022). Is this type of vigilantism the future of cybersecurity?

Insofar as both state-sponsored and extremist abuses of technology are often targeted based on gender, ethnicity, religion, and other manifestations of social hierarchies, the further investigation of these issues is an area in which intersectional approaches are necessary and where, as discussed, research in feminist international relations could benefit from synergies with work in related fields. Though the abolition of abusive practices around cyberarms, state surveillance, and policing may not be feasible, there may be space for feminist innovation and the shaping of feminist futures.

PART III

Futures of Technology, Gender, and Security

6

Resistance, Resilience, and Innovation

In a digital environment that is so often hostile to women and members of other marginalized groups, is there space for resistance and innovation? Many activists and practitioners seem to believe this is the case. Despite widespread concerns about surveillance, privacy, and gender-based violence online, there are signs that innovation is finding inroads. There are also indications that the COVID-19 pandemic has become a tipping point for the adoption of new technologies – with a few caveats. This chapter explores how new technologies are being used to promote feminist goals, including peacebuilding and efforts to combat gender-based violence. In doing so, it draws on case studies and interviews with individuals involved in related projects.

What emerges from this discussion is that technologies including ICT platforms, social media, blockchain, and even AI are being used in service of feminist goals. At the same time, though, these spaces are fragile. Women working in these areas are highly cognisant of the potential for backlash, of biases within the tech industry, and of the role inequalities play in shaping engagements with technology. These inequalities map onto gender, but also race/ethnicity, sexuality, and Global North/South divides. Self-censorship, as alluded to in earlier chapters, is a common coping mechanism for those facing backlash or harassment, but it is a response that limits prospects for transformative change. At the same time, I find that even highly educated and capable women professionals tend to underestimate their own expertise and capacity in ways that map onto gender stereotypes. Importantly, while prior work suggests that men in policy-relevant positions also have knowledge gaps and struggle to understand opaque technologies, this rarely seems to hinder their participation in policy debates (Singer and Friedman 2014). The durability of gendered stereotypes, the pervasiveness of online abuse, and the enduring nature of unequal access to tech all show how more attention and resources must be devoted to cultivating innovation, if we want to see a feminist future in the digital space.

Technologies and peacebuilding

As one practitioner I spoke with put it, 'innovation' can mean either developing new technologies or using existing technologies in new ways.[1] The latter appears to be true for women using ICT in support of peacebuilding. Work on the acceptance of ICT by women peacebuilders suggests that many of these activists have access to relevant technologies long before they decide to use them. Privacy concerns, accessibility and ease-of-use, and the potential cost of accessing services (in particular, data plans for mobile devices) all factor into the likelihood of women adopting technology in their peacebuilding work (Robertson and Ayazi 2019; Buzatu et al 2021).

Colombia

Colombia is one of the contexts in which women have used technology in support of peacebuilding. Much of this work centres on the process of reaching and implementing a peace agreement between the FARC and the government, ending approximately a half-century of civil conflict between these actors. In prior research, I discussed the use of social media by members of the FARC who participated in the negotiation of the 2016 peace accords (Henshaw 2020). In that study, I noted that patterns of adoption were gendered and that women appeared to be both earlier adopters and more successful users of Twitter (the primary platform studied). Compared to their male counterparts, I found that FARC women on Twitter generally reached a larger audience and engaged with a broader range of issues – especially, the relevance of the peace accords to women and LGBTQI+ populations (Henshaw 2020). NGOs including women's groups and peace advocacy groups were also engaged in online campaigning in support of the accords. Yet opponents of the peace process took advantage of the online space too, both before and after the 2016 plebiscite on the peace agreement. Some of these online debates took the form of coordinated disinformation campaigns. Leading up to the 2016 plebiscite on the peace accords, analysts warned that supporters of peace were misrepresenting provisions of the accords, while opponents engaged in fear-mongering, conspiracy-baiting, and outrage campaigns (Alsema 2016).

While some of the disinformation focused on the peace agreement's transitional justice and disarmament, demobilization, and reintegration provisions, disinformation about provisions of the accord related to gender and LGBTQI+ rights was widespread. Prior disputes about sex education and youth surveys on sexuality and gender identity had galvanized conservative leaders in the country – including faith leaders and prominent conservative politicians (Rondón 2017). This pre-existing political network subsequently mobilized against the peace agreement, relying on discourse about 'gender ideology'. As a political buzzword, 'gender ideology' speaks not only to concerns about gender, but also about anxieties over feminism, diversity, and the expansion of LGBTQI+ rights. The movement against 'gender ideology' is politically relevant throughout Latin America and in other countries where the concept has been taken up by religious leaders (Corredor 2019). In Colombia, use of the term evokes fears that parents are being deprived of power over their children's education (especially, related to sex and sexuality), that children are being encouraged to experiment sexually, that Christian populations are being persecuted for their adherence to conservative beliefs, and that the country is moving towards socialism (Rondón 2017; Bohórquez Oviedo 2021). Bohórquez Oviedo (2021) notes that social media and ICTs – especially WhatsApp – were essential conduits for the campaign against the peace accords. In these spaces, disinformation was able to flourish facilitated both by the reach of social media and by the use of private messaging groups, which deterred possibilities for debate or content moderation. Moreover, the campaign against 'gender ideology' reportedly engaged foreign consultants and private companies in its efforts to disseminate targeted disinformation via Facebook, Twitter, and Instagram (Bohórquez Oviedo 2021).

Based on interviews with feminist and LGBTQI+ advocates, Bohórquez Oviedo (2021) suggests that these groups, while actively engaged in informing the public about the accord, lacked effective counter-strategies to respond to gendered (and homophobic) disinformation in the lead-up to the 2016 vote. However, since the 2016 vote and especially in the wake of the COVID-19 pandemic, social media and ICTs have become important tools for those monitoring implementation of the peace accords. For some, the ability to attend and participate in meetings remotely has mitigated the cost and inconvenience of travelling to meet with other advocates or government officials (*Women's Peace and Security in the Digital Age* 2021). This can be especially true for women living in remote/rural areas. Of course, there are also tradeoffs. COVID-19 created an imperative for many advocates to get online quickly if they wanted to remain connected to others. As a result, many embraced platforms that were free and easy to use – but less secure (*Women's Peace and Security in the Digital Age* 2021). Given that hundreds of social leaders and activists have been killed or displaced since 2016, the fear of targeted harassment is very real. A report by the International Crisis Group (2020) indicated that armed groups were circulating hit lists of activists online, and that women and LGBTQI+ activists faced heightened risks of harassment or violence from these groups.

The Philippines

Peacebuilding in Mindanao, in The Philippines, demonstrates the use of social media by women activists while also highlighting connections between women and youth. The conflict in this region, much like Colombia's civil conflict, is protracted and has involved a patchwork of armed groups engaged in conflict with the government since the 1960s. This conflict has religious and ethnic dimensions, with the insurgent Moro Islamic Liberation Front the central focus of peace talks culminating in an agreement in 2014. As was the case in Colombia, women have been highly organized and deeply involved in the peace movement. This organizing was often intersectional, with the peace movement including groups for indigenous women, for Muslim women, and for young women (Santiago 2015). Many such groups continue to remain active and engage in both peacebuilding and monitoring of the existing accords. In Mindanao, mobile phones have been used widely to connect activists, and meetings have been coordinated via Facebook and Zoom (*Women's Peace and Security in the Digital Age* 2021). A poll of youth activists from 11 different organizations demonstrates how essential social media has been – particularly for young peace advocates. All of the activists responding to the survey indicated that they found Facebook helpful in in doing peace activism, and two-thirds felt that publicizing their initiatives (including posting about them on Facebook) was important for the success of peace projects (Witting-Acuesa and Cabanes Ragandang 2021).

Young peacebuilders have engaged in social media-based projects to raise intercultural awareness and to counter hate speech (Cabanes Ragandang 2020; Genon 2021). One such project that engaged university students in combating hate speech was run by an all-women leadership team. This project received financial and technical support from Facebook, though its efforts extended to Twitter, Instagram, and offline spaces in the community (Cabanes Ragandang 2020). Project organizers reported that their online efforts received over one million social media engagements in an approximately two-year period, although there was a significant disparity between engagements on Facebook and on other platforms – a fact that speaks to the importance of that platform. In addition to providing free advertising for the project, Facebook is also the social network of choice in The Philippines. Through deals with the country's main telecommunications provider, most users can access Facebook without incurring data costs (Cabanes Ragandang 2020). This arrangement hearkens back to the discussion of Facebook's 'Free Basics' plan in India and similar arrangements throughout the Global South, introduced in Chapter 3. These plans give Facebook significant power over determining whose messages matter.

Navigating the hegemony of Facebook is only one issue for online peace advocates. Some students involved with this project indicated that they received backlash from those who equated efforts to combat Islamophobia with support for extremist groups (Cabanes Ragandang 2020). It is unclear to what extent resistance to this particular project may have been gendered, however women peace advocates in Mindanao have reported harassment, threats, and monitoring while using social media (*Women's Peace and Security in the Digital Age* 2021). Connectivity could also present unique challenges for women and girls, who could be subjected to harassment in public spaces while attempting to find Internet access (*Women's Peace and Security in the Digital Age* 2021).

Colombia and Mindanao represent just two examples where we can see innovation and risk co-existing in the work of women peace advocates. These are by no means the only places where we can observe this dynamic at work. In Sudan, private Facebook groups were used by women to amplify the message of 2019 protests and to reach women who could not join in person (Robertson and Ayazi 2019). In Ethiopia, women have worked to legitimize discussions about online gender-based violence and to highlight linkages between online and offline manifestations of violence (Gimase Magenya and Shewarega Hussen 2022). In Afghanistan local advocates, with assistance from UN Women, developed an online campaign to raise awareness of women's issues amid their exclusion from peace talks between the United States and the Taliban (Najibullah 2019). Since the Taliban returned to power in 2021, social media continues to be used to cover women's protests and to document abuses by human rights defenders including women.

Other examples show the limitations of relying on technology to promote activism. In the immediate aftermath of the Taliban's takeover, crowdfunding received significant attention as a way to help Afghans, especially women, girls, and LGBTQI+ populations. The sudden influx of attention and donations overwhelmed some crowdfunding sites, offering a cautionary tale of reliance on these outlets. Some US-based LGBTQI+ advocates who organized one fundraiser via GoFundMe complained that their funds (more than US$30,000) were locked by the site after they refused to provide the full names and addresses of their recipient contacts in Afghanistan. The organizers complained that providing these details might risk exposing queer activists in Afghanistan to the Taliban (Lim 2021). A policy update implemented by GoFundMe eventually noted that: 'Due to Taliban control, GoFundMe can no longer transfer money directly to an individual in Afghanistan or release funds that will be transferred to an individual in the country' (GoFundMe 2021). The platform instead encouraged users to donate money via a 'verified nonprofit', and included a list of organizations that provided general humanitarian assistance, medical assistance, and assistance to children – but which did not include women's groups or LGBTQI+ advocacy organizations (GoFundMe 2021).

Other attempts to leverage technology as a form of resistance have encountered barriers. Online education, for example, has been suggested as a means to circumvent Taliban restrictions on women's and girls' access to education. However, the vision of cyberspace as a haven does not always match up with reality. Students, like much of the population, have had to balance study with other challenges – like rising food insecurity (Makoni 2022). Afghanistan has experienced frequent disruptions to both Internet service and the power grid since the Taliban's return to power. Thus, even when there is access, women and girls studying online navigate frequent disruptions and are sometimes limited to studying at off-peak hours (that is, late at night or early in the morning) (Jacinto 2021). The investment required for online learning is another challenge, with some online education providers charging fees and many offering instruction only in English or other non-local languages (Jacinto 2021; Walt 2021). Advocates for online education as a solution, then, must reflect on how opportunity is shaped by gender but also by class, urban–rural divides, and a range of other factors. While some have had success with online learning, it is unclear how much success online educational initiatives have actually had in reaching women.

Creating interventions that promote progress may require close collaboration between developers, institutions, and women activists. One example of such collaborations is the use of AI to support inclusive peace processes. This approach was implemented by the UN's Office of the Special Envoy of the Secretary-General for Yemen (OSESGY) in 2020 as part of its effort to promote dialogue. Prior to the onset of the COVID-19 pandemic, the OSESGY and local women's peace groups exerted pressure on parties involved in the peace talks to include more women in their delegations, with some success (al-Thaibani 2019). Even so, women continued to struggle against the perception that they were not legitimate participants because their lives were not directly impacted by the conflict. Al-Thaibani (2019) discusses how women and youth peacebuilders used radio broadcasts and strategic engagement with traditional media to raise the profile of gender issues. The onset of COVID-19, however, presented new challenges. In June 2020, the OSESGY organized an online forum that was aimed at gauging public opinion on the peace process and assessing the humanitarian situation (including the spread of COVID-19). Over 500 people from across Yemen took part in this event. AI supported the project by providing real-time translation, allowing participants to converse in a variety of local dialects (OSESGY 2020a). Through a partnership with women's organizations, the OSESGY further ensured that women's voices were included. The office estimated that 30–35 per cent of participants in the forum were women (OSESGY 2020b). Though participants, again, faced challenges related to access and bandwidth, some civil society activists who took part in the mass consultations praised the effort for its inclusiveness. The fact that it allowed participants to engage anonymously was further cited as a benefit – particularly for women who attended (OSESGY 2020a).

The range of interventions discussed in this section represent the two dimensions of innovation referenced earlier on in the chapter. For some, innovation takes the form of using tools and technologies that are already familiar in new ways. For others – and especially in the case of AI-enabled approaches – we see emerging technologies being deployed in support of peacebuilding. The outcomes, in some cases, point to hope for resilience and/or resistance. They can also point to how women (and LGBTQI+ communities) can leverage and navigate technologies that were often designed without them in mind. None of this, however, should mitigate the moral burden that falls to technology companies, developers, and states to ensure equitability and accessibility with regard to emerging technologies. As discussed in this and in the next chapter, there are ethical concerns regarding the deployment of emerging technologies in fragile and conflict-affected areas. There are also questions about the personal toll these engagements take on activists and practitioners engaged in the work of gender mainstreaming in peacebuilding and related work.

Stories of feminist innovation: resilience, resistance, and burnout

To better understand the space in which feminist innovation occurs, I conducted interviews with 13 individuals engaged in projects that connected gender, technology, and security, broadly defined. The work of these individuals includes an array of projects, which range from direct support for peace advocacy to P/CVE to the use of ICT tools to counter or document gender-based violence. Their work experiences are also diverse, with some working for large and well-funded organizations in the Global North while others work with smaller advocacy organizations in the Global South.

At the same time, there are some significant commonalities to note. First, all of my interviewees were women. Given the inequalities in the tech profession discussed earlier in the book, I believe this is at once striking and typical of work on gender mainstreaming projects. That is to say, despite the overwhelmingly male nature of the technology workforce, it is primarily women who appear to be shouldering the burden of making technology more equitable and highlighting the need for gendered interventions. At the same time, although my interview pool was diverse in terms of race/ethnicity and nationality, the majority of individuals I spoke with (all but two) were working for organizations based in the Global North (especially the United States, Canada, the United Kingdom, and EU countries). This, too, I believe is reflective of the overall landscape for digital peacebuilding. As my interviewees themselves noted, lack of capacity in the Global South (in terms of both access and safety) remains a limiting factor and sometimes requires local or grassroots organizations to partner with organizations in developed countries. Furthermore, 11 of my 13 interviewees worked for research institutes or NGOs of varying size. Inequalities in funding and/

or institutional capacity, then, also became important factors in shaping interviewees' work experiences and outcomes.

These interviews were conducted between January and March of 2022 and were held via videoconference, in part as a result of the ongoing COVID-19 pandemic. Participants were recruited via email, social media, and snowball sampling. Interviewees responded to a variety of open-ended questions about the nature of their work, any barriers or backlash they had encountered, their sense of how their work has changed over time and/or across different technology platforms (as applicable), and what steps they feel are needed to support their work going forward.[2] Just as the projects these individuals were involved in varied significantly, the specific technologies they engaged with also ranged from social media and Internet forums to mobile phone apps to artificial intelligence and blockchain. Nonetheless, several important themes emerged through these discussions. These include: (1) concerns over the safety and security of those working online; (2) the salience of institutional and/or geographical inequalities; (3) issues regarding transparency, related to both technology providers and the technologies themselves; and (4) a shared sense that, while progress had been made on mainstreaming gender perspectives in tech, more could be done to make the online environment more secure.

Safety and security

Perhaps unsurprisingly, the safety and security of those working on gender-focused projects in technology was an overriding concern. As noted in earlier chapters, prior research on women's engagement with social media suggests that online harassment is pervasive, and causes many women who use these platforms to adopt strategies including self-censorship when engaging online (Amnesty International 2018). Conversations with my interviewees revealed the extent to which women who work with technology are aware of these issues and adapt to avoid them – even when they themselves have not been targeted. While the individuals I spoke with indicated that they had not personally experienced severe harassment in the line of work, four interviewees cited specific examples of female colleagues who had been targeted by harassment campaigns and/or doxing attempts. Several individuals indicated that patterns of harassment at their organizations were gendered. From one P/CVE practitioner:

> '[I]t is well recognized in [our] organization that gender plays an incredibly important role in who gets picked out for that kind of abuse ... there are examples where the authors of the report have primarily been the recipients of abuse, but quickly ... that leads trolls onto the website of the organization and the photos of all of the female members of staff will be picked out, no matter how irrelevant they are to the

work, and they will be shared. They will be talked about. They will be joked about in sexualized ways.'[3]

Interviewees discussed various coping strategies for avoiding or preventing harassment. Among these were limiting the amount of personal information they shared online, making fake social media profiles and/or profiles without their information or photos, monitoring online conversations, and taking steps to find out what personal information about them was discoverable online. In a few cases, interviewees indicated that they gravitated away from publicly accessible spaces and towards smaller or closed groups as a safeguard against harassment. In larger and/or well-funded organizations, support was available for researcher safety. Two individuals at larger NGOs based in the UK and Europe indicated that there was support staff at their organization who conducted some form of 'penetration testing' for them, ensuring their personal information was not easily discoverable.[4] For others, however, their safety was primarily their own responsibility.

The safety landscape also looked different for women in rural locations and/ or in the Global South. Here, the possibility that security threats originated not just from online spaces, but within local households and communities, were real. Two interviewees noted the importance of patriarchal norms in communities where they worked. As noted in Chapter 3, such norms can shape access to devices, but also what women might feel comfortable saying or doing.[5] A practitioner who had been involved in a project in India to bring attention to the security threats facing gig workers discussed how patriarchal norms shaped that work. She noted the difficulty of securing reserved seats for women on a workers' group, which was followed by difficulties finding women to participate:

'[T]he day before [the] meeting, we realize none of the … women we've selected want to turn up … some of them called in sick. The others said, "I don't believe my family is comfortable with my attending what seems like a Union meeting," which it wasn't. … It was one woman who did turn up eventually, and that one woman said she can make it only so long as her husband can join her.'[6]

The potential threat that corrupt or authoritarian governments, too, can pose was raised as an issue:

'I think the lens for analysis tends to be, "let's call out big tech", and I do think there are valid reasons to call out big tech. But I also think … it is equally important to also look at the ways in which the state is increasingly digitizing its processes and what that means for us in terms of our civic rights and also our data and digital rights.'[7]

Two interviewees I spoke with noted that their organizations pre-emptively censored reports based on their research because of concerns over government harassment of local partners or participants.[8]

Dimensions of inequality

The question of who bears responsibility for the safety of women working in this space relates to the theme of inequality. Individuals at larger organizations indicated that the resources available to them included not only basic information security, but also specialized training and/or counselling to deal with the possible mental/emotional health consequences associated with targeted harassment or exposure to extremist/violent content. But access to these services was the exception; only three of my interviewees discussed specifically having access to counselling or trauma-related training through their employer.

Inequalities manifested between larger and smaller organizations, but also across a cultural divide. Global North–South divisions were a significant part of this; a few interviewees also reflected on engagement with indigenous communities. As noted, the majority of my interviewees worked for organizations based in the United States, Canada, the United Kingdom, or European countries, but several of these individuals were involved in projects in the Global South. Multiple interviewees described a similar pattern, where an NGO or local government agency in the Global South would come to them with a partially developed idea but without the technological capability to implement the plan. The organizations based in developed countries then became responsible for contributing funding, procuring the technology, and training recipients on the use of relevant technologies or programmes. Ultimately, the goal was for communities and local/grassroots organizations to become self-sustaining and continue projects themselves, but this did not always work out as expected. One individual worked on a project that trained women in post-conflict contexts on how to use ICTs to document and share their experiences. She recounted that the project had widely varying results. In some countries, women successfully adopted the technology and kept up the project long after her organization had left. However, in other contexts she noted that there was much more of a struggle and that, in her opinion, 'financial motivations' moved projects forward even where there was clearly not adequate local capacity or interest to sustain them.[9]

In other cases, organizations found that it was simply not possible to make partners in the Global South completely self-sustaining. From one individual at a US-based NGO that helped develop a web-based project in Liberia:

> '[O]ne of the issues that we at least identified ... the developers, like, the website developers or the people who kind of run those sites aren't

in Liberia, it's all in Eastern Europe ... so they end up with these really ... ad hoc ways of trying to develop websites or reach out to their population because ... the servers aren't in Liberia, the people who are maintaining them are not in Liberia ... all I can say is if we could get that piece of it more localized, I think it would be so much easier.'[10]

Lack of local knowledge or dialogue further complicated some efforts at creating cross-cultural initiatives. One such example was discussed by an interviewee in Canada who wanted to include First Nations people in an educational programme. Despite creating opportunities, she recounted that it was hard to get people to show up:

'[W]e haven't had a lot of take up, though, because indigenous people were not aware of this opportunity for them and also kind of ... reluctant to participate. But what we have done recently is we have hired an indigenous advisor ... because we realize there are protocols for how you engage with First Nations on their territory and, you know, how knowledge passes and communities operate that we are just not aware of.'[11]

Another example where cultural gaps were evident was in the assessment of 'smart cities' campaigns. Such campaigns use technology to facilitate operations across the municipal level. While not all smart cities initiatives specifically deal with gender, a number of cities (especially in South Asia and Latin America) have tried to use such programmes to tackle gender-based violence. This includes the use of apps and programmes meant to facilitate the reporting of gender-based violence, programmes to reduce sexual harassment on public transit, and mapping initiatives meant to highlight high-crime areas.

While developers and funders in the Global North have championed many of these initiatives, people I spoke with suggested these projects sometimes struggled because they were disconnected from local communities and cultures. One interviewee[12] discussed the example of a smart cities programme in southern India. She noted that the third-party developer involved in the programme effectively used a template, which was an app with a button that allowed women who were experiencing threats or gender-based violence to contact police. When the parties involved in the project reviewed the usage statistics a few months after the rollout, she said they found the service was not used at all. She argued that the funders and developers (individuals outside the region) had failed to understand the gender-, religious-, and caste-based dynamics that made women reluctant to report violence to authorities. As noted elsewhere in this book, in parts of India there are strong stigmas attached to reporting gender-based violence and a tendency to blame victims. This interviewee argued that an app created by in-country developers, which instead used anonymized spatial data to inform users about potential safety risks (that is, flagging areas that may have poor lighting or where other users had reported feeling unsafe) represented a superior approach. I heard of similar struggles with smart cities apps from another US-based interviewee,[13] who had worked on similar projects in parts of the Global South. She alluded to the fact that creating apps or websites for gender-based violence reporting did not resolve the underlying issue that law enforcement was sometimes not responsive to reports. She acknowledged this as a hindrance to the long-term viability of these programmes.

Apart from these issues, even the basics of securing access to Internet- or mobile-based services could be a challenge. This was especially true where organizations were trying to provide outreach and/or connectivity to people in rural areas. In the case of interventions conducted over social media, basic considerations about signal strength, bandwidth, and even reliable access to electricity determined how women interacted with technology and what platforms they could use. One interviewee cited Facebook as a preferred platform for communicating and organizing in the Philippines, a country where Facebook's Free Basics plan (discussed in Chapter 3) was introduced in 2015. This individual noted that Facebook was considered the most widely accessible platform because it could be used on mobile phones even where there was poor signal strength.[14] Literacy issues were another hazard that technological innovators had to navigate. Limited literacy in some communities or, alternatively, the lack of available online content in local languages meant that workarounds were necessary for projects that relied on ICT platforms. These workarounds included a reliance on voice messaging (as opposed to text messaging) functionality, or the use of videoconferencing – which interviewees saw becoming more popular during the COVID-19 pandemic.[15] Still, inequalities around accessibility created tradeoffs with safety and security. As alluded to earlier, some interviewees working on projects in the Global South were aware of the risks of various platforms (especially, with regard to the potential for government censorship), but felt they had to accept the security risks in the name of accessibility.[16]

Transparency

Nearly all of the women I spoke with indicated that they had concerns about the transparency of the technologies they worked with and/or of technology companies. Many also struggled with their own comfort level in using various technologies. I came to believe that this discomfort was gendered. While other authors have noted that political elites (including security/cybersecurity professionals) often don't completely understand the nuances of working with ICTs, this does not prevent them from engaging in debates about cybersecurity, ICT regulation, and so on (Singer and Friedman 2014). By comparison, some women I approached for an interview either turned me down or expressed a reluctance to respond to certain questions because they felt their actual technical knowledge was 'limited' or that they weren't qualified to speak about technology issues. Given that lack of transparency is such a common concern regarding technology (especially, social media or messaging platforms), the frequency with which my interviewees internalized their discomfort – as though these were things that they didn't know, but which were perhaps widely known by others – seemed notable. This comment from an interviewee about working across different social media platforms was emblematic of what I heard from others:

> 'Twitter was only a particular audience because we as an organization hadn't connected enough with, you know local Twitter spheres, if that makes sense. … I have no idea if there's any, like, algorithm stuff that pushes it to like like-minded organizations … and actually I should. … I'm sure it's possible. I really don't know much about tech.'[17]

This individual internalized her lack of knowledge about how Twitter's algorithms work, yet the lack of transparency in these algorithms is generally recognized. Twitter itself has recently funded/conducted research into how its own algorithms work with regard to the amplification of political content (Huszár et al 2021). In a blog post discussing the results of its study, Twitter's Director of Software Engineering and one of its staff researchers noted that: 'certain political content is amplified on the platform. Establishing why these observed patterns occur is a significantly more difficult question to answer as it is a product of the interactions between people and the platform' (Chowdhury and Belli 2021). It is clear that the workings of recommendation algorithms are not completely understood – even by developers – so users should not regard their own lack of understanding as a personal failing.

Other interviewees indicated that they saw tech platforms and/or developers themselves as the cause of issues with transparency and trust. This created some ambiguity about whether these entities – especially, large technology companies – could or should be regarded as partners in feminist innovation.

> 'I got asked, you know, why do we bother working with social media companies? … You know, social media platforms in particular … it's not hard to find examples where they've failed [or] fallen short of those expectations. So it puts us in a quite difficult position just kind of … why do we keep trying with them?'[18]

'[W]e boycotted Facebook. ... I tried to report things ... cases of abuse and harassment. And you try to email or call their support in the country and you're just met with this horrendous lack of sensitivity to what is being reported to gender aspects of violence of the online abuse and all of that.'[19]

'You also see that platforms operating in India are a lot more reluctant to be acting on instances of hate speech or violence than, say, in America. ... Twitter was quick to ban Trump after the January 6 insurrection, but compare it against Indian politicians who used Twitter as the call for action [in the] Delhi riots happening in 2020.'[20]

Some made distinctions between working with large tech companies and small or medium-sized companies, who might have less capacity but greater openness to collaboration.

'For us we actually collaborate more with medium-sized startups ... because we have seen that trend [among larger companies] to go for market opportunities, which in most cases ... the kind of the work that we do, we are working in conflict settings. So that is not the most economically advantageous opportunity for companies.'[21]

Here, too, there was some ambiguity. Another interviewee who worked in P/CVE and dealt with smaller social media and file-sharing platforms discussed a tension working with these providers. She noted that while they were often eager to take measures to de-platform users or content associated with recognized extremist groups, they were more reticent to take action against conspiracies, hate speech, and even violent content that was not clearly associated with a designated extremist organization. She believed the desire of some small platforms to carve out a market niche as free speech havens (especially in the wake of more aggressive content moderation by platforms like Facebook and Twitter) caused them to take advantage of 'loopholes' and grey areas.[22]

Taking action

Ultimately, several interviewees pointed to positive change in the tech industry, especially related to awareness about gender-based harassment and/ or gender inequality. At the same time, almost everyone I spoke with agreed that more could and should be done to mainstream gender perspectives and create more diverse and welcoming spaces online. These recommendations, however, were diverse. Interviewees working in developed countries often saw governments as important allies; one even spoke about the potential benefit of involving more women elected officials in discussions about legislation and regulation.[23] Others were more circumspect about state involvement. Some who had worked on projects in authoritarian countries or countries with severe repression/corruption issues did not see the state as a positive force for regulating online spaces. For some, the COVID-19 pandemic highlighted how state and local governments can abuse technology:

> 'We saw this during COVID, where the state [government] actually put up, like, an Excel [spreadsheet] online with people's addresses. And, you know, numbers and their COVID status. And I remember that being something that we all just kind of paused for a minute and went. Is this really up? Is this really online? And is this something that everyone can access and download and search through?'[24]

Not all issues were unique to developing or non-democratic states. One P/CVE practitioner pointed out that even among some liberal democratic states, she perceived a disinterested attitude towards combating violence against women and gender-based extremism.[25]

Four of my interviewees discussed the potential for international institutions, especially the UN Security Council or other UN agencies, to take a role in highlighting gendered insecurities in the digital space, making recommendations, or assisting small and/or developing states with capacity building in response to online violence against women and gendered extremism. Yet accessibility, elitism, and bureaucracy in international institutions were seen as potential barriers for civil society organizations wanting to engage on these issues. One provided the example of a UN working group on digital technologies which, in her opinion, rejected input or participation from civil society organizations who were doing important work on the targeting of human rights activists.[26] While these individuals generally seemed to agree that addressing gendered security threats in the digital realm should fall within the remit of the WPS Agenda, there was a sense that WPS and online security had yet to fully connect:

> '[T]here is, I think ... this moment where WPS is being recognized as a relevant lens to understanding this. And that combination of gender and security is relevant to what's happening online, because there's been a lot done on security, there's been a lot done on gender. But where the two meet ...? [the interviewee trailed off].'[27]

> '[W]e also do monitoring on General Assembly debates and Security Council open debates of Women, Peace and Security issues. Those kind of issues are the way that Member States, you know, talk about it. We've noticed that they basically mentioned gender whenever there's

an anniversary of the WPS agenda, and so when there isn't … a big anniversary … there isn't really [much said] … which begs the question of is it really substantial? Is it a really meaningful discourse of gender?'[28]

These concerns about the applicability of and/or willingness to apply WPS to online spaces echo larger concerns raised by feminist scholars about the adaptability of WPS to emerging security threats. Shepherd (2021: 119) discusses the idea of 'resolution fatigue' in the WPS community, that is, the view that the agenda is 'a complete and settled policy architecture' that only requires implementation as currently written. This mindset would preclude new Security Council resolutions or instruments specifically dealing with the virtual space. That said, it is fair to say that existing WPS resolutions – especially, UN Security Council Resolution 1325 (2000) and 2242 (2015), which links the WPS Agenda to discussions about violent extremism – should apply as written in the digital realm, as noted by UN officials (Šimonovic 2018). If this is the case, however, discourse on the need for digital policy has largely failed to cascade to member states and to the civil society organizations who provide input for NAPs to implement the WPS Agenda. To date, only seven countries have mentioned 'cyber' (that is, cybersecurity or cybercrime) in their NAPs, and most of these are mentions are just that – mentions, without specific initiatives attached (Hamilton and Shepherd 2020). The two states that most substantially deal with cyber issues in their NAPs are Ireland, whose most recent plan calls for attention to gender imbalance in the technology sector, and Namibia, whose plan calls for attention to gender-based cybercrime (Government of Ireland 2019; Republic of Namibia 2019).[29]

One alternative to allowing states or regional/international organizations to take a lead on regulating online spaces is to allow the technology industry to continue to self-regulate. As noted in the preceding section, although many of my interviewees indicated they had seen some positive progress, there was a shared scepticism about tech platforms' ability to continue in this vein. In some cases, the question was one of companies' willingness to confront issues of gendered security online. In other cases, interviewees seemed to believe the problem had become too large for the industry itself to control:

'I mean the scale of the problem is staggering. … So that … makes me somewhat sad and pessimistic at the state of the kind of interaction of technology and gender in our public life.'[30]

'Black Lives Matter activists, they get taken down and those people get banned, right? Meanwhile, a video of a gang rape is … online for, I think, over a week. … And the problem is, even if the company has a policy they really have to train their staff at all levels.'[31]

Still, amid this conversation there were insights into alternative solutions tech platforms could take which might have some impact while avoiding the high-profile backlash associated with larger efforts to ban users, communities, or content. One point raised by multiple interviewees was the need for tech companies to continue to diversify – and to be transparent about how they treat their own women employees.

> '[T]he technology sector does seem to be growing in terms of some of the influential female voices that are at the top of companies, and they're often very vocal on some of these issues, but I'm not sure I've seen that correlate with an effect on the nature of the environment or on their services for women at large.'[32]

> 'You know, women still remain underrepresented in many dev and tech companies ... and then I'm sure you saw in the news that the gaming industry in particular is ... currently facing accusations of sexual harassment, wage discrimination, public communication and even rape jokes about women in the workforce – and in an industry that's still dominated by men.'[33]

Specific suggestions along these lines included the need for tech companies to hire more women and to publicize and/or take action on gender pay gaps. Alternatively, some interviewees suggested that more data collection, better data collection, or more transparency in reporting was necessary. Some further suggested that this opened possible avenues for multi-stakeholder cooperation:

> 'There are already a lot of women's groups and local groups, and just smaller organizations who are already doing a lot of the work ... like collecting data ... and so what they really emphasize was to really be working with these smaller local groups.'[34]

> 'I don't think we can form really appropriate ... sanctions or responses or asks at the companies without having more information about how they currently work, how their decision-making processes are formed ... we're really working in the dark on at the moment because quantitative stats only take us so far.'[35]

Other suggestions focused on how tech companies might support capacity building for women's organizations who wanted to use ICT platforms and/or for the larger population of users that might be confronting gender-based disinformation and harassment:

'[I]in terms of, like, a softer tool, which I think that [companies] should do is obviously we've seen the advantages of counternarratives and educational campaigns, etc. ... I think it could be targeted more for like misogynistic content or incel content.'[36]

'ICT companies have the capacity to get, for example, lower rates to civil society, grassroots organizations, or to women peacebuilders. And I remember one person said, "Well, in our location they provided this service to teachers over the COVID-19 pandemic. They got connectivity for free. So why can't they do the same for activists?".'[37]

A few proposed solutions to encourage gender mainstreaming circumvented the debate over state/institutional or corporate control altogether. Two participants reflected on the role that educational programmes in technology play in impacting downstream dynamics:

'We used to, before the pandemic, have our [educational programme] where we had students ... it could be any member of the community walk off the street. If you have an interest, you can participate. ... But since the pandemic, unfortunately we've had to pivot to an online delivery mode and that has led to a greater institutionalization ... after this year, I really do want to ... open up the knowledge again.'[38]

'That's what I really hope to see in the future is encouraging everyone to get involved ... it's just, with so much money being pumped in it very quickly can become hard to enter into. ... I've had a lot of women, trans individuals, nonbinary folk ... who already don't feel comfortable in some of these quite heteronormative spaces, and then on top of that try to ask a question ... and that fear of, like, being made fun of or made to feel small.'[39]

Decentralized options to promote inclusion and/or feminist goals, like the use of blockchain technology, were discussed by three interviewees as a solution that could safeguard privacy and place more power in the hands of users. Such solutions allow either the public or small networks of individuals to communicate and manage data. While these technologies have the potential to disrupt existing power relationships, the community of blockchain and cryptocurrency enthusiasts has been described as a hostile space for women (Bowles 2018; Hao 2018; Adams et al 2020). The potential applications and gender dynamics of these technologies are discussed in Chapter 7.

The varied nature of solutions presented here reflects the complexities of pursuing gendered security online. As noted throughout this book, a variety of security threats but also an ever-expanding array of technology providers are involved in this ecosystem. A final point raised by some interviewees was the need to not let technological solutions supplant in-person/offline efforts at peacebuilding and/or confronting violence against women. This topic was salient for some in light of the COVID-19 pandemic, as there was a sense that activists were experiencing burnout. Some also discussed hesitancy about the impact of online advocacy:

> '[Y]ou know, when you are in a [Zoom] room with a bunch of videos turned off, you don't feel that what you're saying is being heard the same way it would be in an in-person discussion.'[40]

> '[W]e should also not aim to move everything just only to the online space ... making this online space better and more inclusive, it will not remove the need for also having that the in-person spaces ... the non-digital spaces for solidarity-building, for movement, building for negotiation, mediation, etc.'[41]

Conclusion

This chapter has sought to explore how technology can be used in innovative ways to promote gendered security. The initiatives discussed in this chapter range from relatively simple solutions, like the use of voice or text messaging, to cutting-edge interventions that rely on AI or blockchain technology (discussed in greater detail in the following chapter). A few key themes emerge from the cases and interviews presented in this chapter. The first of these is that such interventions are possible and can be successful. Especially during the COVID-19 pandemic, technology allowed conversations to continue in a way they may not have otherwise. A second and related point is that it is often women who are leading these efforts. In an industry dominated by men, it was striking to see the proliferation of women-led projects – including several emerging at the grassroots level and/or from the Global South. At the same time, these women are very much aware that they exist in an online ecosystem that was not designed with them in mind. 'Hacking' the technologies available to them – that is, by using existing systems in new ways or by developing their own strategies to ensure their safety – was common.

Even so, inequalities define the space in which innovation takes place. Gender inequalities and norms are one piece of the puzzle, but geography, race/ethnicity, caste, religion, sexuality, age, and an array of other factors shape the terms on which women interact with technology. It would be easy to unwittingly exacerbate these digital divides. As we have seen, innovators in some parts of the world are delving into projects that, to some, may sound like science fiction. These projects rely on technologies that may be largely unfamiliar to members of the general public. Such technologies clearly need to be deployed carefully, and their impacts should be assessed thoroughly. A real concern is what happens when these technologies are deployed to or tested on rural areas, fragile and conflict-affected states, and parts of the Global South. The discussion in this chapter highlights how many of these spaces still struggle with even basic issues relevant to technology use, like access, literacy, and fundamentals of online security. Can we presume that informed consent is truly possible in these communities, where individuals are suddenly thrust into contact with high-tech interventions backed by international organizations or technology startups? The following chapter explores these questions further by examining the gendered deployment of financial technologies.

7

Cryptocurrency, Decentralized Finance, and Blockchain: Gender Issues in Political Economy and Security

In July 2020, Twitter was briefly rocked by a cryptocurrency scam in which hackers, gaining access to the verified accounts of approximately 130 organizations and high-profile individuals, solicited donations of bitcoin with the promise of returning double the donors' money.[1] Though Twitter intervened within the day to stop the spread of these scam messages, estimates suggest the scheme netted the equivalent of over US$100,000 in cryptocurrency transfers (Frenkel et al 2020). Though the hack raises various cybersecurity issues, of note is that, among the individual accounts compromised, it was the accounts of *male* celebrities, technology innovators, and politicians that were targeted to raise money in the scheme. Among lists of known targets only one woman – celebrity Kim Kardashian – was identified (Frenkel et al 2020; Holmes et al 2020).

The demographics of the targets in this scam speak to a bigger question surrounding cryptocurrency and the growing sphere of decentralized finance: Where are the women? As the rise of virtual currencies has accelerated over the past decade – with bitcoin appreciating as much as 8,000 per cent per year in value and becoming more widely accepted as a form of payment (Golumbia 2016) – women have largely been left out of the resulting wealth acquisition. Demographic surveys of cryptocurrency holders suggest that women represent under 13 per cent of all users, while surveys of the general public suggest that women have substantially less awareness about this market than men (ING/Ipsos 2018; Coin Dance 2020). As such, it can be said that the architects of the July 2020 attack on Twitter knew their marks – primarily leveraging the accounts of users that a mostly male target audience would view as aspirational or trustworthy figures.

The gender inequality among cryptocurrency users stands at odds with promises from advocates and developers, who have long sold cryptocurrency as a tool to liberate populations from authoritarian governments, existing social hierarchies, and the instability of traditional currencies in many parts of the world (Vigna and Casey 2015; Golumbia 2016). Cryptocurrency projects carry the promise of reducing inequality by reaching the 'unbanked' populations of the world – particularly women and residents of the Global South – offering new avenues for economic empowerment and security, including in fragile and conflict-affected states (Baldet and Powell 2019). For women, access to cryptocurrency has further been promoted as a means to accrue independent wealth, circumvent discriminatory finance practices, even to escape situations of domestic abuse (Vigna and Casey 2015; Powell and Moncino 2018). Such promises explicitly connect the deployment of these financial technologies to the security issues addressed elsewhere in the book.

To date, evidence suggests that the types of transformative effects promised by crypto developers have failed to materialize. Analysts who refer to blockchain as a 'gender-neutral technology' express frustration over this apparent reluctance of women to get on board – prompting one female investor to take to social media, saying: 'Women, consider crypto. Otherwise the men are going to get all the wealth, again' (Powell and Moncino 2018; Comben 2019).

In this chapter, I argue for a more critical examination of debates about cryptocurrency, development, and gender. In particular, I argue that there is a pressing need for the application of a gendered lens to the rise of decentralized finance (including cryptocurrencies and blockchain) and its promise to empower and elevate women, especially the poor and/or women of the Global South. Beginning with a brief primer on the relevant technologies, proceeding to an overview of relevant literature, and finally touching on specific themes and cases related to gender and cryptocurrency, I argue that the liberatory promise of crypto is flawed in specifically gendered ways. Cryptocurrency has thus far failed to deliver on the promise of participation, the promise of lowering financial barriers, and the promise of empowerment. These shortcomings are driven by the failure to recognize that cryptocurrency development initiatives are built over existing social hierarchies, reinforcing without transforming them.

The discussion is linked to broader theoretical and ethical debates in development discourse. Prior development trends like the financial inclusion movement have been critiqued based on their reliance on neoliberal logics – that is, that initiatives built upon the notion that more interaction with the market coupled with less regulatory oversight are the best solutions to poverty. Debates over cryptocurrency arguably take neoliberal thought a step further, coupling advocacy for more market interaction with the complete removal of any state, institutional, or regulatory oversight – even as it relates to activity as foundational as state backing of currency. Insofar as Golumbia (2016) ties theories of cryptocurrency adoption to libertarian pro-market and anti-institutional principles, I refer to this as a neolibertarian development logic that intertwines suspicion of institutional actors with notions of technological supremacy that see states (especially, states of the Global South) as obstructions to be bypassed. Ultimately, I argue that this conversation calls for feminist critique. This includes greater discussion about ethical practices of inclusion, consent, and the use of experimental financial technologies on marginalized populations. It also relates to security, insofar as the promise of greater economic security underlies both financial inclusion policy and many cryptocurrency-based initiatives. I conclude by examining whether there are openings for change in this system. This includes a closer look at some examples of how the blockchain technology that underlies cryptocurrency is being decoupled from problematic financial systems and deployed in support of progressive initiatives. This culminates in a discussion on how to move forward with these emerging technologies in a more responsible way.

A primer: blockchain, cryptocurrency, and decentralized finance

The term cryptocurrency refers collectively to bitcoin (the first and most well-known cryptocurrency system) and dozens of other cryptocurrencies and tokens that offer various modifications to the system pioneered by bitcoin. A central characteristic of all these cryptocurrencies is that they purport to offer a decentralized monetary system, that is, one that is both digital *and* detached from direct government oversight and regulation. As a substitute, they leverage the underlying model of blockchain technology. First conceptualized by bitcoin founder Satoshi Nakamoto[2] in 2008, blockchain offers a peer-to-peer network through which a central ledger is maintained and reconciled. This practice of storing and reconciling the ledger of cryptocurrency transactions across multiple nodes in a large network is meant to provide a safeguard against fraud, hacking, and the potential for users to double-spend a currency that does not exist in physical form. Blockchain itself has been referred to by various authors as a 'truth machine', a 'revolution', and a way to reduce the 'cost of trust' by relying on 'impregnable cryptography, rather than trust in fallible humans' (Tapscott and Tapscott 2016; Casey and Vigna 2018; Vigna and Casey 2019). 'Decentralized finance' collectively refers to the wider range of financial activity enabled by cryptocurrency use and blockchain technology, including borrowing and lending, movements of currency through exchanges, and the development of self-executing 'smart contracts' using the blockchain system (Alkurd 2020).

The extent to which cryptocurrency is truly 'money' is the subject of ongoing debate. Economists usually envision money as serving three functions: (1) that of a medium of exchange, which can be used to purchase goods; (2) that of a store of value, that is, maintaining value over time; and (3) as a measure of value, offering a baseline against which prices can be compared (Dasgupta 2007; Cleaver 2010). At this point in time, cryptocurrency primarily serves the first function, acting as a medium of exchange that has received varying degrees of acceptance in different parts of the world. The extent to which cryptocurrencies serve the other functions of money – as a store of value or a measure of value – are more debatable. Analysts have argued that price volatility and the limited scale of adoption mean cryptocurrency is unable to truly serve these functions (Vigna and Casey 2015; Golumbia 2016). Though evangelists may argue otherwise, cryptocurrencies remain a risky investment due to wild price fluctuations. Even bitcoin, arguably the most established currency, lost about 80 per cent of its value between 2017 and 2019, only to recover much of that value by late 2020 (Di Salvo 2019). Some cryptocurrencies are also fixed supply currencies, with only a finite amount available, to be released over time. These currencies are (in theory) deflationary; in other words, as long as demand persists, the value of a currency like bitcoin is expected to rise over time. This makes it generally impractical as a reliable store of value and, by extension, as a baseline for determining value. However, in some economies where the value of actual, state-backed money is even more volatile, cryptocurrencies arguably represent an improvement. One clear example of this is in Venezuela, where runaway inflation has prompted the rise of an alternative economy based on cryptocurrency (Chun 2017; Di Salvo 2019).

Such instances bring up relevant points about the decentralized nature of these currencies and their relationship to traditional forms of money. Generally, cryptocurrencies promise both to liberate users from government oversight of money and to mitigate the problem of inflation by controlling the supply of available currency. Analysts have alternatively presented this philosophy as 'extremist' or 'utopian' in nature (Vigna and Casey 2015; Golumbia 2016). Indeed, with the proliferation of digital[3] and cryptocurrencies, variation has expanded along the spectrum of degrees of decentralization and how the amount of currency circulation is managed. Common to most cryptocurrency projects is some form of engagement and oversight by users, founders, and/or developers. Labour is also involved, with those who participate in the blockchain devoting computing resources to its maintenance. These individuals may be compensated in the form of cryptocurrency via a process referred to as mining.[4] However, the rapid expansion of cryptocurrency use in recent years means that mining has become a competitive process, with more parties competing for the finite amounts of currency available through the mining process. Effectively, these systems benefit from large amounts of free labour, increasingly favouring larger actors with more computing power who can succeed in an energy-intensive competition for mining rewards (Baraniuk 2019; Stoll et al 2019).

Applying feminist insights to decentralized finance

What insights can feminist work in international relations and political economy apply to this system? Critical feminist work on political economy since the late 20th century has focused on the reductive treatment of gender in neoliberal thought and the issues caused by the application of neoliberal dogma in Global South contexts. Neoliberalism in development can be seen packaged into ideas like the Washington Consensus, which specified reforms including deficit reduction, trade liberalization, reduced government intervention in the market, lower spending on benefits and public services, privatization, and deregulation as 'best practices' that would foster business growth and competition (Williamson 1993). In theory, the benefits of such reforms were meant to promote transparency and engagement with markets for the benefit of all sectors of society. Critical feminist scholarship on political economy argues that, in reality, the neoliberal development paradigm has failed to realize its promises because it overlooks the salience of gender and other social hierarchies. For women in particular, liberalization has been associated with large-scale movement into insecure, low-wage, and at times dangerous jobs. This, while household gender roles remain unchanged – forcing women to do equal duty at work and home (Griffin 2010; True 2012; Runyan and Peterson 2013).

To the extent that women were 'seen' in neoliberal thought, the dominant view was that the mobilization of women into the workforce was a benefit and a symbol of modernity to which states should aspire (Ellerby 2011). As an example, the mobilization of women into export-oriented production in South Korea in the 1980s was sold to women as a means of becoming full citizens, to families as an extension of women's roles as 'dutiful daughters', and to factory owners as a way of attaining a cheap and docile workforce (Han and Ling 1998; Enloe 2016). The primary beneficiaries of this system were the Western-owned multinationals that benefited from women's labour (Enloe 2016). A generation later, similar ideas were used to mobilize young Chinese women as a force for modernization (Chang 2009). In each case, greater engagement with markets was sold not only as a tool for development, but also as a tool for women's empowerment via this newfound 'freedom' to earn wages. The ignorance of neoliberalism regarding gender power dynamics meant that it failed to envision how these freedoms left women – and particularly women of the Global South – vulnerable to abuses, exploitation, and violence (Griffin 2010; True 2012; Runyan and Peterson 2013).

Some work in critical feminist political economy argues that neoliberalism is deeply reliant upon 'hierarchies that are internalized and institutionalized' in the pursuit of its objectives (Peterson 2003: 8–9). In other words, to borrow from development parlance, neoliberalism's deployment of gender in service of its goals is a feature, not a bug. Men and masculinities also have a distinct role in this process. Scholars have argued that neoliberalism serves a particular notion of hegemonic masculinity that privileges young, able-bodied, and economically successful men (usually, White men in the Global North), who are perceived as more capable of reaching the ideal of being entrepreneurial, competitive, and self-reliant (Cornwall et al 2016). By comparison, neoliberalism sees men who are poor and/or resident in the Global South primarily as obstacles to change, clinging to outdated notions about manual labour, the patriarchal household, and cultural traditions as the roots of masculinity (Ahmed 2008; Cornwall et al 2016; Natile 2020).

Finally, feminist work in international political economy may see decentralized finance as both a continuation of offline social hierarchies and a force for shaping new inequalities. This specifically recalls Peterson's (2003) feminist analysis of the virtual/information economy as a site where power relationships are shaped by decisions about whose knowledge, data, experiences, and so on, can be monetized. The notion that technology is becoming a new axis of inequality brings feminist thought into dialogue with critics of cryptocurrency, who have argued that the system is rooted in logics that promote the moral superiority of technologically capable populations (Golumbia 2016). In the cryptocurrency sector, value arguably centres on those who have the most technological capability and access to engage in development and, by extension, the most existing wealth to invest in expanding the sector. Each of these are, in a global context, areas in which women are disadvantaged due to existing social hierarchies.

'Financial inclusion' and gender hierarchies

Viewed through a feminist lens, the promise of cryptocurrency as a radically transformative system seems dubious. At the same time, discussions about neolibertarianism invite further reflection on how such ideas have moved rapidly towards mainstream acceptance. I argue that there is an obvious connection between neoliberal policies on financial inclusion (FI) and the growth of neolibertarian ideas, in the sense that the former has (unwittingly) set the stage for the latter. Advocated by major institutions including the World Bank, the UN, and the G20, the idea of FI rests on the notion that increasing the depth of financial services in developing communities 'reduces income inequality and poverty and is thus particularly beneficial for the poor' (World Bank 2008). The FI agenda is seen by some as a successor to microcredit – promoting similar ideas about the financialization of the poor while sidestepping the abuses and failures attributed to microcredit (Wichterich 2017; Mader 2018; Natile 2020). While FI as an institutional approach is distinct from the decentralized systems underlying cryptocurrency, one can trace a logical progression from microfinance through FI and ultimately to decentralized finance. Though established players in finance have expressed some need for caution regarding cryptocurrency, an examination of critical perspectives on FI suggests that these same players have primed unbanked (and underbanked) populations to be receptive to decentralized finance. Specifically, critical inquiry suggests that doctrinal neoliberalism coupled with the discourse of FI has rendered these populations more risk-acceptant, valorized technology's role in financialization, and pushed a movement beyond the state. Placing this work into conversation with feminist perspectives further shows how these movements are gendered, at the same time playing into particular stereotypes about men and women in the Global South.

In terms of technology, ideas about FI go hand-in-hand with the application of technologies including big data, psychometric testing, mobile money systems, and surveillance tools. FI appeals to corporate actors by promising both profit *and* data as rewards for more inclusive practice (Gabor and Brooks 2017). Some have argued that international political economy and international relations generally underestimate the relevance of technology in this space and its human impact (Bernards and Campbell-Verduyn 2019). For example, psychometric testing as a requisite for financial services conveys notions about the presumed cognitive capacities of poor populations while also institutionalizing gender stereotypes about how risk and honesty map onto identity (Gabor and Brooks 2017; Bernards 2019). Researchers likewise question the degree to which these technologies are valid predictors of creditworthiness, because they focus on individual behaviours rather than offering a holistic view of potential borrowers' likeliness to succeed in a given venture in a given community (Bernards 2019; Langevin 2019).

This point leads into a further discussion of how technological financialization primes individuals to become more risk acceptant. Assessments of microfinance programmes argue that, in many communities, predatory behaviour by lending agents has led to over-indebtedness (as lenders sought repeat clients) and shaming (as community members were made privy to the lending habits of others) (Martin 2002; Duvendack et al 2011; Gabor and Brooks 2017). Paradoxically, although microcredit borrowers (especially women) were often extended loans on the assumption that they were 'low-risk' clients, intense anxiety over repayment drove this same population towards higher-risk ventures in the hopes of attaining bigger rewards that might eliminate their debt (Duvendack et al 2011; Gabor and Brooks 2017).

When such ventures failed, the result could be exhaustion, crisis, and even suicide – as has been the case in parts of India (Wichterich 2017; Langevin 2019). More recently, studies on FI argue that it perpetuates the same forms of exhaustion because it failed to internalize the lessons of microcredit. FI advocates argue that earlier initiatives failed to work not because their logic was flawed, but because they didn't integrate enough people deeply enough into markets (Mader 2018; Langevin 2019). By this logic, FI strategies are also encouraging traditionally unbanked populations to look beyond the state for solutions to poverty, presenting redistributive policies as anathema to growth and encouraging target populations to embrace a range of 'better than cash' solutions like mobile money services (World Bank 2008; Natile 2020). While these solutions are held out to populations as opportunities, they in fact allow commercially oriented financial actors new entry points into people's everyday lives while raising new barriers to entering the system (for example, costs to access mobile money platforms) (Gabor and Brooks 2017; Rodima-Taylor and Grimes 2019a; Natile 2020).

As noted, cryptocurrency and blockchain technology have a distinct genealogy that – at least initially – organized itself around an ethos of privacy and anti-institutionalism. It may, therefore, seem counterintuitive to suggest that institutional neoliberalism (especially, the FI movement) set the stage for decentralized finance. However, there is direct evidence of institutions leveraging decentralized finance as a tool for FI. In a 2017 report on potential applications of blockchain technology, World Bank experts specifically highlighted blockchain as a potential mechanism to advance FI. This analysis specifically envisioned blockchain as a solution or workaround where existing systems lack secure transaction frameworks, identity verification capabilities, asset verification capabilities (for instance, land registries), and/or affordable products and services (Natarajan et al 2017). In some cases, using blockchain to fill these gaps would allow decentralized systems to perform functions typically associated with the state. While taking a more tenuous view of cryptocurrency, the analysis nonetheless said cryptocurrency 'could be especially relevant for financially excluded and underserved populations', especially when combined with other forms of financial technology (Natarajan et al 2017). In the same year, the World Bank launched a technology and innovation unit including a blockchain lab with the goal of applying this 'disruptive' technology to a variety of use cases, one of which was cross-border payments and FI (Karacaoglu et al 2018).

The World Bank was not alone in positioning blockchain and/or cryptocurrency as the next logical step in FI. The UN's Office of Information and Communications Technology has highlighted blockchain as a force for FI, noting its potential to reach the 'unbanked' and to facilitate microcredit programmes (UN Office of Information and Communications Technology 2018). The United Nations Children's Fund (UNICEF) first experimented with blockchain in 2015 and in 2019 it established a cryptocurrency fund to attract, hold, and disburse donations in cryptocurrency. In the lead-up to the establishment of the fund, UNICEF staff justified the move towards cryptocurrency despite its fluctuating value by appealing to the logics of risk and reward. In particular, there was a presumption that 'crypto-donors' would *a priori* be more comfortable with experimentation and risk and would, therefore, be open to seeing their donations used in riskier ways (Fabian 2018). Thus, we see how logics of technology acceptance, risk acceptance, and even a desire to bypass ineffective state systems move along a pathway from neoliberalism to decentralized finance.[5]

Taking a critical view of development trends illuminates the trajectory of neoliberal development ideology. Placing these ideas into conversation with feminist thought, we further see how this landscape is gendered, classed, and racialized. As was the case with microcredit, FI policies centre poor women and women of the Global South as entrepreneurs in waiting and low-risk targets for financial products (Martin 2002; World Bank 2008; Wichterich 2017). Men of the Global South – especially poor men – are viewed by contrast as undisciplined, untrustworthy, and even potentially violent in their opposition to change (Bedford 2007). Men are presented the possibility of personal enrichment only if they embrace norms of entrepreneurial masculinity and accept the financial technologies that might prove them worthy of investment (Martin 2002; Wichterich 2017; Langevin 2019). While feminist studies of political economy have commented on the gendered impacts of microcredit,[6] the literature broadly suggests a need for more gendered and intersectional assessments of inclusionary development ideologies. While a deeper assessment of institutional approaches to FI is beyond the scope of this chapter, these lessons as applied to cryptocurrency-based approaches should motivate inquiry into how programmes engage with gender roles as they apply to both men and women and how this architecture sees gender interacting with class, race, and Global North/South positionality.

Gender and the failed promises of decentralized finance

The discussion in this chapter offers an entry point for the further exploration of gender and cryptocurrency. Specifically, discussion in the previous section suggests the need to see continuity from neoliberal to neolibertarian thought, to engage with how masculine and feminine gender roles are deployed, and to approach analysis in a way that envisions gender interacting with hierarchies of class and race/ethnicity. Going forward, I apply this analytical lens to three specific 'promises' of decentralized approaches to development. These are the promise of participation, the promise of lowering financial barriers, and the promise of empowerment. Each of these are present in the discourse of cryptocurrency advocates, as already noted, and each also to some extent aligns with the broader and interrelated discourse of FI. In each case, I argue that a gendered analysis further illuminates the failure of the system to produce transformative results.

The promise of participation

Discussions about gender and cryptocurrency are notable mostly for the extent to which they deny that gender hierarchies shape the system. Points like 'gender-neutral', 'no barriers to entry,' and 'bitcoin does not know your name or gender' have been used to reassure investors that cryptocurrency markets are a truly level playing field where women have an equal chance to participate (Vigna and Casey 2015; Comben 2019). Yet the realities of the sector tell a much different story. Though engagement with cryptocurrency by women has grown over time – expanding from an estimated 3 per cent of users in 2008, to 9.1 per cent in 2019, to 12.3 per cent in 2020 (Comben 2019; Coin Dance 2020) – their participation in the sector has remained very low. Even to the extent that women are holders or users of cryptocurrencies, it is likely that they hold very little of the available wealth. Among the known mega-rich of bitcoin holders (those whose holdings were estimated at US$10 million or more) after the boom year of 2013, all identified individuals were male (Wile 2013). A 2018 Forbes list of the richest people in cryptocurrency likewise included no women and was dominated by White and East Asian men (Ambler et al 2018). The predominant success of early adopters means that the greatest known concentration of wealth is in the hands of individuals working in technology and finance – areas where women are historically underrepresented (Bowles 2018).

The experience of women in the field illustrates how the cryptocurrency industry has become deeply entwined with masculinity, especially the norm of the entrepreneurial, tech-savvy male investor/developer. Several women profiled in stories about cryptocurrency have decried the market as being, at best, characterized by a 'bro culture', and at worst dominated by sexual harassment and exclusionary practices. In 2018, the North American Bitcoin Conference hosted only three female speakers (out of a total of 87), and held its official social event at a strip club (Bowles 2018; Hao 2018). Women in the industry have complained of sexual harassment during job interviews and of being confused for spokesmodels rather than experts at events (Bowles 2018). While some women have responded to the culture by creating their own event spaces, some have found that even events marketed as being 'for women' are co-opted by men looking to gain a financial edge (Adams et al 2020; Frizzo-Barker 2020). Ultimately, these dynamics lead women to feel unable to assert themselves (Hao 2018). These linkages between gender inequality, masculinity, and cryptocurrency recall the discussion of neoliberal, hegemonic masculinities explored earlier in the chapter. In an environment that is dominated by men and which values wealth, entrepreneurialism, and self-reliant or anti-establishment thought, it is in many ways unsurprising that gender hierarchies have taken root.[7]

In addition to being underrepresented among cryptocurrency users and investors, women are underrepresented as entrepreneurs and developers – those individuals most responsible for shaping the rules of the new economic system. Drawing on publicly available survey data, Hao (2018) concluded that while women represent about 23 per cent of the workforce engaged in the cryptocurrency sector, they represent only 14 per cent of project founders and just 7 per cent of professional investors. For women engaged in the workforce, she finds they are more concentrated in areas like marketing and fundraising than in coding and development (Hao 2018). Statistics like these expose the fallacy of crypto as a gender-neutral sector where women have an equal opportunity to contribute.

The promise of lowering financial barriers

Taking the conversation into the realm of development, cryptocurrency projects have promised to meet the needs of the world's poor by lowering financial barriers, especially the costs associated with the global movement of money. This speaks specifically to the migrant labour force and the transmission of money through remittances. While remittances are a force in the global economy – reaching an all-time high of US$689 billion globally in 2018 (World Bank 2019) – under current financial systems a significant portion of this total is lost due to transaction fees, fraud, and/or theft.[8] Furthermore, there is evidence that experiences with remittances are gendered in specific and important ways. Research published by UN Women suggests that migrant women transmit a larger portion of their income as remittances than do migrant men, but that women also pay more in fees to remit money – a problem related to low financial literacy and reduced access to money transfer systems (Azam et al 2020). Though discourse about remittances emanating from governments and institutions tends to centre the stereotypical image of the male breadwinner/remittance-sender, the participation of women in migrant labour and the remittance system challenges gender roles by increasing women's economic importance and changing power dynamics within families (Kunz 2008; Lopez-Ekra et al 2011; Petrozziello 2011; Lam and Yeoh 2018). This being the case, an examination of remittances offers the chance to leverage insights in multiple areas, moving into a realm where we can envision the interaction of gender with Global North/South hierarchies as well as the interrelationship of gendered development policies and gender issues in security (Parashar 2016).

Various cryptocurrency projects have promised to mitigate inequality and promote development by offering significantly lower transaction fees and secure platforms that can be accessed without much technological know-how and investment. The startup 37Coins is a case study in the cryptocurrency's promise to transform remittances, as well as in how that promise is racialized and gendered. 37Coins is notable in part because the public faces of the project were women. One of these, Songyi Lee, was a former employee of a development NGO who became the project's chief marketer and co-founder, alongside the venture's two male co-founders. The second woman was 'Fatima', a Malian refugee with whom Lee had contact through her development work. As told by Lee, Fatima was a mother of five living in a refugee camp. Her husband lived and worked in a neighbouring country, but because the couple were disconnected from the banking system, the only way for her to receive remittances was for him to give cash to individuals – sometimes strangers – headed in the direction of the family, in the hopes that they would pass the money to Fatima. This sometimes resulted in money being lost or stolen (CoinSummit London 2014 – Start-up Showcase – 37 Coins 2014; Vigna and Casey 2015). Upon relating Fatima's story, Lee and a friend conceived the idea of using cryptocurrency to facilitate the fast and safe movement of remittances (Vigna and Casey 2015). Though Fatima had no voice in the project, she became the symbolic face of 37Coins, with her image used in promotional materials as embodiment of the project's promise to change lives. By leveraging Fatima as the archetypal female recipient – dependent on transmissions from her husband – the project replicates stereotypes widespread in remittance discourse (Kunz 2008). (Note that it also leverages tropes of masculinity referenced earlier, in particular of Fatima's husband as the typical male labourer who relies on old ways of doing things and jeopardizes his family as a result.) Fatima's image became a gendered, racialized, and classed depiction of cryptocurrency's promise. However, as it turns out, women like Fatima would never actually be served by the project.

Lee and the project's other co-founders proposed to make remittances easier and more secure through the creation of a system to send funds in the form of bitcoin by text message (SMS). By focusing on SMS, the founders of 37Coins argued that their project had the potential to reach a population not currently served by cryptocurrency – that is, the vast number of cell phone users in the Global South who have access to SMS but lack access to mobile Internet. In a presentation for potential investors in 2014, Lee estimated that 96 per cent of the world's population would be able to use the service, saving remittance senders a potential US$43.4 billion in transaction fees versus traditional money transfer services (CoinSummit London 2014; 37Coins 2015). While small fees would be a part of the system, founders argued that these fees would be minimized by the use of

SMS and a reliance on local gateways, which would ensure the transfer of money from sender to recipient and create a digital wallet for the recipient if necessary (CoinSummit London 2014; 37Coins 2015). In their pitch, the founders referenced an aim of working with local 'partners' who could convert received bitcoin into local currency (presumably, at an additional fee), but this was not addressed in detail.

The model advanced by 37Coins' founders was received with enthusiasm. The project was featured in Paul Vigna and Michael J. Casey's (2015) best-selling book *The Age of Cryptocurrency* and was funded by a well-known Silicon Valley accelerator for cryptocurrency projects. Yet, within eight months of the publication of Vigna and Casey's book, the project announced it was ceasing operations (37Coins 2015). In its closing announcement, representatives for the venture cited the inability 'to deliver a quality product', the rise of competing ventures, and issues attracting reliable partners outside the United States (37Coins 2015). Lee, in a later interview, stated that the project's staffing and funding was never sufficient to match its objectives and that the technology to meet the project's core objectives did not exist (Community at Klaytn 2019). Although there seems to be little publicly available feedback from those who actually used the service (perhaps further suggesting demand-side issues), comments from a few individuals who claimed to have used 37Coins and its related SMS wallet service indicate that concerns over the security of the system, errors in using the system, and lost funds were issues.[9]

Beyond these technical concerns, 37Coins never lived up to its promise to reach individuals like Fatima: Users in underdeveloped and conflict-affected states. At the time of its 2014 pitch, Lee stated the project was up and running in 25 countries. However, the majority of these were in *developed* countries, including the United States, Canada, Australia, New Zealand, Japan, South Korea, and a number of European states. Only two countries in Latin America (Chile and Colombia) and just three in Africa (South Africa, Zimbabwe, and Equatorial Guinea) had established service. Vigna and Casey (2015) state that 37Coins chose its markets based on a need to establish initial operations in areas where users were tech-savvy and had an awareness of bitcoin. But this itself exposes how women and populations in the Global South face a paradox. These populations are expected to develop knowledge about cryptocurrency as a prerequisite for participating in crypto-based remittance systems, yet they cannot acquire that knowledge specifically because the developers of these systems don't view them as worthy of investment. In particular, the fetishization of women of the Global South as vulnerable subjects in need of technologies developed and funded by players in the Global North stands in contrast to the ease with which women like Fatima are discarded when they are not immediately perceived as profitable.[10]

Various other startups promising to revolutionize the transmission of remittances have likewise failed to realize the promise of lowering transaction costs. Payment provider Ripple launched in 2012 as a for-profit venture with an associated cryptocurrency (XRP) that promised, among other things, to drastically lower the costs of remittances. By 2018, Ripple's RippleNet enterprise blockchain was active in over 40 countries and claimed access to a potential US$2 billion in inflows (Ripple 2018). However, Ripple encountered a host of problems in realizing the promise of low-cost remittances. Unlike traditional blockchains, which are fully decentralized and monitored by system users, RippleNet relies on partnerships with financial institutions to maintain its blockchain. This, combined with Ripple's for-profit model, leaves it open to critiques that it is neither revolutionary, nor philanthropic, nor fully decentralized (Vigna and Casey 2015; Arisandi 2019). Ripple's impact on remittances costs further seems to have been modest. By mid-2020 it claimed to power about 7 per cent of remittances between the United States and Mexico (Waters 2020). But with the global economic downturn in 2020 as a result of the COVID-19 crisis, the World Bank estimated a drop in remittances of about 20 per cent globally, and sales of Ripple's cryptocurrency stalled (Waters 2020; World Bank 2020). In the midst of this crisis, Ripple announced a strategic 'pivot' away from cross-border payments towards more commercial ventures.[11] This move arguably represents another example of cryptocurrency remittance projects being torn between profit motive and promises to underserved populations, ultimately deciding in favour of profit.

Big-picture thinking on transforming remittances appears to have run up against the hard realities of entrenched financial systems, profit motives, and a market not fully receptive to the technology. Yet the elusive promise of changing the remittance market continues to draw substantial amounts of investment for new cryptocurrency startups, even when they are fundamentally recycling business models that have already failed. Much has been written on the similarities between for-profit Ripple and Stellar, a non-profit with one of the same co-founders that has a similar mission and its own associated cryptocurrency (Vigna and Casey 2015; Arisandi 2019; Pirus 2019). The idea of crypto-via-SMS transfers proposed by 37Coins has also found new life in a Venezuelan startup called DashText, which promised to reach Venezuela's rural poor by facilitating the movement of the Dash cryptocurrency. In an informal pitch in 2018 to the Dash community, the developers behind DashText indicated they had not heard of 37Coins and were unable to respond to questions about how their model would be different. Regardless, in a straw poll 86 per cent of Dash community users surveyed supported the concept, which received in excess of 100 Dash (US$20,000 in 2018) in startup funds.[12] DashText's own statistics indicate difficulty in attaining wider adoption of the service, as the service remains more heavily used in Venezuela than in all other countries combined,[13] suggesting its use for cross-border remittances remains low (DashText 2020). At the time of this writing, the service does not appear to collect or report gender-disaggregated data on its impact.

The promise of empowerment

A final issue to explore is cryptocurrency's promise to empower women in developing countries. This again speaks to how women of the Global South are centred as a population that stands to benefit from decentralization. A test case for this has been the use of cryptocurrencies to fund projects meant to empower women in Afghanistan. The utility of cryptocurrency in this sphere has been argued on multiple grounds. The most frequently invoked justifications are that cryptocurrency can allow women build wealth by paying them in a currency more stable than local currency (the afghani) and that it allows them to challenge patriarchal social practices that limit women's ability to control their own wealth (Vigna and Casey 2015; Baldet and Powell 2019; Rome 2019). However, these altruistic concerns have sometimes overshadowed more instrumental reasons for the emphasis on cryptocurrency. A closer examination shows that, in the case of employment, paying Afghan women in cryptocurrency saved employers money in foreign transaction fees while also allowing them to control how women spent their earnings. As with microcredit, financial inclusion, and other similar development trends, initiatives using decentralized finance conceive of women's empowerment as an instrumental rather than rights-based framework for advancement. In other words, they seek to enhance the status of women primarily by making them financial assets to their families. Again, this raises not only moral and philosophical questions about these projects, but also calls into question how they deploy discourse about feminine *and* masculine gender roles in ways that are racialized and classed.

Various initiatives aimed at women's empowerment in Afghanistan (some with overlapping founders, donors, and/or staff), have engaged with cryptocurrencies. One early initiative that received significant attention was the Women's Annex Foundation (WAF). This organization was co-founded by two Afghan women with backgrounds in technology, in cooperation with an Italian businessman who ran the online video service Film Annex.[14] The WAF provided technology training and employment to women, who populated content for its website online. As of 2014, the organization connected an estimated 50,000 girls to technology and the Internet via its 11 computer media labs and paid an estimated 2,000 Afghan women as content creators (Keyson and Stevens 2014; Macheel 2014). Macheel (2014) estimates that the average woman employed by WAF earned the equivalent of US$250 to $400 per month. As payments were made from overseas in

US dollars, the venture encountered problems transferring funds because of the lack of money transfer services available in Afghanistan and high fees charged by those that did operate in the country (Macheel 2014; Vigna and Casey 2015; Rome 2019). As a workaround, a system of payment via bitcoin was introduced.

The system of payment via cryptocurrency was presented as having several advantages. The venture's co-founders and various analysts noted that paying women in cryptocurrency allowed them to avoid having to open bank accounts, which in Afghanistan requires significant documentation and – sometimes – the approval of male relatives (Macheel 2014; Vigna and Casey 2015). Coverage of WAF and other, subsequent ventures involving the payment of Afghan women via bitcoin also claim this payment system was more secure than cash (Macheel 2014; Baldet and Powell 2019). This is somewhat debatable. One analysis of cryptocurrency-based programmes in Afghanistan says: 'You can take your [cryptocurrency] wallet with you, and you can hold this wallet – it's not really a physical wallet; it's just on your phone, or you can even write it out on a piece of paper if you want. Nobody can really take that away from you, right?' (Baldet and Powell 2019). Yet a phone or a piece of paper literally can be taken away by someone else. Given that one major objection to cash payments was that women could easily be robbed or have the money taken by family members, it is unclear how payment in cryptocurrency fully resolves that issue (Macheel 2014). Possession of bitcoin and other cryptocurrencies are not necessarily tied to one's identity, but rather to a private alphanumeric access key. If unauthorized parties can gain access to the key, for example because it is written on a piece of paper, they have access to those funds.[15] Beyond this, though, the repeated advocacy for cryptocurrency as a way to help Afghan women evade or circumvent male family members – presented as controlling and surveilling forces who can be foiled via their own lack of technological aptitude – replicates the same stereotypes repeated elsewhere about the backward, untrustworthy men of the Global South.

A practical issue with cryptocurrency payments to Afghan women was the lack of available opportunities for them to spend the bitcoin they earned. The co-founders of WAF acknowledged that usability was an issue for their employees, as few retailers within Afghanistan accepted bitcoin, and overseas retailers that accepted bitcoin often would not ship product to Afghanistan (Macheel 2014; Vigna and Casey 2015; Rome 2019). To get around this, the WAF and Film Annex opened their own shop, effectively meaning that employees who were paid in bitcoin were limited to spending it at a company store. The store offered inventory including mobile and Skype credit, gift cards, and some technology items (Macheel 2014; Vigna and Casey 2015). These items are arguably not necessities, and the limitations on how bitcoin can be used and spent would seem to undermine advocates' promises of financial freedom – replicating the very financial control they promised to help women escape. Take, for example, statements made by and about Film Annex's founder in Vigna and Casey's *The Age of Cryptocurrency*, regarding the payment of Afghan women:

> He wants the [Afghan] girls to spend it [their income] on technology, such as Mozilla's forthcoming $25 smartphone, which they can convert into a camera and a tool for producing better video and blog content. He is trying to turn the Film Annex website into its own, self-enclosed bitcoin economy …
>
> 'The belief I have is that if you lock these people into this new economy, they will make that new economy as efficient as possible. If you start giving people opportunities to get out of the economy, they will just cut it down.' (Vigna and Casey 2015: 204–207)

None of this is to suggest that those associated with WAF or the Film Annex intentionally acted in bad faith with regard to their employees. Indeed, the founders consistently express a concern for the safety of their employees. However, the overriding philosophy behind these ventures, that is, that women are empowered by becoming wage-earners and that they should be empowered because they will, in turn, contribute to the economy, places an instrumentalist view of women above rights-based justifications to empowerment. Feminist work has strongly criticized this neoliberal approach to 'empowerment', that is, the notion that promoting gender equality is worthwhile primarily as a means to an end – be it peace, security, or prosperity – rather than as a moral imperative (Ellerby 2017; Parisi 2020). This notion that 'if she's making money, she is more likely to be protected by her brothers, because she's an asset to the family instead of a second-class citizen' (Vigna and Casey 2015: 207) repeats and enshrines neoliberal logics about human value, while presenting men (and, especially, poor men of the Global South) as incapable of philosophical or moral support for women's rights.

Indeed, the degree to which bitcoin-based ventures into women's empowerment improved women's lives in sustainable ways is unclear. By 2017, the WAF had re-branded as the non-profit Digital Citizen Fund, with a larger mission to teach digital and financial literacy to women (2017 IIC Winner: Digital Citizen Fund (Technology Access) 2017). While the Digital Citizen Fund and some other NGOs continue to accept bitcoin donations to fund their aims of women's empowerment, the future for such initiatives remains unclear in the wake of the Taliban's return to power in the country.

Blockchain for good? Alternative futures for the decentralized web

The foregoing analysis demonstrates how cryptocurrency and the larger sector of decentralized finance have thus far failed to deliver on their promises of gender-inclusive development and social transformation. Despite the promise of decentralized financial models as a force for leaving behind social hierarchies of the past, cryptocurrency-based initiatives have failed to promote the participation of, lower financial barriers for, or empower women. A closer examination of each of these areas further highlights the need for analysis that sees gender as a force interacting with hierarchies of race/ethnicity, class, and geographic location. Projects discussed in the previous sections deploy narratives that engage with masculinity, Global North/South encounters, and socioeconomic status in problematic and/or simplistic ways. Each of the examples discussed challenges the notion of cryptocurrency as a gender-neutral innovation, illustrating instead how an emerging technology, harnessed to the same unequal social structures, global hierarchies, and neoliberal/neolibertarian philosophy, fails to produce transformative change in spite of good intentions. Decentralized approaches to development suffer from the paradox of offering targeted benefits to women while denying foundational principles of feminist and critical thought like the salience of gender and other social hierarchies. They also belong to a larger lineage of neoliberal and market-oriented solutions that have fostered risk-acceptance, technological surveillance, and economic insecurity in the Global South. In so doing, these cases only reinforce a central argument of feminist international relations: that is, that no phenomenon in our societies is ever truly gender-neutral (Harding 1986; Runyan and Peterson 2013).

Does this suggest that blockchain, cryptocurrency, and decentralized finance are destined to perpetuate harm in the global context? One can argue otherwise. Some organizations and ventures are decoupling blockchain technology from cryptocurrency and/or fully decentralized systems in ways that open new possibilities. Projects that view blockchain as an archival technology see secure record-keeping, rather than wealth acquisition, as a primary goal. Advocates for the wider use of blockchain as a means of safeguarding, for example, land titles, educational credentials, identity records, and health records see blockchain as a way of recentring power relationships. In such a system, decentralized networks of trust would supplement governmental record-keeping, safeguarding against the potential that cyberattacks, regime change, or misconduct by state actors might compromise critical information (Lemieux 2019).

We have already seen such solutions implemented. In the former Soviet space, blockchain has been used to supplement weak record-keeping systems and to protect data from Russian cyberattacks (Rodima-Taylor and Grimes 2019b). In Hong Kong, decentralized publishing systems run off blockchain technology were used to preserve records related to the 2019 protests – information that was at risk of censorship by China (Hui 2021). The Ethereum blockchain was used by activists in China (possibly in connection with the #MeToo movement) to preserve a letter from a student accusing her university of covering up a sexual assault (Hui 2021). Yet these systems still pose new questions. One is, who runs the blockchain? Whether a blockchain is permissioned (that is, administered by a select few) or permissionless (that is, open to anyone) has ramifications for privacy and control. There is also the question of authority, as simply establishing a blockchain does not give information stored on it the force of law (Lemieux 2019).[16]

UN agencies have recently grappled with these questions while experimenting with the use of blockchain in humanitarian aid distribution. Blockchain-based experiments by the World Food Programme (WFP) and UN Women aim to use technology to establish and safeguard identity. The Building Blocks programme was established with the goal of providing secure identity verification for displaced persons in refugee camps in Jordan, Bangladesh, and Lebanon. Combining biometric data (iris scans) with a blockchain-based network, the goal was to facilitate faster, more reliable, and entirely electronic disbursements of aid payments. The use of blockchain is meant to safeguard against tampering and to ensure that the network would be resilient to the destruction or seizure of individual nodes (Al Saqqaf nd; WFP 2020a, 2020b).

The Building Blocks programme attempted to model best practices in the use of technology in multiple ways. First, the programme was carefully piloted and evaluated before being scaled up. Second, established civil society actors were engaged in project execution and assessment. Third, monitoring and evaluation frameworks mainstreamed a gender perspective through the involvement of UN Women (this was especially true in Jordan, where the pilot project had a component aimed especially at women). Fourth, programme assessments were also conducted by independent experts. Finally, both UN Women and the WFP issued public reports at the conclusion of the pilot, offering some transparency and public accountability (Awan and Nunhuck 2020; WFP 2020a; UN Women Jordan 2021).

Impact studies showed a number of positive benefits to the programme. At a practical level, the use of blockchain eliminated the need to share data with or pay transfer fees to financial service providers as part of the process (Al Saqqaf nd; Awan and Nunhuck 2020). Women who participated in the programme indicated that they felt the system was safer and gave them more control over their funds (UN Women Jordan 2021). Compared to the previous system of cash transfer, in which women would receive disbursements via envelopes with physical cash, the blockchain-based system was viewed as lending more safety, dignity, and normalcy to the process (Al Saqqaf nd; Awan and Nunhuck 2020; UN Women Jordan 2021). UN Women also engaged in digital literacy outreach as part of the pilot, in the hopes of reducing the impact of the digital gender divide (UN Women Jordan 2021).

Still, despite the beneficial results, innovators who wish to integrate emerging technology into relief and recovery efforts still face a number of hurdles. First among these are questions of informed consent. While UN Women worked to incorporate data and financial literacy training into the Building Blocks pilot, this training largely focused on the use of mobile phones to access and use funds (UN Women Jordan 2021). Deeper conversations about data privacy, the nature of blockchain, and other more technical matters do not appear to have been a part of this programme. Outside assessments of Building Blocks and similar initiatives note the problem of achieving informed consent from populations that, for a number of reasons, may be less technically literate (Awan and Nunhuck 2020; Cheesman 2022). Cheesman (2022), in an ethnography of blockchain-based development programmes, finds that programmes like these have proliferated in the developing world in part because of the perception that countries in the Global South are a blank slate, that is, places that are technology vacuums, but which are also seen as willing to accept technology (with few questions asked) in their quest for development. Developers see these populations as willing to experiment technologically, yet simultaneously as too backward to fully understand the solutions being deployed. This creates important ethical dilemmas. In the case of the Building Blocks programme, Awan and Nunhuck (2020) note that Jordan lacks robust data protection laws, meaning that no legal safeguards outside of the UN existed as a recourse if data is mishandled or misused. Since the WFP was, at one point, the only node on the blockchain, this further created transparency problems (Al Saqqaf nd). Ultimately, WFP staffers who worked on the project admitted that blockchain was not the only technological solution available to administer the programme. They cite the publicity benefits and the potential for creating partnerships as motivations to use this technology (Al Saqqaf nd). The notion that the potential for strategic partnerships was placed before accessibility or transparency should be a cause for reflection.

Similarly, the nature of blockchain technology leaves other questions unanswered. Since records on the blockchain are permanently part of the blockchain, there is no right to be forgotten. It is unclear what happens to data when the humanitarian operations end, or what recourse there is for someone who believes their data is incorrect or has been misappropriated.[17] As relevant as these questions are for humanitarian aid distribution, they might arguably be more pressing if blockchain were used to store records related to criminal convictions, gender identity, or sensitive health records. Long-term, ensuring the viability of blockchain technology remains another concern. While cryptographic techniques are currently used to secure blockchain data, advances in quantum computing threaten to render today's cryptography obsolete – perhaps by as early as the late 2020s (Fedorov et al 2018). Put another way, although computer scientists are working on making more resilient blockchain technology for the future, any blockchain data that exists today may be at-risk long term if systems cannot be upgraded.

Clearly, the impact of these technologies requires more study. In the case of the Building Blocks programme, we have some gender analysis because of the UN's internal mandates for gender mainstreaming in monitoring and assessment. Private programmes that promise gendered benefits from cryptocurrency or blockchain use would not necessarily be held to the same standards. This is an important stipulation. While current international policy frameworks for gender mainstreaming are far from ideal, they still present a baseline and offer some mechanisms for accountability. The movement of international development initiatives towards decentralized finance may bypass established practices related to issues like gender mainstreaming, civil society consultation, and even environmental protections, routing development funds into a system with little oversight and expertise. As we have seen, this system frequently fails to see and understand gender and interlinked social hierarchies, beyond the application of crude stereotypes. Furthermore, the current system rewards those who move fast and pitch well – resulting in programmes that repeat earlier failures without adequate reflection, and/or programmes that yield unintended consequences.

At the same time, ignoring the existence of decentralized finance will not change the fact that it exists. Critics have at times regarded decentralized finance, cryptocurrencies, and blockchain as curiosities or passing fads. As this chapter illustrates, these technologies are in fact becoming mainstreamed into the work of significant international and multinational actors. If developers truly wish to make this technology part of a more inclusive future, an ethic of responsible engagement must emerge. This would entail the adoption of an industry standard emphasizing the importance of diversity and meaningful action to address complaints of gender-based discrimination and harassment. It would entail developing projects through consultation with civil society, experts, and the local knowledge base. Especially where projects take place in the Global South, participatory practice and informed consent are particularly important to making projects more closely resemble partnerships, rather than financial experiments. Ideally, we would also expect to see the adoption of best practices regarding gender mainstreaming, such as the collection of gender-disaggregated data and the analysis of gender in programme design. Politically, implementing these changes might further entail some tradeoffs to the fully decentralized model, including the introduction of mechanisms for industry-wide oversight and accountability. While purists in the decentralized finance community would likely object to these conditions, one could argue that the 'decentralization' in decentralized finance is already eroding as international organizations, corporations, and major players in global finance increasingly move in to this space.

Researchers may additionally have a role to play, as there is more that remains to be explored. This research, while centring a feminist perspective, leaves space for a variety of other possible avenues for inquiry. Among these are postcolonial approaches, intersectional analysis, and analyses based on environmental concerns associated with the technology. To the extent that new developments continue to arise, this work should represent a call to 'consider crypto' as a force in global political economy and to engage on this topic in a critical way, bringing a diversity of insights to bear on these developments.

8

Conclusion

Throughout the process of writing this manuscript, the involvement of technology in international politics has become ever more visible. These encounters range from the hopeful, to the unexpected, to the frightening, to the absurd.

In Afghanistan, the Taliban's return to power in 2021 was widely documented on social media with discourse that took on a strange, bimodal quality. On the one hand, international media played to the image of the Taliban as a band of backward luddites, who posed a significant danger (especially to women and girls) but who were simultaneously incapable of running the new, modern Afghanistan that decades of international aid had created. Early stories and social media updates from Associated Press portrayed young Taliban fighters as 'awestruck' by 'modern office buildings', shopping malls, 'plush furniture', and gym equipment (Associated Press 2021; Gannon 2021). A video of Taliban fighters cheerfully attempting to navigate elliptical machines and other equipment at a gym in the presidential palace was widely circulated online and became a source of mockery (Lock 2021). Yet these narratives sat alongside serious reflection about the fate of biometric databases that contained information on millions of Afghans, including many who had worked with US forces and other international agencies (Guo and Noori 2021; Klippenstein and Sirota 2021). Commentators rightfully questioned the damaging effects of allowing these materials to fall into the wrong hands and pondered whether this was a reflection on the judiciousness of collecting this information in the first place.

In El Salvador, President Nayib Bukele oversaw the adoption of bitcoin as a national currency on par with the US dollar in 2021. Early reports suggested that the bitcoinization of the country was marred by popular discontent, technical issues, volatility, and fraud. The government-sponsored Chivo platform, which promised an electronic wallet and a small amount of startup funds to all Salvadorans who created an account, was plagued with reliability issues. The lure of free money further incentivized fraud, as criminals used stolen identities to create accounts (Gerard 2021; McDonald 2022). Protests accompanying the bitcoin rollout in autumn 2021 demonstrated citizens' concerns about financial instability – but also about rising authoritarianism and the rapid, top-down way in which bitcoin was being deployed (Pineda 2021). These fears appeared somewhat justified, with bitcoin's value falling from US$69,000 in November 2021 to below US$37,000 in January 2022 – all as Salvadoran President Nayib Bukele took to Twitter to brag he was 'buying the dip',[1] that is, investing still more of the country's money in cryptocurrency. Bukele's more lavish promises for the country's future included the creation of a 'Bitcoin City' at the base of a volcano. The city would act as a tax haven and a site for geothermal-powered crypto mining. These plans led to headlines comparing Bukele to a villain from a James Bond movie (Duckett 2021). One early analysis of El Salvador's bitcoinization found that, similar to the examples discussed in Chapter 7, the adoption of cryptocurrency made little impact on the remittance market. Bukele's promise that bitcoin adoption would reach an unbanked underclass also seemed dubious, as the authors found that citizens who were 'banked, more educated, younger, and male' were the most likely adopters of bitcoin (Alvarez et al 2022). The pie-in-the-sky promises associated with bitcoinization further distracted from very real issues in El Salvador, like allegations the Bukele government had bought off gang leaders to reduce the country's crime rate or the revelation that the government was using Pegasus spyware to surveil journalists and individuals active in civil society (as discussed in Chapter 5) (Sherman 2021; Amnesty International 2022).

In the United States, the Supreme Court's 2022 decision in *Dobbs* v *Jackson Women's Health Organization* overturned the Constitutional right to abortion established in the 1973 case of *Roe* v *Wade*. Concerns about potential criminal penalties for women seeking abortions (or for doctors performing them) almost immediately turned to warnings about electronic surveillance. Investigative journalists reported that data brokers were selling location information on visits to family planning centres, data that had been harvested from smartphone users (Cox 2022). A website run by Texas Right to Life, which collected tips on illegal abortions, was shut down after the hosting company found it violated rules on data harvesting (Perlroth 2021b). Abortion rights advocates reported that, even in parts of the country where abortion remained legal, anti-abortion protesters used hidden cameras, data aggregators, and fake wi-fi networks to try and dupe or intimidate people seeking abortions (Ohlheiser 2022). The combination of more high-tech policing and weak data privacy laws combined to create new and gendered security risks in the wake of the Supreme Court's ruling.

The Russian invasion of Ukraine in early 2022 further showed how ICTs can prove a double-edged sword in times of conflict. On the one hand, communications technology proved to be a lifeline for some. Ukrainian academics, security forces, and government officials were able to use technology as a platform to reach audiences abroad, informing them about events in the country and the situation on the ground. NGOs like Human Rights Watch were able to use ICTs to reach individuals in conflict zones and to document evidence of war crimes perpetrated by Russian soldiers, while developers experimented with blockchain as a means of preserving evidence (Horowitz 2022; Human Rights Watch 2022). At the same time, however, the digital space became the site of an information war waged by Russia against its own citizens. Faced with attempts by major social media platforms to curtail its disinformation campaigns, Russia deployed what some analysts referred to as a new Iron Curtain, cutting Russians off from platforms that had sought to curtail the reach of its information warfare (Timberg et al 2022).

The Russian government's move drew obvious comparisons to China's long-standing censorship practices. This is hardly surprising, as Russian President Vladimir Putin and Chinese leader Xi Jinping have in the past articulated similar views on cyber sovereignty, that is, the prerogative of states to territorialize and regulate the Internet, including restrictions on any speech they choose to censor (Bandurski 2022). The notion that we are moving towards a future in which states, willingly assisted by corporations, use technology as a force to uphold authoritarianism strikes at the heart of cyber-utopian ideas about the Internet as a force for decentralization and/ or democratization. It is a vision of the future that should deeply unsettle thinkers across a range of critical perspectives.

What role has gender played in the deployment of new technologies? For one, we have witnessed that the rapid digitization of government and society during the COVID-19 pandemic has left many people behind. We are only beginning to understand the long-term gendered impacts of COVID-19. UN agencies have called attention to a 'shadow pandemic' of violence against women and girls, a situation exacerbated by lockdowns, unemployment, and women's inequitable access to information and crisis response via communications technologies (UN Women et al 2021). Despite advancements in ICT, women also found themselves disproportionately squeezed out of the labour force during the pandemic. Experts in the United States attributed gendered trends in unemployment to the lack of childcare, the concentration of women (especially, women of colour) in care work and customer-facing positions, but also to the spread of remote learning among school-aged children (Boesch and Phadke 2021). Online learning frameworks that, ironically, were intended to make education more accessible to children during the crisis ended up becoming one more burden for mothers – who disproportionately took on the demands of supervising remote or homeschooling efforts (Petts et al 2021). One more example to support the argument that new technologies, deployed without critical insight into existing hierarchies, reproduce old power structures in new ways.

Technology thus both shapes and is shaped by international politics, global hierarchies, and dimensions of inequality. Yet the gender dimensions of this dynamic remain underexplored. In the introductory chapter of this book, I noted that feminist international relations/security studies has been a relative latecomer to discussions about digital rights and digital politics. But exclusion can be a two-way street. For instance, in 2022 the organizers of a set of panels on Technology and Politics for the annual meeting of the American Political Science Association (APSA) shared a word cloud to social media, which aggregated over 150 key words from over 100 papers submitted for the event. While some themes relevant to the Global South appeared in the graphic, no terms related to gender, women, feminist international relations, sexuality, or queer studies were evident.[2] The *Journal of Information Technology and Politics*, the official journal of APSA's Information Technology and Politics section, similarly published no articles dealing specifically with gender between 2019 and 2021.[3] In the online portion of the 2022 International Studies Association Convention, 28 panels dealt with themes related to technology or digital politics but just three included papers that touched on gender issues (primarily, gender-based extremism). By comparison, six panels included papers dealing with race/ethnicity or religion and technology. As I hope this book demonstrates, it is possible to have critical and feminist discussions about technology and politics. However, it seems these dialogues are not taking place in the discipline of international relations.

We can therefore stand to grow collaboration and critical interventions. This book has sought to provide some insight into how. Some takeaways include (but are not limited to) the following:

- *There is a need to seek cross-disciplinary alliances for the study of technology and (in)security*. Today, conversations about technology and politics are scattered across silos with many names: FSS, critical data studies, surveillance studies, Black feminist technology studies, science and technology studies, and human–computer interaction, just to name a few. Insofar as many of the issues raised in this text – privacy, surveillance, harassment – are cross-cutting, they provide opportunities to work towards co-liberation. Researchers should be encouraged to build on one another's work and to link scholarship to public engagement – but that requires finding spaces for collaboration. More thought needs to be devoted to how we can broaden conversations in ways that might lead to change.
- *Transforming data use and data ethics is key for change*. The preceding chapters have identified many of the concerning and biased ways in which data is used as a tool for power. There are ways to resist. Institutional solutions like the right to erasure (or, the right to be forgotten)[4] and data portability[5] laws are innovations in the legal realm that deserve further study. But

the points raised in Chapter 2 regarding co-production, ownership, transparency, and accountability should also shape data collection processes in ways that re-centre notions of power and ownership.
- *Technology companies, developers, and states all have unmet responsibilities with regard to security and equitability.* As discussed throughout this book, technology companies and developers are (rightly) the focus of many conversations about the inequalities and insecurities created by technology. By centring and encoding worldviews that are androcentric and/or centred in the Global North, the industry fails to anticipate or respond to the way products are weaponized against marginalized groups. At the same time, though, states must also be held to account for the abuses of technology. This book has shown how states engage in abusive practices (especially, with regard to data and surveillance) that are part of a historical continuity. States have also largely abdicated their responsibility for digital protection at the level of the citizen. Neoliberal development mindsets have created an environment in which all of us who engage with technology take on the daily labour of protecting ourselves from cybercrime and/or cybersecurity threats. A critical analysis should question how we got here and how this landscape drives the movement to decentralize currency, record-keeping, and other functions of governance.
- *More technology will not solve the problems technology created without transformative change.* Benjamin (2019) warns of the potential for technological fixes to become substitutes for systemic change. For this reason, civil society engagement (and, potentially, academic research) are important centres of accountability. Here, too, cross-disciplinary and cross-cutting conversations on gendered and intersectional harms are necessary. The more we raise consciousness around these issues, the more effective we can be as advocates and allies.

In the remainder of this concluding chapter, I offer brief insight into potential future areas for research, including several issue areas that I did not have adequate space to explore in the book. I also reflect on the development of a feminist ethic for research on technology and politics, inspired by critical work introduced in the preceding chapters. I ultimately close with a call to create more space for this work, leveraging feminist curiosity and feminist innovation in creating a path forward.

A few more things: new research agendas for feminist international relations

As with any research project, there is too little space to explore every facet of a given issue. My choice to focus on certain technologies in this book – social media, messaging services, blockchain, big data – is by no means meant to suggest that these are the only technologies or issues that matter. For feminist scholars of technology and politics, there is a great deal more to say. This section briefly introduces some additional issue areas where I believe feminist intervention is called for.

Cyberwar, cybersecurity, and the cyber arms trade

Despite starting this book with a vignette about the weaponization of technology, I have not offered an in-depth assessment of cyberwar or cybersecurity as it has been conceptualized by mainstream (that is, positivist and empirical) international relations during the past two decades. This is a realm where international relations theorists have borrowed heavily from military discourse by envisioning cyberspace as a war-fighting 'domain', and a realm where states are perceived as the central actors (Lynn 2010; Nye 2010; Walt 2010). While there is much space for feminist and critical intervention in such a debate, there are a few obvious contributions that a gender lens could bring to this discourse. First, feminist theories could be brought to bear on the very framing of cyberwar as a concept, and how cybersecurity has been militarized through this discourse. Second, a critical and feminist intervention could be made into the cyberwar discourse of harm and magnitude. Theorists sceptical about the scale of cyberwar have conceptualized harm largely in terms of measuring such a conflict's potential to cause death (Libicki 2011; Gartzke 2013; Rid 2013). A feminist intervention might highlight – as I have in these pages – the range of serious harms short of death that sustained cyberattacks and disinformation campaigns can cause, as well as how those harms are gendered, racialized, and weaponized according to social hierarchies.

Finally, feminist theories – alongside critical work – are well-positioned to question the level of analysis at which cyberwar discourse in international relations takes place, questioning why the state is positioned as the referent (or provider) of security and calling upon the discipline to place human security at the centre of discussions. As the discussion in Chapters 5 and 6 shows, states do not always function as the guarantors of security in the digital space. They have leveraged technology to create new threats against groups including journalists, human rights defenders, and leaders in civil society groups. They have also failed to protect their citizens from a daily barrage of cyberattacks and cybercrime, instead struggling to protect their own systems while leaving individuals responsible for the daily labour of, for example, deleting spam, changing passwords, installing updates, monitoring our credit reports for fraud, and using two-factor authentication and biometric credentialling on our devices. The state likewise fails to provide meaningful security for many marginalized groups because it fails to create inclusive spaces, sidelining women and others who are uniquely vulnerable to insecurity. The same male-default thinking that Cohn (1987) highlighted in nuclear security decades ago has arguably reproduced itself in the fields of technology and cybersecurity. Industrywide, less than one in five cybersecurity professionals are women and the majority report encountering some form of bias or harassment (Poster 2018). Perlroth (2021a) notes the absence of women in the history of cyberarms development and, echoing Cohn's reflections on nuclear security, she wonders how greater inclusion might have impacted the development of norms and cultures around cyberconflict. What feminist and critical interventions would call for is, at the very least, a fundamental re-centring of cybersecurity as a human security issue and an accompanying call for inclusive practice at all levels of cybersecurity practice.

Migration and carceral technology

This is another area in which feminist analysis benefits from dialogue with postcolonial scholarship and work on race/ethnicity and technology. Chapter 5 explored the uses of technology in surveillance and policing, and how these practices are gendered and racialized. Technology is also being deployed in similarly problematic ways through systems of migration and asylum-seeking. Activists from within the technology industry protested the involvement of players like Microsoft, Dell, Amazon, Google, and Palantir in contracts with US government agencies, in light of US policies on family separation and immigration bans on majority-Muslim countries (Frenkel 2018). While this visible action during crisis is laudable, it is unclear to what extent there is sustained vigilance and calls for accountability around the everyday use of technology in immigration practice. Reports from watchdog groups suggest that, even prior to the institution of family separation policies, software from Palantir was being used to facilitate the arrest of parents and family members of unaccompanied minors apprehended at the US border. In spite of the fact that few arrests led to convictions, activists argued that the practice was a means to harass migrant families using fines and the legal process (Biddle and Devereaux 2019).

The electronic monitoring of migrants and asylum seekers further deploys carceral tools of surveillance against vulnerable populations in damaging ways (Benjamin 2019). Countries including the United States and the United Kingdom have engaged in such practices. Legal scholars and activists alike have questioned these practices, noting that the use of ankle monitors causes pain, anxiety, and stigma; the use of such devices is especially contraindicated for survivors of physical and sexual abuse (Pittman 2020; Bhatia 2021). Bhatia (2021) further notes that states including the United Kingdom label the use of these technologies as administrative rather than punitive, allowing agencies to circumvent the oversight of courts in when and how they are used.

Critical inquiry can further contrast how technology facilitates some forms of migration, even while it suppresses others. The COVID-19 pandemic introduced a new wave of interest in 'digital nomad'-ism and e-citizenship arrangements. As populated cities entered lockdown and many professional work arrangements became remote work, many individuals with means sought out ways to move (temporarily or permanently) to less populous or more palatable parts of the world. Rural areas, less-populous countries, and parts of the Global South especially have viewed digital nomads as a potential lifeline. Dozens of countries including Brazil, the Bahamas, Costa Rica, Spain, Iceland, Estonia, Portugal, and Cape Verde offer some form of incentive (usually, extended-stay visas) to those who meet income and proof-of-work requirements and who are willing to pay associated fees (Ledsom 2022; Mari 2022). Estonia further offers an 'e-Residency' programme which, in exchange for fees, taxes, and an initial investment, allows business owners access to banking and government services. The country claimed 85,000 e-Residents as of 2022 (Republic of Estonia nd). The contrast between the freedom of movement extended to digitally engaged upper- and middle-class professionals and the technological surveillance imposed on migrants and asylum seekers reveals how technology stands to uphold but also deepen inequalities and insecurities.

Labour ethics

The issue of labour in technology has cast a shadow throughout this book. From discussions about gender inequality in the technology industry, to discussions of microwork and the gig economy, there is more space for feminist intervention in discussions of technological labour. Feminist political economy scholarship introduces readers to key concepts in gendered labour, like stereotyping, flexibilization, and devaluation (Peterson 2010; Runyan and Peterson 2013). In each case, these concepts can be applied to the information economy. Stereotyping plays a role in shaping the pipeline for the tech industry, coding the sector as a realm of men and masculinity while erasing the historical importance of women's contributions. Stereotyping plays a role in how we define what types of work are inside and outside of the technology sector and, related to that, how we perceive low- and high-skilled work. Chapter 6 demonstrated the ways in which women professionals engaged in feminist innovation sometimes undersell their expertise in technology. In fields where technology is applied to professions coded as female, like the position of instructional designers in education, women may find their contributions devalued (Bond et al 2021).

Without fully interrogating the systems that create devaluation, we risk perpetuating this process. The explosion of digital literacy programmes for girls and programmes to teach girls to code – presented around the world as well-intentioned efforts for empowerment and diversification – should call for sustained attention to the outcomes of these programmes. Do they really represent a pathway to high-paying, high-prestige professions, or will they again prompt employers to reassess the value of work as the gender balance changes – the same dynamic we observed as computing moved from a majority female to a majority male industry? Arguably, we have already observed how some tech labour becomes devalued as work moves from the Global North to the Global South. This comes via the explosion of gig labour markets to do the ghost work of content moderation and training AI. As a large, English-speaking labour force in the Global South emerges to take these jobs, tasks have been devalued to sub-minimum wage levels (Gray and Suri 2019). The work likewise becomes hyper-flexibilized, parceled out into microtasks and performed with no job security, using equipment and energy paid for by the worker, and without any guarantee that the worker will actually be paid (Gray and Suri 2019). The result – a global underclass doing tasks like training sophisticated weapons systems for pennies at a time (McCallum 2020) – underscores the absurdities of the information economy. Yet we see this absurdity only if we render that labour visible. This question of labour has implications for the research process, too, especially where we see an increasing reliance on microwork platforms and systems like Amazon's Mechanical Turk (mTurk) by cash-strapped researchers looking for subject pools. From a feminist perspective, it is enough to say that these labour dynamics are worthy of further exploration at the junction of FSS and feminist international political economy.

Accessibility and disability

While I have sought to explore the intersecting nature of gender and other social hierarchies in technology and politics, I believe much more can be said about how disability and accessibility figure into this equation. Within political science at large, disability is an understudied source of inequality (Clifford Simplican 2021). This omission should become even more pronounced in light of the COVID-19 pandemic. Disability advocates rightly questioned why remote work and schooling arrangements that were once called unreasonable accommodations suddenly (and rapidly) became possible for all at the onset of the pandemic (Bohra and Willingham 2021). Correspondingly, one can ask why such accommodations just as frequently vanished even before the pandemic ended, forcing many to choose between their health and their work.

Disability, in addition to being a political issue, is a gendered issue. Though disability is a heterogeneous category, on a global scale women are considered more likely than men to be living with a disability (UN Women 2018a). While social stigma is a common experience among the disabled, gender shapes the experience of stigmatization in different ways (Gerschick 2000). Women living with disabilities are less likely to participate in the workforce than disabled men, they also earn less money and report more stress/depression when they do work (Gerschick 2000; Brown and Moloney 2019). For women of minority ethnic/racial groups, these inequalities are heightened (Maroto et al 2019). Violence against the disabled is another matter of significant concern and, as shown in Chapter 4, disability intersects with gender, ethnicity, and sexuality to shape the experience of online abuse. Responding to these issues should be a priority, yet researchers with disabilities have also found an unwelcoming space in the technology sector (Ymous et al 2020). Disabled populations, much like women and residents of the Global South, have become a reference point for discussions about closing the 'digital divide'. This again furthers the notion that more exposure to more systems is a normative good. Yet disability scholars point out that technologies are often designed for – but without the input of – referent populations. This, in turn, fosters mistrust, rejection, and fear of technology (Goggin 2017). It may even deepen divides within disabled communities, as developers emphasize accessibility in certain areas more than others (Blanck 2016; Goggin 2017).

Making gender visible: towards a feminist ethic for research on technology and politics

Cyberwar, migration and carceral culture, labour relations, and the intersectional study of disability are just a few of the many avenues available to feminist scholars who wish to engage in the critical study of technology and politics. But how should we, as researchers, approach exploration of these topics? In Chapter 1, I invoked FSS as my underpinning approach to this text. In doing so, I adopt the axiology of FSS work including its call to define 'security' broadly, its commitment to bring to the fore the gendered nature of security/insecurity, its reflection on the diverse and intersectional nature of gender, and its openness to interdisciplinary dialogue (Stern and Wibben 2014). Alongside that, I invoked themes of feminist international relations research more broadly, including its call for methodological pluralism, an understanding of the interrelated nature of security and development, and a commitment to highlight and hopefully improve the lived experiences of women and other marginalized communities (Tickner 2006; Weldon 2006; Elias and Rai 2015).

I hope that I have succeeded in upholding these values. At the same time, I would suggest that engaging in interdisciplinary conversations about technology suggests some further ethical commitments that FSS or feminist international relations scholars should embrace. Among these are the need to more closely embrace the concepts of privacy and refusal in our work. The data privacy concerns brought to the fore by the COVID-19 pandemic – as noted in Chapters 2 and 6 – are unlikely to go away. The privacy of health data especially is a gendered issue, as the use of technology for menstrual tracking, fertility tracking, and similar applications raises privacy concerns. Prior research in feminist international relations has celebrated the notion of refusal, including the refusal to participate in exclusionary citation and/ or knowledge production practices (Zalewski 2006; Duriesmith 2020). We could carry this even further, into a respect for resistance to techno-determinism. As noted by my interlocutors in Chapter 6, feminist innovation does take place – but in a landscape that is highly unequal. There is thus a sentiment that we should safeguard against making digital spaces the sole or default site for activism. The right of subjects to engage in feminist/ queer/decolonial/anti-racist resistance to the expansion of technology in our day-to-day lives should be recognized. This should be a theme in our work, but also in our methodology. Especially with the growth of interest in digital fieldwork, online ethnography, and similar methods, we must respect resistance to these practices and reflect upon who is resisting them, why, and what the consequences may be for those who seek to disengage from these dominant trends.

Similarly, as noted earlier, feminist work may play an important role in engaging in disciplinary conversations about labour ethics in research and the creep of computational research. While computational social science can have value, the discussions of encoded bias throughout this work may call upon us to reflect on whether these methods are receiving adequate scrutiny. At a minimum, the move towards computational social science and 'big data'-engaged research arguably solidifies existing structures of institutional privilege. While code may be freely shared, creating or harvesting data can be an expensive enterprise – as is procuring the computing technology to store and process it (D'Ignazio and Klein 2020). Who benefits from this system? What ethical standards and safeguards do we have? How do the expectations of transparency for computational social science researchers stack up to those imposed upon human subjects researchers or other research methods?

At the same time, the expansion of gig work into research practice should become another site of feminist resistance. Sociological and anthropological scholarship highlights the many unresolved ethical issues engaged in the use of microwork and gig work platforms. These include issues of wage theft, identity fraud, child labour, the potential for vicarious trauma, and the predatory expansion of microwork into fragile and conflict-affected contexts (Gray and Suri 2019; McCallum 2020; Hao and Hernández 2022). Gig workers interviewed by McCallum (2020) specifically expressed resistance to being used as research subjects. Still, academic journals in the social sciences accept and publish research conducted using these platforms. At professional meetings, I have heard early career scholars justify the use of gig work/ghost work on the basis of it being low cost and easily accessible to those lacking research funding. This is perhaps a sign that we should resist the expansion of this practice while educating researchers about the ethical issues.[6]

I conclude this final chapter with a reflection on my own position as a researcher. At many points in the writing process, I questioned why I should be the one to write this book. Not unlike the interviewees profiled in Chapter 6, I questioned my qualifications to write on this topic in spite of my daily engagement with ICTs and even my professional experience (in an earlier phase of my career) in coding and web design. It is this easy to question one's right to engage on questions of technology, politics, and policy. Where we create a mythology or mystique around certain forms of labour and ennoble those who perform it, we lay the groundwork for new hierarchies and sources of inequality. Part of my aim in writing this book is to demystify these forces and to encourage greater engagement from a more diverse range of voices.

At the same time, I must acknowledge the privilege that allowed me to undertake this work during a global pandemic. As an established researcher, as a person with a living wage, as someone with education and access to many technologies, and as a resident of a developed country, avenues for research were open to me that may have been closed to others during this crisis. We must be cognisant of the opportunities provided by technology but also of its limitations. The expansion of technology in and of itself should not be seen as a normative good. Technology, when applied in the political realm, does not represent progress by default; while it may hold the potential to bring people together and to challenge social hierarchies, realizing that vision requires us to name the power dynamics at play, to render them visible through our work, and to resist technological advances that encode the biases of the past.

Notes

Chapter 1

1. Prominent examples include the portrayal of Kim Jong-il by actor Bobby Lee on *MadTV*, his depiction as a puppet in the 2014 movie *Team America: World Police*, and Korean-American comedian Margaret Cho's performance as Kim Jong-il on the TV series *30 Rock*.
2. Myers (2011) also sees particular elements of these portrayals as emphasizing the importance of racial purity, defining North Koreans in opposition to other Asian peoples.
3. Perlroth (2021a), for example, discusses the allegation that the operation codenamed Aurora, an unprecedented Chinese attack on Google in 2010, was ordered by a Politburo member who found something unflattering in Google search results about himself.
4. Though revenge porn may not be native to the online environment, it has unquestionably thrived in the online space. See, for example, Tsoulis-Reay (2013) on the early development of online communities devoted to the sharing of nonconsensual pornography.
5. 'Web 3.0' has variously been used to refer to the decentralized web (as I use it here) and the 'Semantic Web', which engages AI to carry out sophisticated tasks, automating much of the work that humans do online (Berners-Lee et al 2001). Though elements of the Semantic Web have been incorporated into today's environment, some commentators today argue that the idea of the Semantic Web is unattainable in the current environment (Target 2018).
6. As discussed in Chapter 2, one form of exclusion is the omission of transgender, nonbinary, intersex, and other populations outside the gender binary. Throughout the chapters that follow, I seek to discuss gender in a way that calls these populations back into being. This is a nod to queer, trans, and non-Western scholarship that calls for seeing beyond gender binaries as a decolonial act (Driskill 2010; Aizura et al 2014; Dutta and Roy 2014).

Chapter 2

1. This is not to overlook the fact that the disabled, LGBTQI+ populations, and other marginalized groups are also impacted by data gaps. See, for example, the discussion in Criado-Perez (2019) on the relationship between gender and disability.
2. For more on this, see Chapter 5.
3. Interestingly, some authors provide a different set of 'Vs'. Gill (2021) identifies five Vs: volume, variety, velocity, value, and veracity.
4. One article reports that, by April 2020, the Nicaraguan government had received 26,000 total rapid testing kits from the Central American Bank for Economic Integration, falling far short of the recommendation that the country test 10,000 people weekly (Miranda Abuerto 2020; Perez Arguello and Kennon 2020). Though the country had access to additional, slower testing methods, the country's health ministry was at one time only testing about 50 people per day nationwide.
5. Original text in Spanish has been translated by the author.

6. See, for example, resolutions 1888 (2009), 1960 (2010), 2122 (2013), 2242 (2015), and 2467 (2019).
7. The goals were set to be in place from 2000 to 2015 and were subsequently replaced by the Sustainable Development Goals.
8. The US Women, Peace, and Security Index compiled by the Georgetown Institute for Women, Peace, and Security is one example.
9. Many of the indicators reported by the World Bank are aggregated from UN agencies. Some of these may, in turn, rely on self-reporting from states – a matter suggesting the need for further critical engagement.
10. Child marriage (more specifically, girl marriage) is another factor impacting education rates for girls.
11. These statistics, reported in World Bank Open Data, originate from UNICEF.
12. The global index was developed by GIWPS and the Peace Research Institute of Oslo (PRIO) (GIWPS/PRIO 2019).
13. Indeed, it is worth noting that, in addition to the large-scale and cross-national projects discussed, new data on gender issues in a variety of specific contexts are now available, including the prevalence of female combatants and supporters in armed conflict, the use of girl soldiers, women in diplomacy, and women in political protests (Cohen and Nordås 2014; Henshaw 2016; Towns and Niklasson 2017; Wood and Thomas 2017; Haer and Böhmelt 2018; ACLED 2020).
14. The Trans Legal Mapping Report compiled by the International Lesbian, Gay, Bisexual, Trans and Intersex Association demonstrates the complexity of even defining 'recognition', with de facto and de jure forms of recognition/prohibition often co-existing in the same spaces and with significant subnational variation in law and practice (ILGA 2019).
15. The Karim-Hill scales report a margin of error for each measurement, meaning that states cannot be definitively ranked. WomenStats multivariate scales, by their nature, provide an indication of rank.
16. This is a trichotomous variable scales 0–2 based on the existence of federal legislation and constitutional guarantees.
17. Indeed, the US decision in *Dobbs* v *Jackson Women's Health Organization* in 2022, which reversed the findings of *Roe* v *Wade* by declaring that there is no constitutional right to abortion in the United States, represents the foremost example of the Supreme Court removing what it once had considered a Constitutional right. A discussion of the privacy and surveillance implications of this case can be found in the Conclusion.
18. Karim and Hill (2018) indeed note that primary and secondary education are weighted highly in their index, while the relationship to the male-female ratio of PhD completion is more dubious.
19. I gratefully acknowledge my co-panellists and fellow attendees at the 2021 FemQuant workshop and the 2022 ISA Annual Convention for their early reflections on this chapter. In particular, the discussion in this chapter incorporates insights offered by Daniel Hill, S. Laurel Weldon, and Sara Rose Taylor.
20. As of this writing, several prominent journals in political science/international relations have publication guidelines with provisions for special data features or research notes, which are intended for the introduction of new datasets. Examples include *Journal of Peace Research* and *International Studies Quarterly*.
21. I reflect here on my own involvement in data production frameworks and the limitations of the resultant data, as discussed in earlier work (Henshaw 2017).
22. See also Chapter 5.

Chapter 3

1. This includes 'computing and mathematical' occupations as defined by the US Bureau of Labor Statistics.
2. This figure includes marketing professionals as well as founders and developers.
3. Mobile phone access, for example, is one component measure in the GIWPS/PRIO index on Women, Peace, and Security and is classified into the sub-category of women's inclusion. They state '[a]ccess to cellphones is a critical tool for women in developing countries, especially given cellphones' increasing association with digital inclusion. Accumulating evidence demonstrates cellphones' importance for women's agency and self-confidence, safety, and access to markets and income earning opportunities' (GIWPS/PRIO 2018: 4).
4. 'Safety and security' was cited as the number 1 concern of both men and women.
5. Colombia, Egypt, Ghana, India, Indonesia, Kenya, Mozambique, Nigeria, Philippines, and Uganda.
6. See also Chapter 5 for a discussion of this issue.
7. The World Values Survey is a global, academic research effort conducted in over 100 countries since its inception in 1981. The data presented here comes from the most recent wave of the survey, which was conducted in 49 countries and territories between 2017 and 2020 (WVS Association 2020).
8. These measures of trust are also negatively correlated with a country's percentage of female mobile phone subscribers, though these correlations are weaker (Economist Intelligence Unit/Facebook 2020).
9. Including elderly, youth, women, minorities, the disabled, and/or low-income households.
10. Compare this to instances in sub-Saharan Africa, where activists have also suggested that government shutdowns of the Internet are common because shutdowns are one of the few tools governments have at their disposal to manage an otherwise ungovernable space (Gimase Magenya and Shewarega Hussen 2022).
11. This ruling still did not completely end restrictions on services. By early 2021, in the majority of Jammu and Kashmir only slower means of connecting to the Internet were restored, with restrictions still in place on faster connections like 4G (Mir 2021).
12. See also Chapter 6 for interviews with activists working in these areas.
13. There is also the suggestion that Facebook learned from its mistakes in India. Nothias (2020) reports greater consultation between Facebook and local civil society groups in several African countries. The company also now markets the service as one that promotes inclusive solutions, with resources related to maternal and child health and confidential health counselling for women (Facebook 2021a).
14. Access was suspended by the Bangladeshi government in 2020, based on the allegation that the service was being used for criminal activity (TBS Report 2020).
15. Access to services was offered in English and Urdu (Kapadia and Jalil 2017).
16. A few exceptions can be found in Matthews et al (2017), Malnad et al (2020), and Burke et al (2011). In particular, Burke et al (2011) make the argument that young women are also heavily engaged in electronic surveillance of intimate partners, based on a sense that this behaviour is normal or justifiable in a relationship.
17. GIFCT was founded by Facebook, Twitter, Microsoft, and YouTube in 2017. As of 2021 it includes nine additional members.
18. Hashing is an algorithm-driven approach that creates a unique, alphanumeric representation of content which can then be used to track its appearance across platforms without sharing the actual content, in theory facilitating removal.
19. An attempt by Facebook to pilot the use of hashing against revenge porn in Australia in 2017 was widely criticized after the company requested that potential victims proactively

share graphic photos and videos that they believed abusers might use against them (Dickey 2017; Pringle 2018; Romano 2018). As of this writing, Facebook's pilot has expanded to eight countries (Facebook 2021b).

Chapter 4

1. Dogpiling is a form of online harassment where a large number of accounts 'pile on' with criticism of an individual user or post deemed controversial, often with the intent to intimidate or silence.
2. See, for example, Moonshot (2021).
3. Gender attribution in some instances may be dubious, as in the case of anonymous or pseudonymous authors in jihadist magazines, who generally claim to be wives of leaders but whose identity cannot be conclusively proven.
4. UN Security Council Resolution 2242 (2015).
5. Boys aged 8–12 were most often conscripted for indoctrination and military service, while elderly women were usually executed (Al-Dayel and Mumford 2020; Al-Dayel et al 2020).
6. These include the Al-Mahdi Army, Ansar al-Islam, the Al-Nusra Front (an al-Qaeda affiliate), and Islamic State. In terms of homophobic violence, these groups arguably competed with the Iraqi government itself, which allegedly tolerated and/or facilitated homophobic violence after 2003 (IWHR/MADRE 2015; Tschantret 2018).
7. Kilbride (2015) notes that Islamic State violence against third gender communities like the *khawaja sara* or *hijra* – which have some legal and cultural recognition in Pakistan – distinguishes them from the Pakistani Taliban, who accept the existence of these communities.
8. The role of women in conspiracy-based extremism has also drawn significant attention with the rise of QAnon. See, for example, Gillespie (2020); Amarasingam and Argentino (2020).
9. As of this writing, Men Going Their Own Way (MGTOW) communities have been banned from Reddit but can still be found on other major social media platforms, including Facebook and YouTube.
10. Information is current at the time of this writing. See Van Valkenburgh (2021) for a content analysis of the TRP subreddit.
11. The most prolific users of the site posted on average several times daily, while some users posted only once or twice during the observation period.
12. In particular, the authors note that Levine's appointment was a significant topic of discussions in Telegram channels linked to the Proud Boys.

Chapter 5

1. See UN Development Programme (1994).
2. The Mérida Initiative, for example, was a multi-billion dollar agreement involving assistance between the United States, Mexico, and several other countries in Central America and the Caribbean which included training, financial assistance, and funding earmarked for technologies including secure communication systems, scanners, and specialized software for law enforcement agencies (US Department of State 2017). As another example of how high-tech policing becomes transnational, some law enforcement agencies in the US southwest reportedly have access to Central American driver's licence photos and mug shots for use in facial recognition (Garvie et al 2016).

3   Academics will also likely be familiar with Turnitin, the anti-plagiarism software in use at more than half of all universities in the United States, Canada, and the United Kingdom and one-quarter of all US high schools (Wylie 2012; Turner 2014). While Turnitin checks submitted student work against other publications and material available on the Internet, it also uses student work to build its repository. Thus, users who pay for the system are also working to maintain and improve the system continually. Turner (2014) quotes a company vice president as stating that the company's database of content items contained 400 million student papers in 2014, compared to 110 million academic publications. While the company's pricing is not publicized, estimates put the cost of a licence for higher education at about US$2 per student, per year (Wylie 2012). The company was set to be acquired by a publishing conglomerate in 2019 for US$1.75 billion (Johnson 2019).

4   On the surveillance and censorship of ethnic and religious-based movements, see the discussion in Chapter 3 on India. Also Walker et al (2021) on the surveillance of caste-based activist groups in India and Shere and Nurse (2020) on law enforcement agencies' use of surveillance technologies during Black Lives Matter protests in the United States. Some interviews discussed in Chapter 6 also raise related concerns.

5   This list included targets of Pegasus and associated NSO Group tools Kismet and ForcedEntry. The latter of these are 'zero-click' exploits which, unlike Pegasus, do not require targets to click on a link or proactively download the spyware (Scott-Railton et al 2022).

6   Though it has been widely reported that Pegasus does not work on phones with US numbers, other NSO Group tools are reportedly capable of hacking US phones. A number of US citizens including diplomats have also been targeted by Pegasus while living and working abroad (Timberg et al 2021; Bergman and Mazzetti 2022).

Chapter 6

1   Interview 4, January 2022.
2   The plan for this research was approved by the Institutional Review Board (IRB) at Troy University.
3   Interview 1, January 2022.
4   Interview 1, January 2022; Interview 6, January 2022.
5   Interview 8, March 2022; Interview 9, March 2022.
6   Interview 10, March 2022.
7   Interview 11, March 2022.
8   Interview 3, January 2022; Interview 4, January 2022.
9   Interview 3, January 2022.
10 Interview 2, January 2022.
11 Interview 12, March 2022.
12 Interview 11, March 2022.
13 Interview 2, January 2022.
14 Interview 8, March 2022.
15 Interview 8, March 2022; Interview 9, March 2022.
16 Interview 9, March 2022.
17 Interview 3, January 2022.
18 Interview 7, February 2022.
19 Interview 8, March 2022.
20 Interview 10, March 2022.
21 Interview 4, January 2022.
22 Interview 6, January 2022.
23 Interview 1, January 2022.

24 Interview 11, March 2022.
25 Interview 6, January 2022.
26 Interview 9, March 2022.
27 Interview 9, March 2022.
28 Interview 4, January 2022.
29 One of my interviewees also mentioned Canada as an example of a country that is seeking to include gender issues in their national cybersecurity strategy, though these issues are not mentioned in the country's 2017–2022 NAP. Interview 9, March 2022.
30 Interview 1, January 2022.
31 Interview 8, March 2022.
32 Interview 1, January 2022.
33 Interview 7, February 2022.
34 Interview 5, January 2022.
35 Interview 1, January 2022.
36 Interview 6, January 2022.
37 Interview 9, March 2022.
38 Interview 12, March 2022.
39 Interview 13, March 2022.
40 Interview 9, March 2022.
41 Interview 8, March 2022.

Chapter 7

1 Portions of this chapter were originally published as Henshaw, Alexis. 2022. '"Women, Consider Crypto": Gender in the Virtual Economy of Decentralized Finance'. *Politics & Gender*. 1–25. doi:10.1017/S1743923X22000253. © The Author(s), 2022. Published by Cambridge University Press on behalf of the Women, Gender, and Politics Research Section of the American Political Science Association. Reprinted with permission.
2 Satoshi Nakamoto is a pseudonym used by the founder or founders of bitcoin. Despite speculation over the years, it is unclear whether this is one or multiple individuals, or their gender identity.
3 It is worth noting that cryptocurrencies are distinct from the notion of 'virtual' or 'digital' currencies advanced in recent years by states including China and India (John 2020; Jadhav 2021). Projects like China's digital yuan remain fully centralized and do not use blockchain (John 2020). Government control over the ledger raises significant concerns about privacy and surveillance, as it allows the state to more easily track the flow of money.
4 A more complete discussion of 'proof of work' versus 'proof of stake' or 'proof of history' models is beyond the scope of this work, though it suffices to say that not all cryptocurrencies use the competitive mining model associated with 'proof of work' systems. Proponents of blockchain are quick to point out that alternatives to the competitive model are increasingly being adopted and may bring about an end to the discussion over environmental impact. See also Calvão (2018).
5 A valid question, though one beyond the scope of this analysis, is to what extent this economic model remains decentralized once major transnational players like the World Bank, the UN, and an array of transnational financial actors move more deeply into the system. This is another area worth further exploration.
6 See, for example, Ahmed (2008); Keating et al (2010); Dineen and Le (2015); George (2020).
7 See also Chapter 4 for a discussion of the use of cryptocurrencies in support of far-right and gender-based extremism.
8 One recent estimate put remittance loss to fees alone at US$25 billion in 2018 (Elks 2018).

NOTES

9   These comments were sourced from users on Reddit and YouTube who claimed to have interacted with the service. I was unable to verify the identities of these users, however their comments seem generally consistent with the issues identified by the project team.

10 Indeed, it is unclear what happened to Fatima or whether she herself was actually aware of the project or that her family's story was used in its marketing.

11 More recently, Ripple was the subject of legal action by the United States Securities and Exchange Commission, which alleges that Ripple is not a decentralized currency but rather a for-profit company engaged in the unlawful sale of unregistered, digital securities to finance its operation (Securities and Exchange Commission 2020).

12 In Dash's system, 10 per cent of the cryptocurrency mined is reserved for reinvestment into projects developed by the community and voted on by 'masternodes', individuals holding at least 1,000 Dash and a static IP (Prusty 2017: 19–20). The community conversation around DashText and details of the start-up budget can be found on the Dash community forum at www.dash.org/forum/threads/pre-proposal-dash-text-sms-wallets-for-every one-exclusively-for-dash-first-stage-venezuela.39160/ (accessed 4 November 2022).

13 As of this writing, the service is active in Venezuela, Colombia, the United States, Spain, Italy, Mexico, Cuba, Paraguay, Chile, and Peru, but had handled a total of 20 transactions or less in most of these countries. The service does not appear to be active in any African countries, despite identifying this as a target region of interest in its initial pitch. (See Dash community forum, details in note 12.)

14 Italian businessman Francesco Rulli has variously been presented as a partner or co-founder in the venture, although some stories notably omit his involvement entirely, presenting the project as a joint venture of two Afghan women, Fereshteh Forough and Roya Mahboob. Compare, for example, histories appearing in Shah (2012); Keyson and Stevens (2014); Macheel (2014).

15 This is to say nothing of the significant financial loss incurred when parties lose access to their private keys. Recent reports estimate that as much as 20 per cent of all bitcoin in existence is considered 'lost', because it is held in wallets for which the keys have been lost or forgotten (Popper 2021).

16 It should also be mentioned that blockchain technology, in its current form, is not designed to store data like video and audio files. This content would have to be stored off-chain in a separate repository, with blockchain records used to establish ownership and/or a chain of custody (Lemieux 2019).

17 Pugliese (2012) further notes the impact that disability can have on biometric identification. In the case of iris scans, medical research has found that certain surgical procedures (especially cataract surgery), can alter the iris in ways that render them incompatible with pre-surgical scans (Roizenblatt et al 2004). It is unclear how these types of accessibility problems are addressed.

Chapter 8

1   See, for example, https://twitter.com/nayibbukele/status/1484651539587289091 (accessed 4 November 2022).

2   See https://twitter.com/jcanfil/status/1483718554155245569 (accessed 4 November 2022).

3   While 'gender' was employed as a variable in several studies published during this time, most studies treated it as one among many variables.

4   The right to be forgotten was enshrined in EU law in 2014 and allows individuals to curate search engine results by requesting the removal of results that are inaccurate, irrelevant, or that they believe reveal excessive personal information. A study of the five-year impact of the law (conducted by researchers at Google) found that while some individuals did use

the law to pursue erasure of personal information like home addresses, medical records, sexual orientation, ethnicity, or religious or political affiliation, there was widespread confusion over what types of records could be erased (Bertram et al 2019).
5. Data portability refers to a user's right to access and retrieve stored information from applications, programmes, cloud computing services, and similar environments. This can facilitate a user's ability to migrate between competing platforms (thus fostering competition), but also allows users to see what data may have been passively collected by these services (Benjamin 2019; Null and Schulman 2019). Both the EU and the US state of California have legal requirements related to data portability.
6. The need to push back on the neoliberal academic practices that have steadily reduced funding for early career researchers is also worth noting.

References

2017 IIC Winner: Digital Citizen Fund (Technology Access). 2017. www.youtube.com/watch?v=Bqhuz6TMT7o&feature=emb_logo&ab_channel=MITInitiativeontheDigitalEconomy (accessed 25 January 2021).

37Coins. 2015. 'Thank You'. *Medium.* https://medium.com/@37Coins/thank-you-59baedb13c50 (accessed 7 August 2020).

Abu-Laban, Yasmeen. 2015. 'Gendering Surveillance Studies: The Empirical and Normative Promise of Feminist Methodology'. *Surveillance & Society* 13(1): 44–56.

Access Now/Front Line Defenders. 2022. 'Women Human Rights Defenders Speak out about Pegasus Attacks'. *Access Now.* www.accessnow.org/women-human-rights-defenders-pegasus-attacks-bahrain-jordan/ (accessed 12 February 2022).

Ackerly, Brooke A., Maria Stern, and Jacqui True, eds. 2006. *Feminist Methodologies for International Relations.* 1st edition. Cambridge, UK and New York: Cambridge University Press.

ACLED. 2020. 'Where Are Demonstrations Featuring Women Most Prevalent?'. *Acled Data.* https://acleddata.com/2020/03/06/where-are-demonstrations-featuring-women-most-prevalent/ (accessed 7 April 2020).

Adams, Philippa R., Julie Frizzo-Barker, Betty B. Ackah, and Peter Chow-White. 2020. 'Meetups'. In *Blockchain and Web 3.0: Social, Economic, and Technical Challenges,* edited by Massimo Ragnedda and Giuseppe Destefanis. New York: Routledge, pp 48–61.

Ahmed, Azam, and Nicole Perlroth. 2017. 'Using Texts as Lures, Government Spyware Targets Mexican Journalists and Their Families'. *The New York Times.* www.nytimes.com/2017/06/19/world/americas/mexico-spyware-anticrime.html (accessed 10 February 2022).

Ahmed, Fauzia Erfan. 2008. 'Microcredit, Men, and Masculinity'. *NWSA Journal* 20(2): 122–155.

Aizura, Aren Z., Carsten Trystan Cotton, Carla Balzer, Marcia Ochoa LaGata and Slavador Vidal-Ortiz 2014. 'Introduction'. *TSQ: Transgender Studies Quarterly* 1(3): 308–319.

Al-Dayel, Nadia, and Andrew Mumford. 2020. *ISIS and Their Use of Slavery.* The Hague: International Centre for Counter-Terrorism – The Hague.

Al-Dayel, Nadia, Andrew Mumford, and Kevin Bales. 2020. 'Not Yet Dead: The Establishment and Regulation of Slavery by the Islamic State'. *Studies in Conflict & Terrorism* 45(11): 1–24.

Al Saqqaf, Walid. nd. 'Ep. 143 – UN World Food Programme on the Blockchain'. https://insureblocks.com/ep-143-un-world-food-programme-on-the-blockchain/ (accessed 5 April 2022).

Alkurd, Ibrahim. 2020. 'Council Post: A Guide To Decentralized Finance'. *Forbes*. www.forbes.com/sites/theyec/2020/10/16/a-guide-to-decentralized-finance/ (accessed 22 January 2021).

Allyn, Bobby. 2021. '"Lex Luthor of the Internet": Meet the Man Keeping Far-Right Websites Alive'. *NPR.org*. www.npr.org/2021/02/08/965448572/meet-the-man-behind-epik-the-tech-firm-keeping-far-right-websites-alive (accessed 8 July 2021).

Alsema, Adriaan. 2016. 'Colombia's Most Important Vote in Recent History Marred by Disinformation'. *Colombia Reports*. https://colombiareports.com/amp/colombias-important-vote-recent-history-marred-disinformation/ (accessed 20 January 2022).

Alsuwaida, Nouf. 2016. 'Women's Education in Saudi Arabia'. *Journal of International Education Research* 12(4): 111–118.

al-Thaibani, Kawkab. 2019. *Agents for Change: Women as Grassroots Peacebuilders in Yemen*. Vale City: Women4Yemen Network. www.academia.edu/49510283/Agents_for_Change_Women_as_Grassroots_Peacebuilding_in_Yemen (accessed 31 August 2022).

Alvarez, Fernando E., David Argente, and Diana Van Patten. 2022. *Are Cryptocurrencies Currencies? Bitcoin as Legal Tender in El Salvador*. Cambridge, MA: National Bureau of Economic Research.

Aly, Anne, and Jason-Leigh Striegher. 2012. 'Examining the Role of Religion in Radicalization to Violent Islamist Extremism'. *Studies in Conflict & Terrorism* 35(12): 849–862.

Amarasingam, Amarnath, and Marc-André Argentino. 2020. 'The QAnon Conspiracy Theory: A Security Threat in the Making?'. *Combating Terrorism Center at West Point*. https://ctc.usma.edu/the-qanon-conspiracy-theory-a-security-threat-in-the-making/ (accessed 10 December 2020).

Ambler, Pamela, Angel Au-Yeung, Grace Chung, Jeff Kauflin, Alex Konrad, Laura Shin et al. 2018. 'The Richest People in Cryptocurrency'. *Forbes*. www.forbes.com/richest-in-cryptocurrency/ (accessed 30 July 2020).

Amnesty International. 2018. *Toxic Twitter: A Toxic Place for Women*. London: Amnesty International.

Amnesty International. 2022. 'Amnesty International Verifies Use of Pegasus Spyware against Journalists in El Salvador'. *Amnesty International*. www.amnesty.org/en/latest/news/2022/01/el-salvador-pegasus-spyware-surveillance-journalists/ (accessed 8 February 2022).

REFERENCES

Amnesty International India. 2020. *Troll Patrol India: Exposing Online Abuse Faced by Women Politicians in India*. Bengaluru: Indians for Amnesty International Trust. https://decoders.blob.core.windows.net/troll-patrol-india-findings/Amnesty_International_India_Troll_Patrol_India_Findings_2020.pdf (accessed 31 March 2021).

AP. 2021. 'India Restores 4G Mobile Internet in Kashmir after 18-Month Ban'. *NBC News*. www.nbcnews.com/news/world/india-restores-4g-mobile-internet-kashmir-after-18-month-ban-n1256930 (accessed 5 February 2022).

Argentino, Marc-André, Blyth Crawford, Florence Keen, and Hannah Rose. 2021. *Far From Gone: The Evolution of Extremism in the First 100 Days of the Biden Administration*. London: International Centre for the Study of Radicalisation.

Arisandi, Fifi. 2019. 'Ripple vs Stellar: The History, Rivalry, and Future'. *Medium*. https://medium.com/@fifiarisandi_/ripple-vs-stellar-the-history-rivalry-and-future-53de6a6f5add (accessed 14 August 2020).

Armstrong, Charles K. 2002. 'The Origins of North Korean Cinema: Art and Propaganda in the Democratic People's Republic'. *Acta Koreana* 5(1): 1–20.

Armstrong, Gary, and Clive Norris. 1999. *The Maximum Surveillance Society: The Rise of CCTV*. New York: Routledge.

Asmann, Parker. 2021. 'Colombia Report Triples Number of Known False Positives Victims'. *InSight Crime*. https://insightcrime.org/news/report-colombia-false-positives/ (accessed 11 November 2021).

Associated Press. 2021. 'Taliban Fighters Who Rolled into Kabul Appeared Awestruck by the Towering Apartment Blocks, Modern Office Buildings and Shopping Malls: Afghanistan's Cities Have Been Transformed in the Two Decades since a U.S.-Led Invasion Drove the Militants from Power'. 17 August. https://apnews.com/article/afghanistan-taliban-then-and-now-82594865156f9fdae9db4ce1c34d8d43?utm_source=Twitter&utm_campaign=SocialFlow&utm_medium=AP (accessed 3 November 2022).

Avant, Deborah. 2004. 'The Privatization of Security and Change in the Control of Force'. *International Studies Perspectives* 5(2): 153–157.

Avant, Deborah, and Kara Kingma Neu. 2019. 'The Private Security Events Database'. *Journal of Conflict Resolution* 63(8): 1986–2006.

Awan, Farah, and Soheib Nunhuck. 2020. 'Governing Blocks: Building Interagency Consensus to Coordinate Humanitarian Aid'. *Journal of Science Policy and Governance* 16(2). www.sciencepolicyjournal.org/uploads/5/4/3/4/5434385/awan_nunhuck_jspg_v16.2.pdf (accessed 3 November 2022).

Azam, Mehtabul, Yana Rodgers, Michael Stewart-Evans, and Inkeri von Hase. 2020. *Migrant Women and Remittances: Exploring the Data from Selected Countries*. New York: UN Women.

Baldet, Amber, and Catherine Powell. 2019. 'Women Revolutionizing Blockchain: Cryptocurrencies for Change'. Presented at the Council on Foreign Relations. www.cfr.org/event/women-revolutionizing-blockchain-cryptocurrencies-change-0 (accessed 29 July 2020).

Ball, Kirstie, Kevin Haggerty, and David Lyon. 2012. 'Introducing Surveillance Studies'. In *Routledge Handbook of Surveillance Studies*, edited by Kirstie Ball, Kevin Haggerty, and David Lyon. Florence, SC: Taylor & Francis, pp 1–12.

Bandurski, David. 2022. 'China and Russia are Joining Forces to Spread Disinformation'. *Brookings*. www.brookings.edu/techstream/china-and-russia-are-joining-forces-to-spread-disinformation/ (accessed 25 April 2022).

Baraniuk, Chris. 2019. 'Bitcoin's Energy Consumption "Equals that of Switzerland"'. *BBC News*. www.bbc.com/news/technology-48853230 (accessed 22 January 2021).

Barkawi, Ban. 2020. 'Six Years on: Yazidi Survivors See "Only Empty Promises" in Aftermath of Massacre'. *Reuters*. www.reuters.com/article/iraq-war-yazidis-idINL8N2DW0XI (accessed 7 January 2021).

Basu, Soumita. 2016. 'The Global South Writes 1325 (Too)'. *International Political Science Review* 37(3): 362–374.

Basu, Soumita, and Paul Kirby, eds. 2020. 'Women, Peace and Security: A Critical Cartography'. In *New Directions in Women, Peace and Security*, edited by Soumita Basu, Paul Kirby, and Laura Shepherd. Bristol: Policy Press, pp 1–28.

BBC News. 2021. 'Peace Court: Colombia Army "behind 6,400 Extrajudicial Killings"'. *BBC News*. www.bbc.com/news/world-latin-america-56112386 (accessed 11 November 2021).

Bearman, Christopher J. 2005. 'An Examination of Suffragette Violence'. *The English Historical Review* 120(486): 365–397.

Bedford, Kate. 2007. 'The Imperative of Male Inclusion: How Institutional Context Influences World Bank Gender Policy'. *International Feminist Journal of Politics* 9(3): 289–311.

Bell, Christine, Sanja Badanjak, Robert Forester, Astrid Jamar, Kevin McNicholl, Kathryn Nash et al. 2019. *PA-X Codebook, Version 1*. Edinburgh: Political Settlements Research Programme, University of Edinburgh. www.peaceagreements.org/wsearch?WggSearchForm%5Bregion%5D=&WggSearchForm%5Bcountry_entity%5D=&WggSearchForm%5Bname%5D=&WggSearchForm%5Bcategory_addressed%5D%5B%5D=70&WggSearchForm%5Bcategory_addressed%5D%5B%5D=71&WggSearchForm%5Bcategory_mode%5D=any&WggSearchForm%5Bagreement_text%5D=&s=Search+Database (accessed 11 November 2021).

Benjamin, Ruha. 2019. *Race After Technology: Abolitionist Tools for the New Jim Code*. 1st edition. Medford, MA: Polity.

Berger, J.M., and Jonathon Morgan. 2015. *The ISIS Twitter Census*. Washington, DC: The Brookings Institution.

Bergman, Ronen, and Mark Mazzetti. 2021. 'Israeli Companies Aided Saudi Spying Despite Khashoggi Killing'. *The New York Times*. www.nytimes.com/2021/07/17/world/middleeast/israel-saudi-khashoggi-hacking-nso.html (accessed 12 February 2022).

Bergman, Ronen, and Mark Mazzetti. 2022. 'The Battle for the World's Most Powerful Cyberweapon'. *The New York Times*. www.nytimes.com/2022/01/28/magazine/nso-group-israel-spyware.html (accessed 10 February 2022).

Bernards, Nick. 2019. 'The Poverty of Fintech? Psychometrics, Credit Infrastructures, and the Limits of Financialization'. *Review of International Political Economy* 26(5): 815–838.

Bernards, Nick, and Malcom Campbell-Verduyn. 2019. 'Understanding Technological Change in Global Finance through Infrastructures'. *Review of International Political Economy* 26(5): 773–789.

Berners-Lee, Tim, James Hendler, and Ora Lassila. 2001. 'The Semantic Web'. *Scientific American*. www.scientificamerican.com/article/the-semantic-web/ (accessed 15 February 2021).

Bertram, Theo, Elie Bursztein, Stephanie Caro, Hubert Chao, Rutledge Chin Feman, Albin Gustafsson et al. 2019. 'Five Years of the Right to Be Forgotten'. In *Proceedings of the 2019 ACM SIGSAC Conference on Computer and Communications Security*. London: ACM, pp 959–972.

Beteta, Hanny Cueva. 2006. 'What Is Missing in Measures of Women's Empowerment?' *Journal of Human Development* 7(2): 221–241.

Bhandari, Vrinda. 2021. *What's Sex Got to Do with It? Mapping the Impact of Questions of Gender and Sexuality on the Evolution of the Digital Rights Landscape in India*. Delhi: Internet Democracy Project. https://internetdemocracy.in/reports/whats-sex-got-to-do-with-it-mapping-the-impact-of-questions-of-gender-and-sexuality-on-the-evolution-of-the-digital-rights-landscape-in-india/ (accessed 31 March 2021).

Bhatia, Monish. 2021. 'Racial Surveillance and the Mental Health Impacts of Electronic Monitoring on Migrants'. *Race & Class* 62(3): 18–36.

Biddle, Sam, and Ryan Devereaux. 2019. 'Peter Thiel's Palantir was Used to Bust Relatives of Migrant Children, New Documents Show'. *The Intercept*. https://theintercept.com/2019/05/02/peter-thiels-palantir-was-used-to-bust-hundreds-of-relatives-of-migrant-children-new-documents-show/ (accessed 8 February 2022).

Black, Edwin. 2012. *IBM and the Holocaust: The Strategic Alliance Between Nazi Germany and America's Most Powerful Corporation*. Expanded edition. Washington, DC: Dialog Press.

Blanck, Peter. 2016. *eQuality: The Struggle for Web Accessibility by Persons with Cognitive Disabilities*. Reprint edition. Cambridge: Cambridge University Press.

Blee, Kathleen M. 2008. *Women of the Klan: Racism and Gender in the 1920s*. Berkeley, CA: University of California Press.

Boateng, Godfred O., Torsten B. Neilands, Edward A. Frongillo, Hugo R. Melgar-Quiñonez, Sera L. Young et al. 2018. 'Best Practices for Developing and Validating Scales for Health, Social, and Behavioral Research: A Primer'. *Frontiers in Public Health* 6. www.frontiersin.org/articles/10.3389/fpubh.2018.00149/full (accessed 18 March 2021).

Boesch, Diana, and Shilpa Phadke. 2021. 'When Women Lose All the Jobs: Essential Actions for a Gender-Equitable Recovery'. *Center for American Progress*. www.americanprogress.org/article/women-lose-jobs-essential-actions-gender-equitable-recovery/ (accessed 1 February 2022).

Bohórquez Oviedo, Ángela María. 2021. 'Weaponizing Gender: The Campaign against "Gender Ideology" in the Colombian Peace Plebiscite'. Doctoral Dissertation. University of Delaware.

Bohra, Neelam, and A.J. Willingham. 2021. 'Remote Work Made Life Easier for Many People with Disabilities. They Want the Option to Stay'. *CNN*. www.cnn.com/2021/08/10/health/remote-work-disabilities-pandemic-wellness-trnd/index.html (accessed 8 February 2022).

Bond, Jeremy, Kathryn Dirkin, Alexa Jean Tyler, and Stefanie Lassitter. 2021. 'Ladders and Escalators: Examining Advancement Obstacles for Women in Instructional Design'. *The Journal of Applied Instructional Design* 10(2). https://edtechbooks.org/jaid_10_2/examining_advancemen (accessed 1 February 2022).

Bowles, Nellie. 2018. 'Women in Cryptocurrencies Push Back Against "Blockchain Bros"'. *The New York Times*. www.nytimes.com/2018/02/25/business/cryptocurrency-women-blockchain-bros.html (accessed 30 July 2020).

Brand, Dalana. 2019. 'Inclusion & Diversity Report September 2019'. https://blog.twitter.com/en_us/topics/company/2019/inclusion-and-diversity-report-september-2019.html (accessed 29 March 2021).

Brown, Robyn Lewis, and Mairead Eastin Moloney. 2019. 'Intersectionality, Work, and Well-Being: The Effects of Gender and Disability'. *Gender & Society* 33(1): 94–122.

Browne, Simone. 2012. 'Race and Surveillance'. In *Routledge Handbook of Surveillance Studies*, edited by Kirstie Ball, Kevin Haggerty, and David Lyon. Florence, SC: Taylor & Francis, pp 72–80.

Browning, Kellen, and Taylor Lorenz. 2021. 'Pro-Trump Mob Livestreamed Its Rampage, and Made Money Doing It'. *The New York Times*. www.nytimes.com/2021/01/08/technology/dlive-capitol-mob.html (accessed 24 August 2021).

REFERENCES

BSR. 2021. *Human Rights Assessment: Global Internet Forum to Counter Terrorism*. London: Business for Social Responsibility. https://gifct.org/wp-content/uploads/2021/07/BSR_GIFCT_HRIA.pdf (accessed 10 August 2021).

Buolamwini, Joy, and Timnit Gebru. 2018. 'Gender Shades: Intersectional Accuracy Disparities in Commercial Gender Classification'. *Proceedings of Machine Learning Research* 81: 1–15.

Burke, Sloane C., Michele Wallen, Karen Vail-Smith, and David Knox. 2011. 'Using Technology to Control Intimate Partners: An Exploratory Study of College Undergraduates'. *Computers in Human Behavior* 27(3): 1162–1167.

Burton, Anthony Glyn, Greg Elmer, and Stephen J. Neville. 2020. 'Zoom-Bombings Disrupt Online Events with Racist and Misogynist Attacks'. *The Conversation*. http://theconversation.com/zoom-bombings-disrupt-online-events-with-racist-and-misogynist-attacks-138389 (accessed 12 November 2020).

Buzatu, Anne-Marie, Agnieszka Fal-Dutra Santos, Dinah Lakehal, Panthea Pourmalek, Michaela Zelenanska. 2021. *Women, Peace, and Security and Human Rights in the Digital Age: Opportunities and Risks to Advance Women's Meaningful Participation and Protect Their Rights*. Policy Brief. Global Network of Women Peacebuilders/ICT4Peace Foundation. https://gnwp.org/wp-content/uploads/PolicyBriefGNWP-2021c.pdf (accessed 3 November 2022).

Bytes for All Bangladesh. 2022. 'BDOSN Survey on Gender Based Online Violence (GBV) in Bangladesh: What It Tells about Our Internet Environment?'. www.bytesforall.org/bytesforall-bangladesh-survey-on-gender-based-online-violence-gbv-in-bangladesh-what-it-tells-about-our-internet-environment/ (accessed 27 April 2022).

Cabanes Ragandang, Primitivo. 2020. 'Social Media and Youth Peacebuilding Agency: A Case From Muslim Mindanao'. *Journal of Peacebuilding & Development* 15(3): 348–361.

Calvão, Filipe. 2018. 'Crypto-Miners: Digital Labor and the Power of Blockchain Technology'. *Economic Anthropology* 6(1): 123–134.

Caprioli, Mary. 2000. 'Gendered Conflict'. *Journal of Peace Research* 37(1): 51–68.

Caprioli, Mary. 2004. 'Feminist IR Theory and Quantitative Methodology: A Critical Analysis'. *International Studies Review* 6(2): 253–269.

Caprioli, Mary, and Mark A. Boyer. 2001. 'Gender, Violence, and International Crisis'. *Journal of Conflict Resolution* 45(4): 503–518.

Carletti, Laura, Derek McAuley, Dominic Price, Gabriella Giannachi and Steve Benford. 2013. 'Digital Humanities and Crowdsourcing: An Exploration'. Annual Conference of Museums and the Web, Portland, OR. https://ore.exeter.ac.uk/repository/bitstream/handle/10871/17763/Digital?sequence=2 (accessed 3 November 2022).

Carter Olson, Candi S. 2021. '"To Ask Freedom for Women": The Night of Terror and Public Memory'. *Journalism & Mass Communication Quarterly* 98(1): 179–199.

Casey, Michael J., and Paul Vigna. 2018. 'In Blockchain We Trust'. *MIT Technology Review*. www.technologyreview.com/2018/04/09/3066/in-block chain-we-trust/ (accessed 22 January 2021).

CCRI. 2021. 'Frequently Asked Questions'. *Cyber Civil Rights Initiative*. www.cybercivilrights.org/faqs/ (accessed 15 February 2021).

CDCA. 2020. 'Live from Nicaragua: Coronavirus Update'. Presented at the Online and Managua, Nicaragua, 25 June 2020.

Chandran, Rina, and Maya Gebeily. 2021. 'Analysis: From Middle East to India, Women "Violated" in Pegasus Hack'. *Reuters*. www.reuters.com/article/tech-women-surveillance-idUSL8N2P91KX (accessed 12 February 2022).

Chang, Leslie T. 2009. *Factory Girls: From Village to City in a Changing China*. New York: Random House.

Chanlett-Avery, Emma, Liana W. Rosen, John W. Rollins, and Catherine A. Theohary. 2017. *North Korean Cyber Capabilities: In Brief*. CRS Report for Congress. Washington, DC: Congressional Research Service. www.ncnk.org/sites/default/files/CRS_DPRK_Cyber.pdf (accessed 15 February 2021).

Charmes, Jacques, and Saskia Wieringa. 2003. 'Measuring Women's Empowerment: An Assessment of the Gender-Related Development Index and the Gender Empowerment Measure'. *Journal of Human Development* 4(3): 419–435.

Chatterjee, R., P. Doerfler, H. Orgad, S. Havron, J. Palmer, D. Freed et al. 2018. 'The Spyware Used in Intimate Partner Violence'. In *2018 IEEE Symposium on Security and Privacy (SP)*, pp 441–458.

Cheesman, Margie. 2022. 'Self-Sovereignty for Refugees? The Contested Horizons of Digital Identity'. *Geopolitics* 27(1): 134–159.

Chemaly, Soraya. 2016. 'The Problem with a Technology Revolution Designed Primarily for Men'. *Quartz*. https://qz.com/640302/why-is-so-much-of-our-new-technology-designed-primarily-for-men/ (accessed 12 January 2021).

Chowdhury, Rumman, and Luca Belli. 2021. 'Examining Algorithmic Amplification of Political Content on Twitter'. https://blog.twitter.com/en_us/topics/company/2021/rml-politicalcontent (accessed 23 March 2022).

Chun, Rene. 2017. 'Big in Venezuela: Bitcoin Mining'. *The Atlantic*. www.theatlantic.com/magazine/archive/2017/09/big-in-venezuela/534177/ (accessed 4 October 2020).

REFERENCES

Clarke, Colin, and Liana Turner. 2020. 'The "Incel" Ideology Continues to Build a Strong Following in the Online "Manosphere"'. *GNET*. https://gnet-research.org/2020/04/22/the-incel-ideology-continues-to-build-a-strong-following-in-the-online-manosphere/ (accessed 20 June 2021).

Clausen Nielsen, René. 2014. 'Big Data, Innovation and the Data Revolution'. *UN Data Revolution*. www.undatarevolution.org/data-innovation/ (accessed 3 March 2022).

Cleaver, Tony. 2010. *Economics: The Basics*. New York: Taylor & Francis. http://ebookcentral.proquest.com/lib/troy/detail.action?docID=683999 (accessed 4 October 2020).

Clifford Simplican, Stacy. 2021. 'Politicizing Disability in Political Science, COVID-19, and Police Violence'. *Politics, Groups, and Identities* 9(2): 387–394.

Cockburn, Cynthia. 2017. 'A Continuum of Violence: Gender, War and Peace'. In *The Criminology of War*, edited by Ruth Jamieson. Abingdon: Routledge, pp 357–376.

Cohen, Dara Kay, and Ragnhild Nordås. 2014. 'Sexual Violence in Armed Conflict: Introducing SVAC Dataset 1989–2009'. *Journal of Peace Research* 51(3): 418–428.

Cohn, Carol. 1987. 'Sex and Death in the Rational World of Defense Intellectuals'. *Signs* 12(4): 687–718.

Cohn, Carol. 2006. 'Motives and Methods: Using Multi-Sited Ethnography to Study U.S. National Security Discourses'. In *Feminist Methodologies for International Relations*, edited by Brooke A. Ackerly, Maria Stern, and Jacqui True. New York: Cambridge University Press, pp 91–107.

Cohn, Carol. 2014. 'Women and Wars: A Conceptual Framework'. In *Women and Wars*. Cambridge: Polity Press, pp 1–35.

Cohn, Carol. 2018. 'The Perils of Mixing Masculinity and Missiles'. *The New York Times*. www.nytimes.com/2018/01/05/opinion/security-masculinity-nuclear-weapons.html (accessed 15 February 2021).

Coin Dance. 2020. 'Coin Dance: Bitcoin Statistics'. https://coin.dance/stats (accessed 29 July 2020).

CoinSummit London 2014 – Start-up Showcase – 37 Coins. 2014. www.youtube.com/watch?v=Mau0XFS2L8A (accessed 7 August 2020).

Comben, Christina. 2019. 'Female Engagement in Bitcoin Hits New High as Adoption Grows'. *Bitcoinist*. https://bitcoinist.com/women-in-bitcoin-engagement-new-high/ (accessed 30 July 2020).

Community at Klaytn. 2019. 'Diversity in Blockchain Series #2: Songyi Lee, the Pioneer of Blockchain Diversity'. *Medium*. https://medium.com/klaytn/diversity-in-blockchain-series-2-songyi-lee-the-pioneer-of-blockchain-diversity-571f47ff6bb3 (accessed 7 August 2020).

Cook, Joana, and Gina Vale. 2018. *From Daesh to 'Diaspora': Tracing the Women and Minors of the Islamic State*. London: International Centre for the Study of Radicalisation. https://icsr.info/wp-content/uploads/2018/07/ICSR-Report-From-Daesh-to-%E2%80%98Diaspora%E2%80%99-Tracing-the-Women-and-Minors-of-Islamic-State.pdf (accessed 7 January 2021).

Cornish, Chloe. 2019. 'Yazidi Hostages Traded to Criminals as Isis Loses Ground'. *Financial Times*. www.ft.com/content/cabb2f68-4570-11e9-a965-23d669740bfb (accessed 7 January 2021).

Cornwall, Andrea, Frank G. Karioris, and Nancy Lindisfarne. 2016. *Masculinities under Neoliberalism*. London: Zed Books.

Corredor, Elizabeth S. 2019. 'Unpacking "Gender Ideology" and the Global Right's Antigender Countermovement'. *Signs: Journal of Women in Culture and Society* 44(3): 613–638.

Cowman, Krista. 1996. '"The Stone-Throwing Has Been Forced Upon Us": The Function of Militancy Within the Liverpool W.S.P.U., 1906–14'. *Transactions of the Historic Society of Lancashire and Cheshire* 145: 171–192.

Cox, Joseph. 2022. 'Data Broker SafeGraph Stops Selling Location Data of People Who Visit Planned Parenthood'. *Vice*. www.vice.com/en/article/88gyn5/data-broker-safegraph-stops-selling-location-data-of-people-who-visit-planned-parenthood (accessed 1 September 2022).

Cragin, Kim, and Sara A. Daly. 2009. *Women as Terrorists: Mothers, Recruiters, and Martyrs*. Washington, DC: ABC-CLIO.

Crenshaw, Kimberlé. 1990. 'Mapping the Margins: Intersectionality, Identity Politics, and Violence against Women of Color'. *Stanford Law Review* 43: 1241–1299.

Crenshaw, Kimberlé. 2013. 'Demarginalizing the Intersection of Race and Sex: A Black Feminist Critique of Antidiscrimination Doctrine, Feminist Theory and Antiracist Politics'. In *Feminist Legal Theories*, edited by Karen Maschke. New York: Routledge, pp 23–51.

Criado-Perez, Caroline. 2019. *Invisible Women: Data Bias in a World Designed for Men*. First printing edition. New York: Harry N. Abrams.

D'Anastasio, Cecilia. 2021. 'A Game Livestreaming Site Has Become an Extremist Haven'. *Wired*. www.wired.com/story/dlive-livestreaming-site-extremist-haven/ (accessed 24 August 2021).

Darby, Seyward. 2020. *Sisters in Hate: American Women on the Front Lines of White Nationalism*. London: Hachette.

Dasgupta, Partha. 2007. *Economics: A Very Short Introduction*. Illustrated edition. Oxford and New York: Oxford University Press.

DashText. 2020. 'Dash Text Worldwide Statistics'. *DashText*. https://stats.dashtext.io/ (accessed 14 August 2020).

Data Revolution Group. 2014. *A World That Counts: Mobilising the Data Revolution for Sustainable Development.* New York: United Nations/Independent Expert Advisory Group on a Data Revolution for Sustainable Development. www.undatarevolution.org/wp-content/uploads/2014/12/A-World-That-Counts2.pdf (accessed 2 March 2022).

Davey, Jacob, and Julia Ebner. 2017. *The Fringe Insurgency: Connectivity, Convergence and Mainstreaming of the Extreme Right.* London: Institute for Strategic Dialogue.

Davis, Megan. 2016. 'Data and the United Nations Declaration on the Rights of Indigenous Peoples'. In *Indigenous Data Sovereignty: Toward an Agenda*, edited by Tahu Kukutai and John Taylor. Acton: ANU Press, pp 25–38.

de Córdoba, José and Juan Montes. 2020. 'As Coronavirus Spreads in Nicaragua, Official Denials Amplify Risk'. *Wall Street Journal.* www.wsj.com/articles/as-coronavirus-spreads-in-nicaragua-official-denials-amplify-risk-11590246000 (accessed 25 March 2021).

Demick, Barbara. 2009. *Nothing to Envy: Ordinary Lives in North Korea.* 1st edition. New York: Random House.

Devika, J., Chithira Vijayakumar, Darshana Sreedhar Mini, and Resmi P S. 2019. *Walking on Eggshells: A Study on Gender Justice and Women's Struggles in Malayali Cyberspace.* IT for Change. https://itforchange.net/sites/default/files/1618/Kerala-Report_Righting-Gender-Norms.pdf (accessed 30 March 2022).

deVries, Jacqueline R. 2013. 'Popular and Smart: Why Scholarship on the Women's Suffrage Movement in Britain Still Matters'. *History Compass* 1(1/3): 177–188.

DiBranco, Alex. 2020. 'Male Supremacist Terrorism as a Rising Threat'. https://icct.nl/publication/male-supremacist-terrorism-as-a-rising-threat/ (accessed 17 December 2020).

Dickey, Megan Rose. 2017. 'Facebook Defends Revenge Porn Pilot That Has People Upload Nude Images of Themselves'. *TechCrunch.* https://social.techcrunch.com/2017/11/09/facebook-revenge-porn-pilot-details/ (accessed 1 April 2021).

Digital Rights Foundation. 2019. *Experiences of Online Harassment in Pakistan: Case Studies from the Cyber Harassment Helpline.* Pakistan: Digital Rights Foundation. https://digitalrightsfoundation.pk/wp-content/uploads/2019/01/Research-Work.pdf (accessed 30 March 2021).

D'Ignazio, Catherine, and Lauren F. Klein. 2020. *Data Feminism.* Cambridge, MA: The MIT Press.

Di Meco, Lucina. 2019. *#ShePersisted: Women, Politics, and Power in the New Media World.* Washington, DC: The Wilson Center.

Dineen, Katherine, and Quan V. Le. 2015. 'The Impact of an Integrated Microcredit Program on the Empowerment of Women and Gender Equality in Rural Vietnam'. *The Journal of Developing Areas* 49(1): 23–38.

Di Salvo, Mathew. 2019. 'Why Are Venezuelans Seeking Refuge in Crypto-Currencies?' *BBC News*. www.bbc.com/news/business-47553048 (accessed 4 October 2020).

Diskaya, Ali. 2013. 'Towards a Critical Securitization Theory: The Copenhagen and Aberystwyth Schools of Security Studies'. *E-International Relations*. www.e-ir.info/2013/02/01/towards-a-critical-securitization-theory-the-copenhagen-and-aberystwyth-schools-of-security-studies/ (accessed 16 February 2021).

Doval, Pankaj. 2017. 'Rajan Anandan: "90% of New Net Users Non-English"'. *The Times of India*. https://timesofindia.indiatimes.com/business/india-business/90-of-new-net-users-non-english/articleshow/58371769.cms (accessed 31 March 2021).

DRF. 2020. *Addressing Online Attacks on Women Journalists in Pakistan*. Pakistan: Digital Rights Foundation. https://digitalrightsfoundation.pk/wp-content/uploads/2020/11/Policy-1.pdf (accessed 30 March 2021).

DRF/Hamara Internet. 2021. *Cyber Harassment during the COVID-19 Pandemic in Pakistan*. New York: UN Women/Hamara Internet/Digital Rights Foundation. https://digitalrightsfoundation.pk/wp-content/uploads/2021/02/UN-Policy-Brief-2.pdf (accessed 30 March 2021).

Driskill, Qwo-Li. 2010. 'Doubleweaving Two-Spirit Critiques: Building Alliances between Native and Queer Studies'. *GLQ: A Journal of Lesbian and Gay Studies* 16(1–2): 69–92.

Duckett, Chris. 2021. 'Volcano-Powered Bitcoin City Could Be Bond Villainy or the State of Play in 2021'. *ZDNet*. www.zdnet.com/article/volcano-powered-bitcoin-city-could-be-bond-villainy-or-the-state-of-play-in-2021/ (accessed 8 February 2022).

Duriesmith, David. 2017. *Engaging Men and Boys in the Women, Peace, and Security Agenda: Beyond the 'Good Men' Industry*. London: London School of Economics Centre for Women, Peace, and Security.

Duriesmith, David. 2019. 'Engaging or Changing Men? Understandings of Masculinity and Change in the New "Men, Peace and Security" Agenda'. *Peacebuilding* 8(4): 418–431.

Duriesmith, David. 2020. 'Friends Don't Let Friends Cite the Malestream: A Case for Strategic Silence in Feminist International Relations'. *International Feminist Journal of Politics* 22(1): 26–32.

Dutta, Aniruddha, and Raina Roy. 2014. 'Decolonizing Transgender in India: Some Reflections'. *TSQ: Transgender Studies Quarterly* 1(3): 320–337.

Duvendack, Maren, Richard Palmer-Jones, James G Copestake, Lee Hooper, Yoon Loke and Nitya Rao. 2011. *What Is the Evidence of the Impact of Microfinance on the Well-Being of Poor People?* London: EPPI-Centre, Social Science Research Unit, Institute of Education, University of London. https://ueaeprints.uea.ac.uk/id/eprint/35466/ (accessed 14 September 2021).

Dwoskin, Elizabeth, Tory Newmyer, and Shibani Mahtani. 2021. 'Mark Zuckerberg Was More Involved in Decision Making at Facebook than He Let On'. *The Washington Post.* www.washingtonpost.com/technology/2021/10/25/mark-zuckerberg-facebook-whistleblower/ (accessed 15 November 2021).

Eager, Paige Whaley. 2008. *From Freedom Fighters to Terrorists.* New York: Ashgate.

Ebner, Julia, and Jacob Davey. 2019. *How Women Advance the Internationalization of the Far-Right.* Washington, DC: GWU Program on Extremism. https://extremism.gwu.edu/sites/g/files/zaxdzs2191/f/How%20Women%20Advance%20the%20Internationalization%20of%20the%20Far-Right.pdf (accessed 14 January 2021).

Eck, Kristine, and Sophia Hatz. 2020. 'State Surveillance and the COVID-19 Crisis'. *Journal of Human Rights* 19(5): 603–612.

Economist Intelligence Unit/Facebook. 2020. 'Inclusive Internet Index 2020'. *Inclusive Internet Index 2020.* https://theinclusiveinternet.eiu.com/explore/countries/performance/availability/usage/gender-gap-in-internet-access?highlighted=AZ (accessed 13 November 2020).

Elias, Juanita, and Shirin Rai. 2015. 'The Everyday Gendered Political Economy of Violence'. *Politics & Gender* 11(2): 424–429.

Elks, Sonia. 2018. 'Migrants Losing $25 Billion per Year through Remittance Fees: UN'. *Reuters.* www.reuters.com/article/us-global-migrants-un-idUSKCN1NP2BA (accessed 27 January 2021).

Ellerby, Kara. 2011. 'Engendered Security: Norms, Gender and Peace Agreements'. Dissertation. University of Arizona. http://arizona.openrepository.com/arizona/bitstream/10150/204911/1/azu_etd_11682_sip1_m.pdf (accessed 20 February 2013).

Ellerby, Kara. 2017. *No Shortcut to Change: An Unlikely Path to a More Gender Equitable World.* New York: New York University Press.

Enloe, Cynthia. 1999. *Maneuvers.* Berkeley: University of California Press.

Enloe, Cynthia. 2016. *Globalization and Militarism: Feminists Make the Link.* Lanham, MD: Rowman & Littlefield.

ERA Education Project. 2013. 'Doesn't the 14th Amendment Already Guarantee Women Equal Rights Under the Law?' *ERA Education Project.* https://eraeducationproject.com/doesnt-the-14th-amendment-already-guarantee-women-equal-rights-under-the-law/ (accessed 26 March 2021).

Estermann, Beat. 2014. 'Diffusion of Open Data and Crowdsourcing among Heritage Institutions: Results of a Pilot Survey in Switzerland'. *Journal of Theoretical and Applied Electronic Commerce Research* 9(3): 15–31.

Fabian, Christopher. 2018. 'Un-Chained: Experiments and Learnings in Crypto at UNICEF'. *Innovations: Technology, Governance, Globalization* 12(1–2): 30–45.

Facebook. 2018. 'Free Basics'. *Facebook Connectivity*. https://connectivity.fb.com/free-basics/ (accessed 30 March 2021).

Facebook. 2021a. 'Free Basics: Documentation'. *Facebook for Developers*. https://developers.facebook.com/docs/internet-org/ (accessed 30 March 2021).

Facebook. 2021b. 'NCII Pilot'. *NCII Pilot: Not Without My Consent*. www.facebook.com/safetyv2 (accessed 1 April 2021).

Farzan, Antonia Noori. 2019. 'A Neo-Nazi Unleashed a "Troll Storm". Now He Could Owe His Jewish Victim $14 Million'. *Washington Post*. www.washingtonpost.com/nation/2019/07/16/andrew-anglin-daily-stormer-tanya-gersh-million-verdict/ (accessed 7 July 2021).

Feder, Lester. 2017. 'These Lawyers Have a Case for Charging ISIS with Killing LGBT People'. *BuzzFeed News*. www.buzzfeednews.com/article/lesterfeder/these-lawyers-have-a-case-for-charging-isis-with-killing (accessed 7 July 2021).

Fedorov, Aleksey, Evgeniy Kiktenko, and Alexander Lvovsky. 2018. 'Quantum Computers Put Blockchain Security at Risk'. *Nature* 19 November.

Feminism and Nonviolence Study Group. 1983. *Piecing It Together: Feminism and Nonviolence*. Feminism and Nonviolence Study Group, Bilthoven, 17 November. https://wri-irg.org/en/story/2010/piecing-it-together-feminism-and-nonviolence (accessed 3 November 2022).

FIDH/Kinyat. 2018. *Iraq: Sexual and Gender-based Crimes against the Yazidi Community: The Role of ISIL Foreign Fighters*. Paris: International Federation for Human Rights.

Fischer, Paul. 2015. *A Kim Jong-Il Production: The Extraordinary True Story of a Kidnapped Filmmaker, His Star Actress, and a Young Dictator's Rise to Power*. New York: Flatiron Books.

Fisher, Chris. 2019. 'IBM Quantum: Use Cases'. www.ibm.com/quantum-computing/learn/welcome/ (accessed 24 March 2021).

Fitzgerald, Kelly C. 2020. 'Mapping the Manosphere: A Social Network Analysis of the Manosphere on Reddit'. Master's Thesis. Naval Postgraduate School.

FNIGC. 2016. 'Pathways to First Nations Data and Information Sovereignty'. In *Indigenous Data Sovereignty: Toward an Agenda*, edited by Tahu Kukutai and John Taylor. Acton: ANU Press, pp 139–156.

Foucault, Michel. 2019 [1975]. *Discipline and Punish: The Birth of the Prison*. New York. Penguin.

Fowler, Rowena. 1991. 'Why Did Suffragettes Attack Works of Art?'. *Journal of Women's History* 2(3): 109–125.

Freed, Diana, Jackeline Palmer, Diana Elizabeth Minchala, Karen Levy, Thomas Ristenpart, and Nicola Dell. 2017. 'Digital Technologies and Intimate Partner Violence: A Qualitative Analysis with Multiple Stakeholders'. *Proceedings of the ACM on Human-Computer Interaction* 1(CSCW): 46:1–46:22.

Freed, Diana, Jackeline Palmer, Diana Elizabeth Minchala, Karen Levy, Thomas Ristenpart, and Nicola Dell. 2018. '"A Stalker's Paradise": How Intimate Partner Abusers Exploit Technology'. In *Proceedings of the 2018 CHI Conference on Human Factors in Computing Systems*. New York: Association for Computing Machinery, pp 1–13. https://doi.org/10.1145/3173 574.3174241 (accessed 1 April 2021).

Freedom House. 2019. 'Azerbaijan: Government Must Stop Blackmailing Women Journalists in Response to Criticism'. *Freedom House*. https://freedomhouse.org/article/azerbaijan-government-must-stop-blackmailing-women-journalists-response-criticism (accessed 10 February 2022).

Freedom House. 2020a. 'India: Freedom on the Net 2020 Country Report'. *Freedom House*. https://freedomhouse.org/country/india/freedom-net/2020 (accessed 30 March 2021).

Freedom House. 2020b. 'Myanmar: Freedom on the Net 2020 Country Report'. *Freedom House*. https://freedomhouse.org/country/myanmar/freedom-net/2020 (accessed 25 March 2021).

Freedom House. 2020c. 'Pakistan: Freedom on the Net 2020 Country Report'. *Freedom House*. https://freedomhouse.org/country/pakistan/freedom-net/2020 (accessed 30 March 2021).

Freedom House. 2021. 'Freedom on the Net 2021: India'. *Freedom House*. https://freedomhouse.org/country/india/freedom-net/2021 (accessed 15 November 2021).

Frenkel, Sheera. 2018. 'Microsoft Employees Protest Work with ICE, as Tech Industry Mobilizes Over Immigration'. *The New York Times*. www.nytimes.com/2018/06/19/technology/tech-companies-immigration-border.html (accessed 8 February 2022).

Frenkel, Sheera, Nathaniel Popper, Kate Conger, and David E. Sanger. 2020. 'A Brazen Online Attack Targets V.I.P. Twitter Users in a Bitcoin Scam'. *The New York Times*. www.nytimes.com/2020/07/15/technology/twitter-hack-bill-gates-elon-musk.html (accessed 29 July 2020).

Frizzo-Barker, Julie. 2020. 'Women in Blockchain: Discourse and Practice in the Co-Construction of Gender and Emerging Technologies'. *The 21st Annual Conference of the Association of Internet Researchers*. http://spir.aoir.org/ (accessed 4 April 2022).

Gabor, Daniela, and Sally Brooks. 2017. 'The Digital Revolution in Financial Inclusion: International Development in the Fintech Era'. *New Political Economy* 22(4): 423–436.

Gannon, Kathy. 2021. 'Taliban Encounter Afghan Cities Remade in Their Absence'. *AP NEWS*. https://apnews.com/article/afghanistan-taliban-then-and-now-82594865156f9fdae9db4ce1c34d8d43 (accessed 18 August 2021).

Gartzke, Erik. 2013. 'The Myth of Cyberwar'. *International Security* 38(2): 41–73.

Garvie, Clare, Alvaro Bedova, and Jonathan Frankle. 2016. 'Perpetual Line Up: Unregulated Police Face Recognition in America'. *Georgetown Center on Privacy and Technology*. www.perpetuallineup.org/ (accessed 16 November 2021).

Genon, Lynrose Jane D. 2021. 'Beyond Resistance: Youth in Local Peacebuilding'. In *Youth, Peacebuilding, and Sustainability: Connecting Theory to Practice*, edited by Mary Koren Apas Witting-Acuesa and Primitivo III Cabanes Ragandang. np: Seeds for Mindanao's Advocacy and Youth Leadership (SMAYL), pp 56–77. http://smayl.org/wp-content/uploads/2022/01/SMAYL-Book-Final-1.pdf (accessed 31 March 2022).

George, Nicole. 2020. 'The Price of Peace? Frictional Encounters on Gender, Security and the "Economic Peace Paradigm"'. In *New Directions in Women, Peace and Security*, edited by Soumita Basu, Paul Kirby, and Laura Shepherd. Bristol: Policy Press, pp 41–60.

Gerard, David. 2021. 'Bitcoin Failed in El Salvador: The President Says the Answer is More Bitcoin'. *Foreign Policy*. https://foreignpolicy.com/2021/12/06/bitcoin-city-el-salvador-nayib-bukele/ (accessed 8 February 2022).

Gerschick, Thomas J. 2000. 'Toward a Theory of Disability and Gender'. *Signs* 25(4): 1263–1268.

Geybulla, Arzu. 2019. 'Azerbaijan: Women Journalists Under Pressure'. *IWPR*. https://iwpr.net/global-voices/azerbaijan-women-journalists-under-pressure (accessed 10 February 2022).

Geybulla, Arzu. 2020. 'Government Hits Activists' Online Profiles'. *Index on Censorship* 49(3): 8–10.

Ghittoni, Marta, Lèa Lehouck, and Megan Bastick. 2019. *A Security Sector Governance Approach to Women, Peace and Security*. Geneva: Geneva Centre for Security Sector Governance/OSCE/UN Women. www.dcaf.ch/sites/default/files/publications/documents/GSPolicyBrief_1%20EN%20FINAL_1.pdf (accessed 3 November 2022).

GIFCT. 2019. *Transparency Report: July 2019*. Washington, DC: GIFCT. https://gifct.org/wp-content/uploads/2020/10/GIFCT-Transparency-Report-July-2019-Final.pdf (accessed 1 April 2019).

Gill, Jeff. 2021. 'Political Science is a Data Science'. *The Journal of Politics* 83(1): 1–7.

Gill, Rosalind. 2019. 'Surveillance is a Feminist Issue'. In *Routledge Handbook of Contemporary Feminism*, edited by Tasha Oren and Andrea Lee Press. Abingdon: Routledge.

Gillespie, Eden. 2020. '"Pastel QAnon": The Female Lifestyle Bloggers and Influencers Spreading Conspiracy Theories through Instagram'. *The Feed*. www.sbs.com.au/news/the-feed/pastel-qanon-the-female-lifestyle-bloggers-and-influencers-spreading-conspiracy-theories-through-instagram (accessed 10 December 2020).

Gilmore, Justin. 2019. 'Incels: The New Politics of Indifference'. *Centre for the Analysis of the Radical Right*. www.radicalrightanalysis.com/2019/11/11/incels-the-new-politics-of-indifference/ (accessed 16 December 2020).

Gimase Magenya, Sheena, and Tigist Shewarega Hussen. 2022. 'Feminist Peace for Digital Movement Building in Kenya and Ethiopia: Reflections, Lessons, Hopes, and Dreams'. In *Feminist Conversations on Peace*, edited by Sarah Smith and Keina Yoshida. Bristol: Bristol University Press, pp 63–75.

GIWPS. 2020. *The Best and Worst States to Be a Woman: Introducing the U.S. Women, Peace, and Security Index 2020*. Washington, DC: Georgetown Institute for Women, Peace, and Security. https://giwps.georgetown.edu/wp-content/uploads/2020/10/The-Best-and-Worst-States-to-Be-a-Woman.pdf (accessed 3 November 2022).

GIWPS/PRIO. 2018. *Women Peace and Security Index 2017/18 (Report)*. Washington DC: Georgetown Institute for Women, Peace, and Security. https://giwps.georgetown.edu/wp-content/uploads/2019/11/WPS-Index-Report-2017-18.pdf (accessed 3 November 2022).

GIWPS/PRIO. 2019. 'Women, Peace, and Security Index'. *Women, Peace, and Security Index*. https://giwps.georgetown.edu/the-index/ (accessed 3 November 2022).

Global Voices. 2017. *Free Basics in Real Life: Six Case Studies on Facebook's Internet 'On Ramp' Initiative*. Global Voices. https://advox.globalvoices.org/wp-content/uploads/2017/08/FreeBasicsinRealLife_FINALJuly27.pdf (accessed 31 March 2021).

GoFundMe. 2021. 'GoFundMe Providing Support for Afghanistan'. *GoFundMe*. www.gofundme.com/c/blog/support-for-afghanistan (accessed 21 January 2022).

Goggin, Gerard. 2017. 'Disability and Digital Inequalities: Rethinking Digital Divides with Disability Theory'. In *Theorizing Digital Divides*, edited by Massimo Ragnedda and Glenn W. Muschert. New York: Routledge, pp 63–74.

Goldstein, Jessica M. 2020. '"Revenge Porn" was Already Commonplace. The Pandemic has Made Things Even Worse'. *Washington Post*. www.washingtonpost.com/lifestyle/style/revenge-porn-nonconsensual-porn/2020/10/28/603b88f4-dbf1-11ea-b205-ff838e15a9a6_story.html (accessed 15 February 2021).

Golumbia, David. 2016. *The Politics of Bitcoin: Software as Right-Wing Extremism*. Minneapolis, MN: University of Minnesota Press.

Gordon, Eleanor. 2017. 'Crimes of the Powerful in Conflict-Affected Environments: False Positives, Transitional Justice and the Prospects for Peace in Colombia'. *State Crime Journal* 6(1): 132–155.

Goswami, Ranjit, S.K. De, and B. Datta. 2009. 'Linguistic Diversity and Information Poverty in South Asia and Sub-Saharan Africa'. *Universal Access in the Information Society* 8(3): 219–238.

Government of Ireland. 2019. *Women, Peace and Security: Ireland's Third National Action Plan for the Implementation of UNSCR 1325 and Related Resolutions*. Dublin: Government of Ireland. www.dfa.ie/media/dfa/ourr olepolicies/womenpeaceandsecurity/Third-National-Action-Plan.pdf (accessed 15 February 2021).

Government of the Peoples' Republic of Bangladesh. 2011. *National Women Development Policy*. Dhaka: Ministry of Women and Children Affairs. https://mowca.portal.gov.bd/sites/default/files/files/mowca.por tal.gov.bd/policies/64238d39_0ecd_4a56_b00c_b834cc54f88d/Natio nal-Women%20Development%20Policy-2011English.pdf (accessed 31 March 2021).

Graham, Mark. 2016. 'Facebook is No Charity, and the "Free" in Free Basics Comes at a Price'. *The Conversation*. http://theconversation.com/faceb ook-is-no-charity-and-the-free-in-free-basics-comes-at-a-price-52839 (accessed 30 March 2021).

Gray, Mary L., and Siddharth Suri. 2019. *Ghost Work: How to Stop Silicon Valley from Building a New Global Underclass*. Illustrated edition. Boston, MA: Mariner Books.

Greenberg, Andy. 2022. 'North Korea Hacked Him. So He Took Down Its Internet.' *Wired*. www.wired.com/story/north-korea-hacker-internet-out age/ (accessed 4 February 2022).

Griffin, Penny. 2010. 'Gender, Governance and the Global Political Economy'. *Australian Journal of International Affairs* 64(1): 86–104.

Griset, Pamala, and Sue Mahan. 2002. *Terrorism in Perspective*. Thousand Oaks, CA: SAGE.

GSMA. 2020. *The Mobile Gender Gap Report 2020*. London: Global System for Mobile Communications (GSM) Association. www.gsma.com/mobil efordevelopment/wp-content/uploads/2020/05/GSMA-The-Mobile-Gender-Gap-Report-2020.pdf (accessed 30 March 2021).

Guo, Eileen, and Hikmat Noori. 2021. 'This is the Real Story of the Afghan Biometric Databases Abandoned to the Taliban'. *MIT Technology Review*. www.technologyreview.com/2021/08/30/1033941/afghanistan-biomet ric-databases-us-military-40-data-points/ (accessed 2 November 2021).

Guyan, Kevin. 2022. *Queer Data: Using Gender, Sex and Sexuality Data for Action*. London: Bloomsbury.

Haastrup, Toni, and Jamie Hagen. 2020. 'Global Racial Hierarchies and the Limits of Localization via National Action Plans'. In *New Directions in Women, Peace and Security*, edited by Soumita Basu, Paul Kirby, and Laura J. Shepherd. Bristol: Policy Press, pp 133–153.

Haastrup, Toni, and Jamie J. Hagen. 2021. 'Racial Hierarchies of Knowledge Production in the Women, Peace and Security Agenda'. *Critical Studies on Security*. https://doi.org/10.1080/21624887

Haer, Roos, and Tobias Böhmelt. 2018. 'Girl Soldiering in Rebel Groups, 1989–2013: Introducing a New Dataset'. *Journal of Peace Research* 55(3): 395–403.

Hagen, Jamie. 2016. *Sexual Orientation and Gender Identity as Part of the WPS Project*. London: London School of Economics Centre for Women, Peace, and Security. www.lse.ac.uk/women-peace-security/assets/documents/2016/wps2Hagen.pdf (accessed 3 November 2022).

Haggard, Stephan, and Jon R. Lindsay. 2015. *North Korea and the Sony Hack: Exporting Instability Through Cyberspace*. Manoa: East-West Center. https://scholarspace.manoa.hawaii.edu/bitstream/10125/36444/1/api117.pdf (accessed 3 November 2022).

Haleem, Abid, Mohd Javaid, Ibrahim Haleem Khan, and Raju Vaishya. 2020. 'Significant Applications of Big Data in COVID-19 Pandemic'. *Indian Journal of Orthopaedics* 54: 1–3.

Hamilton, Caitlin, and Laura J. Shepherd. 2020. 'WPS National Action Plans: Content Analysis and Data Visualization, V2'. University of Sydney/LSE Centre for Women, Peace, and Security. www.wpsnaps.org (accessed 3 November 2022).

Hamilton, Caitlin, Nyibeny Naam, and Laura Shepherd. 2020. *Twenty Years of Women, Peace and Security National Action Plans: Analysis and Lessons Learned*. Sydney: University of Sydney. www.wpsnaps.org/app/uploads/2020/03/Twenty-Years-of-Women-Peace-and-Security-National-Action-Plans_Report_Final_Web.pdf (accessed 3 November 2022).

Han, Jongwoo, and L.H.M. Ling. 1998. 'Authoritarianism in the Hypermasculinized State: Hybridity, Patriarchy, and Capitalism in Korea'. *International Studies Quarterly* 42(1): 53–78.

Hao, Karen. 2018. 'The First Rule of Being a Woman in Crypto'. *Quartz*. https://qz.com/1262167/the-first-rule-of-being-a-woman-in-crypto-is-you-do-not-talk-about-being-a-woman-in-crypto/ (accessed 30 July 2020).

Hao, Karen. 2021. 'Deepfake Porn is Ruining Women's Lives: Now the Law May Finally Ban it.' *MIT Technology Review*. www.technologyreview.com/2021/02/12/1018222/deepfake-revenge-porn-coming-ban/ (accessed 15 February 2021).

Hao, Karen, and Andrea P. Hernández. 2022. 'How the AI Industry Profits from Catastrophe'. *MIT Technology Review*. www.technologyreview.com/2022/04/20/1050392/ai-industry-appen-scale-data-labels/ (accessed 25 April 2022).

Harding, Sandra. 1986. *The Science Question in Feminism*. 1st edition. Ithaca: Cornell University Press.

Harlan, Elisa, and Oliver Schnuck. 2021. 'Objective or Biased'. *BR24*. https://web.br.de/interaktiv/ki-bewerbung/en (accessed 27 March 2021).

Hawley, Caroline. 2015. 'Why My Own Father Would Have Let IS Kill Me'. *BBC News*. www.bbc.com/news/magazine-33565055 (accessed 7 July 2021).

Henshaw, Alexis Leanna. 2016. 'Where Women Rebel: Patterns of Women's Participation in Armed Rebel Groups 1990–2008'. *International Feminist Journal of Politics* 18(1): 39–60.

Henshaw, Alexis Leanna. 2017. *Why Women Rebel: Understanding Women's Participation in Armed Rebel Groups*. New York: Routledge.

Henshaw, Alexis Leanna. 2020. '"Peace with a Woman's Face": Women, Social Media, and the Colombian Peace Process'. *Contexto Internacional* 42(3): 515–538.

Henshaw, Alexis, June Eric-Udorie, Hannah Godefa, Kathryn Howley, Cat Jeon, Elise Sweezy, and Katheryn Zhao. 2019. 'Understanding Women at War: A Mixed-Methods Exploration of Leadership in Non-State Armed Groups'. *Small Wars & Insurgencies* 30(6–7): 1089–1116.

Henshaw, Alexis. 2021a. 'Extremism in the Manosphere During the Presidential Transition'. *GNET*. https://gnet-research.org/2021/01/22/extremism-in-the-manosphere-during-presidential-transition/ (accessed 20 June 2021).

Henshaw, Alexis. 2021b. 'Mainstreaming Gender in Research Methods'. In *Teaching Research Methods in Political Science*, edited by Jeffrey Bernstein. Cheltenham: Edward Elgar, pp 222–237.

Hill, Kashmir. 2020. 'The Secretive Company That Might End Privacy as We Know It'. *The New York Times*. www.nytimes.com/2020/01/18/technology/clearview-privacy-facial-recognition.html (accessed 15 November 2021).

Hinnant, Lori, Maya Alleruzzo, and Balint Szlanko. 2016. 'Islamic State Tightens Grip on Captives Held as Sex Slaves'. *AP Explore*. www.ap.org/explore/a-savage-legacy/islamic-state-tightens-grip-on-captives-held-as-sex-slaves.html (accessed 7 January 2021).

Hoffman, Bruce, and Jacob Ware. 2020. 'Incels: America's Newest Domestic Terrorism Threat'. *Lawfare*. www.lawfareblog.com/incels-americas-newest-domestic-terrorism-threat (accessed 16 December 2020).

Hoffman, Bruce, Jacob Ware, and Ezra Shapiro. 2020. 'Assessing the Threat of Incel Violence'. *Studies in Conflict & Terrorism* 43(7): 565–587.

Holmes, Aaron, Paige Leskin, Tyler Sonnemaker, and Charles Davis. 2020. 'Hackers Took over Dozens of High-Profile Twitter Accounts Including Those of Barack Obama, Joe Biden, Elon Musk, Kim Kardashian, and Apple and Used Them to Post Bitcoin Scam Links'. *Business Insider*. www.businessinsider.com/hackers-bitcoin-crypto-cashapp-gates-ripple-coindesk-twitter-scam-links-2020-7 (accessed 29 July 2020).

Hong Fincher, Leta. 2018. *Betraying Big Brother: The Feminist Awakening in China*. London: Verso.

Horgan, John. 2009. 'Deradicalization or Disengagement? A Process in Need of Clarity and a Counterterrorism Initiative in Need of Evaluation'. *International Journal of Social Psychology* 24(2): 291–298.

Horowitz, Julia. 2022. 'A Crypto-based Dossier Could Help Prove Russia Committed War Crimes'. *CNN*. www.cnn.com/2022/06/10/tech/ukraine-war-crimes-blockchain/index.html (accessed 1 September 2022).

Horta Ribeiro, Manoel, Jeremy Blackburn, Barry Bradlyn, Emiliano De Cristofaro, Gianluca Stringhini, Summer Long et al. 2021. 'The Evolution of the Manosphere across the Web'. https://arxiv.org/pdf/2001.07600.pdf (accessed 3 November 2022).

HRGJ/MADRE/OWFI. 2017. *Gender-based Persecution and Torture as Crimes Against Humanity and War Crimes Committed by the Islamic State of Iraq and the Levant (ISIL) in Iraq*. New York: The Human Rights and Gender Justice (HRGJ) Clinic of the City University of New York (CUNY) School of Law/MADRE/The Organization of Women's Freedom in Iraq (OWFI). https://s3.documentcloud.org/documents/4177269/CUNY-MADRE-OWFI-Article-15-Communication.pdf (accessed 4 April 2022).

Huckerby, Jayne, and Fionnuala Ní Aoláin. 2018. 'Gendering Counterterrorism: How to, and How Not to – Part II'. *Just Security*. www.justsecurity.org/55670/gendering-counterterrorism-to-part-ii/ (accessed 10 December 2020).

Hudson, Valerie, Bonnie Ballif-Spanvill, Mary Caprioli, and Chad Emmett. 2014a. *Sex and World Peace*. Revised edition. New York: Columbia University Press.

Hudson, Valerie M., Bonnie Ballif-Spanvill, Mary Caprioli, Chad Emmett, Rose McDermott, and Matthew Stearmer. 2014b. *WomanStats Codebook*. www.womanstats.org/CodebookCurrent.htm (accessed 3 November 2022).

Huete-Pérez, Jorge, and John Hildebrand. 2020. 'Nicaragua's COVID-19 Crisis Demands a Response'. *Science* 369(6502): 385.

Hui, Mary. 2021. 'Hong Kongers Are Using Blockchain Archives to Fight Government Censorship'. *Quartz*. https://qz.com/2008673/hong-kongers-use-blockchain-to-fight-government-censorship (accessed 3 November 2022).

Human Rights Centre. nd. *Ways to Bridge the Gender Digital Divide from a Human Rights Perspective*. Essex: Human Rights, Big Data and Technology Project at the Human Rights Centre of the University of Essex. www.ohchr.org/Documents/Issues/Women/WRGS/GenderDigital/HRBDT_submission.pdf (accessed 29 March 2021).

Human Rights Watch. 2022. 'Ukraine: Apparent War Crimes in Russia-Controlled Areas'. *Human Rights Watch*. www.hrw.org/news/2022/04/03/ukraine-apparent-war-crimes-russia-controlled-areas (accessed 25 April 2022).

Hurlburt, Heather, Elizabeth Weingarten, Alexandra Stark, and Elena Souris. 2019. *The 'Consensual Straitjacket': Four Decades of Women in Nuclear Security*. Washington, DC: New America. http://newamerica.org/political-reform/reports/the-consensual-straitjacket-four-decades-of-women-in-nuclear-security/ (accessed 29 May 2020).

Huszár, Ferenc, Sofia Ira Ktena, Conor O'Brien, Luca Belli, Andrew Schlaikjera, and Moritz Hardt. 2021. *Algorithmic Amplification of Politics on Twitter*. Twitter. https://cdn.cms-twdigitalassets.com/content/dam/blog-twitter/official/en_us/company/2021/rml/Algorithmic-Amplification-of-Politics-on-Twitter.pdf (accessed 3 November 2022).

Hutchinson, Susan. 2020. 'Financing Da'esh with Sexual Slavery: A Case Study in Not Gendering Conflict Analysis and Intervention'. *Journal of Global Security Studies* 5(2): 379–386.

IBM. 2021. 'Big Data Analytics'. www.ibm.com/analytics/hadoop/big-data-analytics (accessed 24 March 2021).

Ibtasam, Samia, Lubna Razaq, Maryam Ayub, Jennifer Webster, Syed Ishtiaque Ahmed and Richard Anderson. 2019. '"My Cousin Bought the Phone for Me. I Never Go to Mobile Shops": The Role of Family in Women's Technological Inclusion in Islamic Culture'. *Proceedings of ACM Human-Comput. Interaction* 3: CSCW, Article 46.

IFF. 2016. 'Campaigns and Projects'. *Internet Freedom Foundation*. https://internetfreedom.in/campaigns/ (accessed 31 March 2021).

ILGA. 2019. *Trans Legal Mapping Report*. 3rd edition. Geneva: International Lesbian, Gay, Bisexual, Trans, and Intersex Association. https://ilga.org/downloads/ILGA_World_Trans_Legal_Mapping_Report_2019_EN.pdf (accessed 3 November 2022).

Imran, Syed Tajamul, and Mohd Tahir Ganie. 2020. 'Surviving the Occupation'. *Adi Magazine*. https://adimagazine.com/articles/surviving-the-occupation/ (accessed 5 February 2022).

ING/Ipsos. 2018. *Cracking the Code on Cryptocurrency*. ING/Ipsos. https://think.ing.com/uploads/reports/ING_International_Survey_Mobile_Banking_2018.pdf (accessed 3 November 2022).

Ingram, Kiriloi M. 2021. 'An Analysis of Islamic State's Gendered Propaganda Targeted Towards Women: From Territorial Control to Insurgency'. *Terrorism and Political Violence*. https://doi.org/10.1080/09546553.2021.1919637

International Crisis Group. 2020. *A Course Correction for the Women, Peace, and Security Agenda*. Crisis Group Special Briefing No. 5. London and Brussels: International Crisis Group.

IPU. 2016. *Sexism, Harassment and Violence against Women Parliamentarians*. Geneva: Inter-Parliamentary Union. http://archive.ipu.org/pdf/publications/issuesbrief-e.pdf (accessed 3 November 2022).

Isaac, Mike, and Kellen Browning. 2020. 'Fact-Checked on Facebook and Twitter, Conservatives Switch Their Apps'. *The New York Times*. www.nytimes.com/2020/11/11/technology/parler-rumble-newsmax.html (accessed 8 July 2021).

ITU. 2019. 'Bridging the Gender Divide'. www.itu.int/en/mediacentre/backgrounders/Pages/bridging-the-gender-divide.aspx (accessed 13 November 2020).

IWHR/MADRE. 2015. *Dying to Be Free: LGBT Human Rights Violations in Iraq*. New York: The International Women's Human Rights Clinic at the City University of New York (CUNY) School of Law/MADRE. https://tbinternet.ohchr.org/Treaties/CESCR/Shared%20Documents/IRQ/INT_CESCR_CSS_IRQ_21554_E.pdf (accessed 3 November 2022).

Jacinto, Leela. 2021. 'Online Education Is the Only Hope for Afghan Schoolgirl, but It's a Slog'. *France 24*. www.france24.com/en/asia-pacific/20211012-online-education-is-the-only-hope-for-afghan-schoolgirl-but-it-s-a-slog (accessed 21 January 2022).

Jadhav, Rajendra. 2021. 'India Proposes Law to Ban Cryptocurrencies, Create Official Digital Currency'. *Reuters*. www.reuters.com/article/us-india-cryptocurrency-lawmaking-idUSKBN29Z0EX (accessed 1 February 2021).

Jamison, Amelia, David Broniatowski, Mark Dredze, Anu Sangraula, Michael Smith and Sandra Quinn. 2020. 'Not Just Conspiracy Theories: Vaccine Opponents and Proponents Add to the COVID-19 "Infodemic" on Twitter'. *Harvard Kennedy School Misinformation Review* 1(3). https://misinforeview.hks.harvard.edu/article/not-just-conspiracy-theories-vaccine-opponents-and-pro-ponents-add-to-the-covid-19-infodemic-on-twitter/ (accessed 3 November 2022).

Jammu and Kashmir Coalition of Civil Society. 2020. *Kashmir's Internet Siege: An Ongoing Assault on Digital Rights*. Jammu and Kashmir Coalition of Civil Society. https://jkccs.net/report-kashmirs-internet-siege/ (accessed 3 November 2022).

Janetsky, Megan. 2020. 'Violence against Women up amid Latin America COVID-19 Lockdowns'. *Al Jazeera*. www.aljazeera.com/features/2020/4/20/violence-against-women-up-amid-latin-america-covid-19-lockdowns (accessed 16 November 2020).

Jankowicz, Nina, Jillian Hunchak, Alexandra Pavliuc, Celia Davies, Shannon Pierson and Zoë Kaufmann. 2021. *Malign Creativity: How Gender, Sex, and Lies Are Weaponized Against Women Online*. Washington, DC: The Wilson Center. www.wilsoncenter.org/publication/malign-creativity-how-gender-sex-and-lies-are-weaponized-against-women-online?utm_medium=social&utm_source=twitter.com&utm_campaign=wilson (accessed 25 January 2021).

Jansson, Ina-Maria. 2020. 'Creating Value of the Past through Negotiations in the Present: Balancing Professional Authority with Influence of Participants'. *Archival Science* 20(4): 327–345.

John, Alun. 2020. 'Explainer: How Does China's Digital Yuan Work?' *Reuters*. www.reuters.com/article/us-china-currency-digital-explainer-idUSKBN27411T (accessed 1 February 2021).

Johnson, Britney, Ben Rydal Shapiro, Betsy DiSalvo, Annabel Rothschild and Carl DiSalvo. 2021. 'Exploring Approaches to Data Literacy Through a Critical Race Theory Perspective'. https://dl.acm.org/doi/pdf/10.1145/3411764.3445141 (accessed 3 November 2022).

Johnson, Sydney. 2019. 'Turnitin to Be Acquired by Advance Publications for $1.75B'. *EdSurge*. www.edsurge.com/news/2019-03-06-turnitin-to-be-acquired-by-advance-publications-for-1-75b (accessed 15 November 2021).

Jones, Christopher. 2021. 'Law Enforcement Use of Facial Recognition: Bias, Disparate Impacts to People of Color, and the Need for Federal Legislation'. *North Carolina Journal of Law & Technology* 22(4): 777–815.

Kaku, Michio. 2011. *Physics of the Future: How Science Will Shape Human Destiny and Our Daily Lives by the Year 2100*. New York: Penguin.

Kapadia, Faisal, and Mahnoor Jalil. 2017. *Free Basics in Pakistan*. Global Voices. https://advox.globalvoices.org/wp-content/uploads/2017/07/PAKISTAN.pdf (accessed 31 March 2021).

Karacaoglu, Yusuf, Stela Mocan, and Rachel Alexander Halsema. 2018. 'The World Bank Group's Technology and Innovation Lab, From Concept to Development'. *Innovations: Technology, Governance, Globalization*, November: 18–28.

Karim, Sabrina, and Daniel Hill. 2018. 'The Study of Gender and Women in Cross-National Political Science Research: Rethinking Concepts and Measurements'. Unpublished working paper. www.womanstats.org/KarimHillGenderEqualityArticleApr2018.pdf (accessed 3 November 2022).

Karimi, Ali. 2019. 'Surveillance in Weak States: The Problem of Population Information in Afghanistan'. *International Journal of Communication* 13: 4778–4793.

Katwala, Amit. 2020. 'Quantum Computing and Quantum Supremacy, Explained'. *Wired UK*. www.wired.co.uk/article/quantum-computing-explained (accessed 24 March 2021).

Keating, Christine, Claire Rasmussen, and Pooja Rishi. 2010. 'The Rationality of Empowerment: Microcredit, Accumulation by Dispossession, and the Gendered Economy'. *Signs: Journal of Women in Culture and Society* 36(1): 153–176.

Kent, Susan Kingsley. 1990. *Sex and Suffrage in Britain 1860–1914*. New York: Routledge.

Keyson, Lauren, and Dana Stevens. 2014. 'Fereshteh Forough Is Fascinated by Bitcoin'. *Disruptive Technologists*. https://disruptivetechnologists.com/2014/08/fereshteh-forough-is-fascinated-by-bitcoin/ (accessed 25 January 2021).

Kilbride, Erin. 2015. 'The Forgotten: Pakistan's Transgender Population, and the Islamic State'. *E-International Relations*. www.e-ir.info/2015/01/07/the-forgotten-pakistans-transgender-population-and-the-islamic-state/ (accessed 18 January 2015).

King-Close, Alexandria. 2016. 'A Gender Analysis of Cyber War'. Master's Thesis. Harvard Extension School. https://dash.harvard.edu/bitstream/handle/1/33797321/KING-CLOSE-DOCUMENT-2016.pdf?sequence=1 (accessed 3 November 2022).

Kirby, Paul, and Laura J. Shepherd. 2016. 'The Futures Past of the Women, Peace and Security Agenda'. *International Affairs* 92(2): 373–392.

Kirchgaessner, Stephanie. 2021. 'New Evidence Suggests Spyware Used to Surveil Emirati Activist Alaa Al-Siddiq'. *The Guardian*. www.theguardian.com/world/2021/sep/24/new-evidence-suggests-spyware-used-to-surveil-emirati-activist-alaa-al-siddiq (accessed 10 February 2022).

Klasen, Stephan. 2006. 'UNDP's Gender-related Measures: Some Conceptual Problems and Possible Solutions'. *Journal of Human Development* 7(2): 243–274.

Klasen, Stephan, and Dana Schüler. 2011. 'Reforming the Gender-Related Development Index and the Gender Empowerment Measure: Implementing Some Specific Proposals'. *Feminist Economics* 17(1): 1–30.

Klippenstein, Ken, and Sara Sirota. 2021. 'The Taliban Have Seized U.S. Military Biometrics Devices'. *The Intercept*. https://theintercept.com/2021/08/17/afghanistan-taliban-military-biometrics/ (accessed 1 November 2021).

Koskela, Hille. 2012. '"You Shouldn't Wear That Body": The Problematic of Surveillance and Gender'. In *Routledge Handbook of Surveillance Studies*, edited by Kirstie Ball, Kevin Haggerty, and David Lyon. Florence, SC: Taylor & Francis, pp 49–56.

Kreps, Sarah. 2020. *Social Media and International Relations*. New York: Cambridge University Press.

Kronstadt, K. Allen. 2020. *Kashmir: Background, Recent Developments, and U.S. Policy*. Washington, DC: Congressional Research Service.

Krook, Mona Lena. 2020. *Violence against Women in Politics*. 1st edition. New York: Oxford University Press.

Kshetri, Nir. 2020. 'The Lack of Women in Cybersecurity Leaves the Online World at Greater Risk'. *The Conversation*. http://theconversation.com/the-lack-of-women-in-cybersecurity-leaves-the-online-world-at-greater-risk-136654 (accessed 15 February 2021).

Kukutai, Tahu, and John Taylor. 2016. 'Data Sovereignty for Indigenous Peoples: Current Practice and Future Needs'. In *Indigenous Data Sovereignty: Toward an Agenda*, edited by Tahu Kukutai and John Taylor. Acton: ANU Press, pp 1–24.

Kunz, Rahel. 2008. '"Remittances Are Beautiful"? Gender Implications of the New Global Remittances Trend'. *Third World Quarterly* 29(7): 1389–1409.

Kunzelman, Michael. 2021. 'Neo-Nazi Website Founder Accused of Ignoring $14M Judgment'. *AP NEWS*. https://apnews.com/article/technology-race-and-ethnicity-montana-courts-1554c9a9254449b75018cee56317c557 (accessed 8 July 2021).

Lam, Theodora, and Brenda S.A. Yeoh. 2018. 'Migrant Mothers, Left-behind Fathers: The Negotiation of Gender Subjectivities in Indonesia and the Philippines'. *Gender, Place & Culture* 25(1): 104–117.

The Lancet. 2020. 'Expression of Concern: Hydroxychloroquine or Chloroquine with or without a Macrolide for Treatment of COVID-19: A Multinational Registry Analysis'. *The Lancet* 395(10240): e102.

Langevin, Marie. 2019. 'Big Data for (Not so) Small Loans: Technological Infrastructures and the Massification of Fringe Finance'. *Review of International Political Economy* 26(5): 790–814.

Lankov, Andrei. 2007. 'Surfing Net in North Korea'. *koreatimes*. www.koreatimes.co.kr/www/nation/2021/02/166_13540.html (accessed 15 February 2021).

Ledsom, Alex. 2022. 'The Newest European Country Launching a Digital Nomad Visa'. *Forbes*. www.forbes.com/sites/alexledsom/2022/02/02/the-new-large-eu-country-offering-a-digital-nomad-visa/ (accessed 8 February 2022).

Lehane, Orla, David Mair, Saffron Lee, and Jodie Parker. 2018. 'Brides, Black Widows and Baby-Makers; or Not: An Analysis of the Portrayal of Women in English-Language Jihadi Magazine Image Content'. *Critical Studies on Terrorism* 11(3): 505–520.

Lemieux, Victoria L. 2019. 'Blockchain and Public Record Keeping: Of Temples, Prisons, and the (Re)Configuration of Power'. *Frontiers in Blockchain* 2. www.frontiersin.org/article/10.3389/fbloc.2019.00005 (accessed 31 March 2022).

Liang Lin, Jie. 2017. 'Antifeminism Online: MGTOW (Men Going Their Own Way)'. In *Digital Environments: Ethnographic Perspectives Across Global Online and Offline Spaces*, edited by Urte Undine Frömming, Steffen Köhn, Samantha Fox, and Mike Terry. Bielefeld: Transcript Verlag.

Libicki, Martin C. 2011. 'Cyberwar as a Confidence Game'. *Strategic Studies Quarterly* 5(1): 132–147.

Lim, Clarissa-Jan. 2021. 'Organizers of a GoFundMe to Help Queer and Trans Afghans Say the Platform Won't Allow Them to Access the Money'. *BuzzFeed News*. www.buzzfeednews.com/article/clarissajanlim/gofundme-fundraiser-afghanistan-queer-trans (accessed 21 January 2022).

Ling, Qi, and Sara Liao. 2020. 'Intellectuals Debate #MeToo in China: Legitimizing Feminist Activism, Challenging Gendered Myths, and Reclaiming Feminism'. *Journal of Communication* 70: 895–916.

Linthicum, Kate. 2021. 'Nicaragua Activist Fights a Coronavirus Cover-Up'. *Los Angeles Times*. www.latimes.com/world-nation/story/2020-06-04/nicaraguan-activist-sees-coronavirus-pandemic-as-opportunity (accessed 24 March 2021).

Lock, Samantha. 2021. 'Video Shows Taliban Soldiers Working out in Presidential Palace Gym'. *Newsweek*. www.newsweek.com/taliban-soldiers-working-out-gym-presidential-palace-kabul-video-1620017 (accessed 18 August 2021).

Lokshina, Tanya. 2017. 'Authorities in Southern Russia Scared of Feminism'. *Human Rights Watch*. www.hrw.org/news/2017/08/14/authorities-southern-russia-scared-feminism (accessed 11 February 2022).

Lopez-Ekra, Sylvia, Christine Aghazarm, Henriette Kötter, and Blandine Mollard. 2011. 'The Impact of Remittances on Gender Roles and Opportunities for Children in Recipient Families: Research from the International Organization for Migration'. *Gender & Development* 19(1): 69–80.

Lovett, Ray. 2016. 'Aboriginal and Torres Strait Islander Community Wellbeing: Identified Needs for Statistical Capacity'. In *Indigenous Data Sovereignty: Toward an Agenda*, edited by Tahu Kukutai and John Taylor. Acton: ANU Press, pp 213–232.

Lynn, William. 2010. 'Defending a New Domain: The Pentagon's Cyberstrategy'. *Foreign Affairs* 89(5): 97–108.

Lyon, David. 2007. *Surveillance Studies: An Overview*. Cambridge, MA: Polity.

Ma, Kevin C., and Marc Lipsitch. 2021. 'Big Data and Simple Models Used to Track the Spread of COVID-19 in Cities'. *Nature* 589(7840): 26–28.

Mac, Ryan, Caroline Haskins, and Logan McDonald. 2020. 'Clearview AI's Facial Recognition Tech is Being Used by the Justice Department, ICE, and the FBI'. *BuzzFeed News.* www.buzzfeednews.com/article/ryanmac/clearview-ai-fbi-ice-global-law-enforcement (accessed 15 November 2021).

Macheel, Tanaya. 2014. 'How Bitcoin Helps Afghan Girls Achieve Financial Freedom'. *CoinDesk.* www.coindesk.com/how-bitcoin-helps-afghan-girls-achieve-financial-freedom (accessed 25 January 2021).

MacKenzie, Megan. 2009. 'Securitization and Desecuritization: Female Soldiers and the Reconstruction of Women in Post-Conflict Sierra Leone'. *Security Studies* 18(2): 241–261.

MacKenzie, Megan. 2010. 'Securitizing Sex?' *International Feminist Journal of Politics* 12(2): 202–221.

MacKenzie, Megan. 2012. *Female Soldiers in Sierra Leone: Sex, Security, and Post-Conflict Development.* New York: New York University Press.

Mader, Philip. 2018. 'Contesting Financial Inclusion'. *Development and Change* 49(2): 461–483.

Madhok, Sumi, and Shirin Rai. 2012. 'Agency, Injury, and Transgressive Politics in Neoliberal Times'. *Signs* 37(3): 645–669.

Magnet, Shoshana, and Rachel E. Dubrofsky. 2015. 'Introduction'. In *Feminist Surveillance Studies*, edited by Shoshana Magnet and Rachel E. Dubrofsky. Durham, NC: Duke University Press, pp 1–20.

Maher, Sanam. 2020. *A Woman Like Her: The Story Behind the Honor Killing of a Social Media Star.* Portland, OR: Melville House.

Makoni, Abbianca. 2022. '"Code to Inspire" Founder Uses Crypto to Help Tech Students in Afghanistan on the Brink of Hunger Side-Step US Sanctions'. *POCIT. Telling the Stories and Thoughts of People of Color in Tech.* https://peopleofcolorintech.com/front/code-to-inspire-founder-uses-crypto-to-help-tech-students-in-afghanistan-on-the-brink-of-hunger-side-step-us-sanctions/ (accessed 21 January 2022).

Malnad, Megha, Parimala, Nagina, and Tasneem Mewa. 2020. *Use of Mobile Phones by Vulnerable Communities: A Survey of Gay Men and Sex Workers in Karnataka.* Bengaluru: Sangama/CIS-India. https://cis-india.org/internet-governance/MobilePhones_GayMen_SexWorkers_Karnataka (accessed 31 March 2021).

Margolin, Devorah, and Charlie Winter. 2021. *Women in the Islamic State: Victimization, Support, Collaboration, and Acquiescence.* Washington, DC: Program on Extremism/The George Washington University. https://isisfiles.gwu.edu/downloads/3484zg88m?locale=en (accessed 7 July 2021).

Mari, Angelica. 2022. 'Brazil Changes Visa Rules to Attract Digital Nomads'. *ZDNet.* www.zdnet.com/article/brazil-changes-visa-rules-to-attract-digital-nomads/ (accessed 8 February 2022).

Mariano, Willoughby, and J. Scott Trubey. 2020. '"It's Just Cuckoo": State's Latest Data Mishap Causes Critics to Cry Foul'. *ajc*. www.ajc.com/news/state--regional-govt--politics/just-cuckoo-state-latest-data-mishap-causes-critics-cry-foul/182PpUvUX9XEF8vO11NVGO/ (accessed 25 March 2021).

Maroto, Michelle, David Pettinicchio, and Andrew C. Patterson. 2019. 'Hierarchies of Categorical Disadvantage: Economic Insecurity at the Intersection of Disability, Gender, and Race'. *Gender & Society* 33(1): 64–93.

Martin, Randy. 2002. *Financialization of Daily Life*. Philadelphia, PA: Temple University Press.

Mason, Corinne, and Shoshana Magnet. 2012. 'Surveillance Studies and Violence Against Women'. *Surveillance & Society* 10(2): 105–118.

Mattheis, Ashley, and Charlie Winter. 2019. *'The Greatness of Her Position': Comparing Identitarian and Jihadi Discourses*. London: International Centre for the Study of Radicalisation. https://icsr.info/wp-content/uploads/2019/05/ICSR-Report-%E2%80%98The-Greatness-of-Her-Position%E2%80%99-Comparing-Identitarian-and-Jihadi-Discourses-on-Women.pdf (accessed 3 November 2022).

Matthews, Tara, Kathleen O'Leary, Anna Turner, Manya Sleeper, Jill Palzkill Woelfer, Martin Shelton et al. 2017. 'Stories from Survivors: Privacy & Security Practices When Coping with Intimate Partner Abuse'. *Proceedings of the 2017 CHI Conference on Human Factors in Computing Systems*, pp 2189–2201. http://dl.acm.org/citation.cfm?id=3025875 (accessed 1 April 2021).

Mayhall, Laura E. Nym. 2003. *The Militant Suffrage Movement: Citizenship and Resistance in Britain, 1860–1930*. Oxford: Oxford University Press.

McArdle, Terence. 2017. '"Night of Terror": The Suffragists Who Were Beaten and Tortured for Seeking the Vote'. *Washington Post*. www.washingtonpost.com/news/retropolis/wp/2017/11/10/night-of-terror-the-suffragists-who-were-beaten-and-tortured-for-seeking-the-vote/ (accessed 20 June 2021).

McCahill, Mike. 2002. *The Surveillance Web*. London: Willan.

McCallum, Jamie K. 2020. *Worked Over: How Round-the-Clock Work is Killing the American Dream*. New York: Basic Books.

McDonald, Michael D. 2022. 'El Salvador Hires AlphaPoint to Fix Bitcoin Digital Wallet Bugs'. *Bloomberg.com*. www.bloomberg.com/news/articles/2022-02-07/el-salvador-hires-alphapoint-to-fix-bitcoin-digital-wallet-bugs (accessed 8 February 2022).

McMahon, Robert, and Isabella Bennett. 2011. 'U.S. Internet Providers and the "Great Firewall of China"'. *Council on Foreign Relations*. www.cfr.org/backgrounder/us-internet-providers-and-great-firewall-china (accessed 15 November 2021).

Mehra, Mandeep R., Frank Ruschitzka, and Amit N. Patel. 2020. 'Retraction: Hydroxychloroquine or Chloroquine with or without a Macrolide for Treatment of COVID-19: A Multinational Registry Analysis'. *The Lancet* 395(10240): 1820.

Mehran, Weeda, Dominika Imiolek, Lucy Smeddle, and Jack Springett-Gilling. 2020. 'The Depiction of Women in Jihadi Magazines: A Comparative Analysis of Islamic State, Al Qaeda, Taliban and Tahrik-e Taliban Pakistan'. *Small Wars & Insurgencies*. DOI: 10.1080/09592318.2020.1849898

Mersch, Max, and Richard Muirhead. 2020. 'What Is Web 3.0 and Why It Matters'. *Medium*. https://medium.com/fabric-ventures/what-is-web-3-0-why-it-matters-934eb07f3d2b (accessed 13 February 2021).

Mhajne, Anwar. 2021. 'A Human Rights Approach to U.S. Cybersecurity Strategy'. *Carnegie Council*. www.carnegiecouncil.org/publications/articles_papers_reports/a-human-rights-approach-to-us-cybersecurity-strategy (accessed 1 February 2022).

Mir, Shakir. 2021. 'Internet Restrictions in J&K Are Undermining the Supreme Court's Orders'. *The Wire*. https://thewire.in/rights/jammu-kashmir-4g-internet-supreme-court (accessed 31 March 2021).

Miranda Abuerto, Wilfredo. 2020. 'Nueva orden del Minsa: Hacer solo "50 muestras diarias" de covid-19'. *Confidencial*. https://confidencial.com.ni/coranavirus-en-nicaragua/nueva-orden-del-minsa-hacer-solo-50-pruebas-diarias-de-covid-19/ (accessed 25 March 2021).

Mitew, Teodor, and Travis Wall. 2017. 'Swarm Networks and the Design Process of a Distributed Meme Warfare Campaign'. *First Monday* 22 (5–7): 1–33.

Moaveni, Azadeh. 2015. 'ISIS Women and Enforcers in Syria Recount Collaboration, Anguish and Escape'. *The New York Times*. www.nytimes.com/2015/11/22/world/middleeast/isis-wives-and-enforcers-in-syria-recount-collaboration-anguish-and-escape.html (accessed 7 January 2021).

Moaveni, Azadeh. 2019. *Guest House for Young Widows: Among the Women of ISIS*. New York: Random House.

Moonshot. 2021. *Understanding and Preventing Incel Violence in Canada*. London: Moonshot CVE. https://moonshotteam.com/preventing-incel-violence-in-canada/ (accessed 3 November 2022).

Moore, Lisa Jean, and Paisley Currah. 2015. 'Legally Sexed: Birth Certificates and Transgender Citizens'. In *Feminist Surveillance Studies*, edited by Shoshana Magnet and Rachel E. Dubrofsky. Durham, NC: Duke University Press, pp 58–78.

Moyn, Samuel. 2018. 'Opinion: The Alt-Right's Favorite Meme Is 100 Years Old'. *The New York Times*. www.nytimes.com/2018/11/13/opinion/cultural-marxism-anti-semitism.html (accessed 11 January 2021).

Mukerjee, Subhayan. 2016. 'Net Neutrality, Facebook, and India's Battle to #SaveTheInternet'. *Communication and the Public* 1(3): 356–361.

REFERENCES

Myers, B.R. 2011. *The Cleanest Race: How North Koreans See Themselves and Why It Matters*. Reprint edition. New York: Melville House.

Najibullah, Farangis. 2019. 'Afghan Women Drawing #MyRedLine for Peace with the Taliban'. *Radio Free Europe/Radio Liberty*. www.rferl.org/a/myredline-the-afghan-women-who-won-t-accept-taliban-peace-at-any-cost/29972913.html (accessed 21 January 2022).

Natarajan, Harish, Solvej Krause, and Helen Gradstein. 2017. *Distributed Ledger Technology (DLT) and Blockchain*. Washington, DC: World Bank Group. https://openknowledge.worldbank.org/bitstream/handle/10986/29053/WP-PUBLIC-Distributed-Ledger-Technology-and-Blockchain-Fintech-Notes.pdf?sequence=5&isAllowed=y (accessed 3 November 2022).

Natile, Serena. 2020. *The Exclusionary Politics of Digital Financial Inclusion: Mobile Money, Gendered Walls*. New York: Routledge.

NBC News. 2014. 'North Korea Furious Over Kim Jong Un Parody Dance Video'. *NBC News*. www.nbcnews.com/news/asian-america/north-korea-furious-over-kim-jong-un-parody-dance-video-n162786 (accessed 15 February 2021).

Nicas, Jack. 2021. 'Parler, a Social Network That Attracted Trump Fans, Returns Online'. *The New York Times*. www.nytimes.com/2021/02/15/technology/parler-back-online.html (accessed 8 July 2021).

NIST. 2015. *NIST Big Data Interoperability Framework: Volume 1, Definitions*. Washington, DC: US Department of Commerce. https://bigdatawg.nist.gov/_uploadfiles/NIST.SP.1500-1.pdf (accessed 24 March 2021).

Noble, Safiya Umoja. 2018. *Algorithms of Oppression: How Search Engines Reinforce Racism*. Illustrated edition. New York: New York University Press.

Noble, Safiya Umoja, and Brendesha M. Tynes. 2016a. 'Introduction'. In *The Intersectional Internet: Race, Sex, Class, and Culture Online*, edited by Safiya Umoja Noble and Brendesha M. Tynes. Bern: Peter Lang, pp 1–19.

Noble, Safiya Umoja, and Brendesha M. Tynes, eds. 2016b. *The Intersectional Internet: Race, Sex, Class, and Culture Online*. Bern: Peter Lang.

Nothias, Toussaint. 2020. 'Access Granted: Facebook's Free Basics in Africa'. *Media, Culture & Society* 42(3): 329–348.

NSO Group. 2021a. 'NSO News: Cyber Intelligence Sector Leader NSO Group Unveils the Industry's First "Transparency and Responsibility Report"'. www.nsogroup.com/Newses/cyber-intelligence-sector-leader-nso-group-unveils-the-industrys-first-transparency-and-responsibility-report/ (accessed 3 November 2022).

NSO Group. 2021b. *Transparency and Responsibility Report 2021*. Hersliya: NSO Group. www.nsogroup.com/wp-content/uploads/2021/06/ReportBooklet.pdf (accessed 3 November 2022).

Null, Eric, and Eric Schulman. 2019. 'The Data Portability Act: More User Control, More Competition'. *New America*. http://newamerica.org/oti/blog/data-portability-act-more-user-control-more-competition/ (accessed 8 February 2022).

Nye, Joseph. 2010. *Cyberpower.* Cambridge, MA: Harvard Kennedy School, Belfer Center. www.belfercenter.org/sites/default/files/legacy/files/cyberpower.pdf (accessed 3 November 2022).

O'Brien, Luke. 2017. 'The Making of an American Nazi'. *The Atlantic.* www.theatlantic.com/magazine/archive/2017/12/the-making-of-an-american-nazi/544119/ (accessed 7 July 2021).

Observatorio Ciudadano. 2020. '¿Quiénes somos?' *Observatorio Ciudadano COVID-19 Nicaragua.* https://observatorioni.org/quienes-somos/ (accessed 25 March 2021).

OECD. 2018. *Bridging the Digital Gender Divide: Include, Upskill, Innovate.* Paris: OECD. www.oecd.org/digital/bridging-the-digital-gender-divide.pdf (accessed 4 November 2022).

Ohlheiser, Abby. 2022. 'Anti-Abortion Activists Are Collecting the Data They'll Need for Prosecutions Post-Roe'. *MIT Technology Review.* www.technologyreview.com/2022/05/31/1052901/anti-abortion-activists-are-collecting-the-data-theyll-need-for-prosecutions-post-roe/ (accessed 1 September 2022).

O'Malley, Roberta Liggett, Karen Holt, and Thomas J. Holt. 2020. 'An Exploration of the Involuntary Celibate (Incel) Subculture Online'. *Journal of Interpersonal Violence* 37(7–8): NP4981–NP5008..

O'Neil, Cathy. 2016. *Weapons of Math Destruction: How Big Data Increases Inequality and Threatens Democracy*. Reprint edition. New York: Crown.

Onyesoh, Joy, Madeleine Rees, and Catia C. Confortini. 2020. 'Feminist Challenges to the Co-Optation of WPS: A Conversation with Joy Onyesoh and Madeleine Rees'. In *New Directions in Women, Peace and Security*, edited by Soumita Basu, Paul Kirby, and Laura J. Shepherd. Bristol: Policy Press, pp 233–245.

Oracle. nd. 'What Is Big Data?'. www.oracle.com/big-data/what-is-big-data/ (accessed 24 March 2021).

OSESGY. 2020a. 'Cutting-Edge Tech in the Service of Inclusive Peace in Yemen'. *OSESGY.* https://osesgy.unmissions.org/cutting-edge-tech-service-inclusive-peace-yemen (accessed 20 January 2022).

OSESGY. 2020b. 'UN Special Envoy's Office for Yemen Concludes First Online Mass Consultations'. *OSESGY.* https://osesgy.unmissions.org/un-special-envoy%E2%80%99s-office-yemen-concludes-first-online-mass-consultations (accessed 21 January 2022).

Papadamou, Kostantinos, Savvas Zannettou, Jeremy Blackburn, Emiliano De Cristofaro, Gianluca Stringhini and Michael Sirivianos. 2020. 'Understanding the Incel Community on YouTube'. https://arxiv.org/pdf/2001.08293.pdf (accessed 4 November 2022).

Paprocki, Kasia. 2016. '"Selling Our Own Skin": Social Dispossession through Microcredit in Rural Bangladesh'. *Geoforum* 74: 29–38.

Parashar, Swati. 2016. 'Feminism and Postcolonialism: (En)Gendering Encounters'. *Postcolonial Studies* 19(4): 371–377.

Parashar, Swati. 2019. 'The WPS Agenda: A Post-Colonial Critique'. In *The Oxford Handbook of Women, Peace, and Security*, edited by Jacqui True and Sara E. Davies. Oxford: Oxford University Press. www.oxfordhandbooks.com/view/10.1093/oxfordhb/9780190638276.001.0001/oxfordhb-9780190638276-e-46 (accessed 27 September 2020).

Parisi, Laura. 2020. 'Canada's New Feminist International Assistance Policy: Business as Usual?'. *Foreign Policy Analysis* 16(2): 163–180.

Parker, Kim. 2021. 'What's behind the Growing Gap between Men and Women in College Completion?' *Pew Research Center*. www.pewresearch.org/fact-tank/2021/11/08/whats-behind-the-growing-gap-between-men-and-women-in-college-completion/ (accessed 3 March 2022).

Peacock, Donna, and Alastair Irons. 2017. 'Gender Inequalities in Cybersecurity: Exploring the Gender Gap in Opportunities and Progression'. *International Journal of Gender, Science, and Technology* 9(1): 25–44.

Pearson, Elizabeth. 2018. 'Online as the New Frontline: Affect, Gender, and ISIS-Take-Down on Social Media'. *Studies in Conflict & Terrorism* 41(11): 850–874.

Perez Arguello, Maria Fernandez, and Isabel Kennon. 2020. 'Nicaragua's Response to COVID-19 Endangers Not Only Its Own People, but Also Its Neighbors'. *Atlantic Council*. www.atlanticcouncil.org/blogs/new-atlanticist/nicaraguas-response-to-covid-19-endangers-not-only-its-own-people-but-also-its-neighbors/ (accessed 25 March 2021).

Perlroth, Nicole. 2016. 'How Spy Tech Firms Let Governments See Everything on a Smartphone'. *The New York Times*. www.nytimes.com/2016/09/03/technology/nso-group-how-spy-tech-firms-let-governments-see-everything-on-a-smartphone.html (accessed 10 February 2022).

Perlroth, Nicole. 2021a. *This Is How They Tell Me the World Ends: The Cyberweapons Arms Race*. London: Bloomsbury Publishing.

Perlroth, Nicole. 2021b. 'TikTok Users and Coders Flood Texas Abortion Site With Fake Tips'. *The New York Times*. www.nytimes.com/2021/09/03/technology/texas-abortion-law-website-tiktok.html (accessed 1 September 2022).

Perrigo, Billy. 2020. 'Supreme Court Orders Review of Internet Shutdown in Kashmir'. *Time.* https://time.com/5762751/internet-kashmir-supreme-court/ (accessed 31 March 2021).

Perry, John. 2020. 'NicaNotes: Covid-19: On the Decline in Nicaragua as Its Critics Fall Silent'. *Alliance for Global Justice.* https://afgj.org/nicanotes-covid-19-on-the-decline-in-nicaragua-as-its-critics-fall-silent (accessed 25 March 2021).

Petersen, J.K. 2012. *Introduction to Surveillance Studies.* Boca Raton, FL: Taylor & Francis.

Peterson, V. Spike. 1992. 'Transgressing Boundaries: Theories of Knowledge, Gender, and International Relations'. *Journal of International Studies* 21(2): 183–206.

Peterson, V. Spike. 2003. *A Critical Rewriting of Global Political Economy: Integrating Reproductive, Productive and Virtual Economies.* New York: Routledge.

Peterson, V. Spike. 2010. 'Informalization, Inequalities and Global Insecurities'. *International Studies Review* 12(2): 244–270.

Peto, Andrea, and Weronika Grzebalska. 2016. 'How Hungary and Poland Have Silenced Women and Stifled Human Rights'. *The Conversation.* http://theconversation.com/how-hungary-and-poland-have-silenced-women-and-stifled-human-rights-66743 (accessed 11 February 2022).

Petrozziello, Allison J. 2011. 'Feminised Financial Flows: How Gender Affects Remittances in Honduran–US Transnational Families'. *Gender & Development* 19(1): 53–67.

Petts, Richard J., Daniel L. Carlson, and Joanna R. Pepin. 2021. 'A Gendered Pandemic: Childcare, Homeschooling, and Parents' Employment during COVID-19'. *Gender, Work & Organization* 28(S2): 515–534.

Phelan, Alexandra. 2017. 'Insurgent Feminism and Colombia's New Peace'. *Australian Institute of International Affairs.* www.internationalaffairs.org.au/australianoutlook/insurgent-feminism-colombias-new-peace/ (accessed 21 June 2021).

Pineda, Wilfredo. 2021. 'Salvador Street Protest Breaks out against Bitcoin Adoption'. *Reuters.* www.reuters.com/world/americas/salvador-street-protest-breaks-out-against-bitcoin-adoption-2021-09-07/ (accessed 8 February 2022).

Pion-Berlin, David, and Miguel Carreras. 2017. 'Armed Forces, Police and Crime-Fighting in Latin America'. *Journal of Politics in Latin America* 9(3): 3–26.

Pirus, Benjamin. 2019. 'Why Stellar Is Giving Away $124 Million In Cryptocurrency'. *Forbes.* www.forbes.com/sites/benjaminpirus/2019/09/09/why-stellar-is-giving-away-124-million-in-cryptocurrency/ (accessed 14 August 2020).

Pittman, Julie. 2020. 'Released into Shackles: The Rise of Immigrant E-Carceration'. *California Law Review* 108(2).

Ponder, Crissinda. 2020. 'Survey: Nearly Half of Americans Working From Home'. *LendingTree*. www.lendingtree.com/home/mortgage/lendingtree-survey-nearly-half-of-americans-working-from-home/ (accessed 27 March 2021).

Popper, Nathaniel. 2021. 'Lost Passwords Lock Millionaires Out of Their Bitcoin Fortunes'. *The New York Times*. www.nytimes.com/2021/01/12/technology/bitcoin-passwords-wallets-fortunes.html (accessed 25 January 2021).

Poster, Winifred R. 2018. 'Cybersecurity Needs Women'. *Nature* 555(7698): 577–580.

Powell, Catherine, and Maiya Moncino. 2018. 'Cryptocurrencies for Change: Why We Need Women on the Blockchain'. *Council on Foreign Relations*. www.cfr.org/blog/cryptocurrencies-change-why-we-need-women-blockchain (accessed 29 July 2020).

Prasad, Revati. 2018. 'Ascendant India, Digital India: How Net Neutrality Advocates Defeated Facebook's Free Basics'. *Media, Culture & Society* 40(3): 415–431.

Priest, Dana, Craig Timberg, and Souad Mekhennet. 2021. 'Private Israeli Spyware Used to Hack Cellphones of Journalists, Activists Worldwide'. *Washington Post*. www.washingtonpost.com/investigations/interactive/2021/nso-spyware-pegasus-cellphones/ (accessed 12 February 2022).

Pringle, Ramona. 2018. 'Send Us Your Naked Photos to Help Block Revenge Porn, Facebook Invites Users'. *CBC*. www.cbc.ca/news/technology/facebook-revenge-porn-measures-1.4687659 (accessed 1 April 2021).

Prusty, Narayan. 2017. *Building Blockchain Projects*. Birmingham: Packt Publishing.

Puar, Jasbir K. 2007. *Terrorist Assemblages*. Durham, NC: Duke University Press.

Pugliese, Joseph. 2012. *Biometrics: Bodies, Technologies, Biopolitics*. London: Taylor & Francis.

Rabiul Karim, K.M., and Chi Kong Law. 2013. 'Gender Ideology, Microcredit Participation and Women's Status in Rural Bangladesh'. *International Journal of Sociology and Social Policy* 33(1/2): 45–62.

Rafail, Patrick, and Isaac Freitas. 2019. 'Grievance Articulation and Community Reactions in the Men's Rights Movement Online'. *Social Media + Society* 5(2): 2056305119841387.

Randall, Vicky. 2002. 'Feminism'. In *Theory and Methods in Political Science*, edited by David Marsh and Gerry Stoker. New York: Palgrave Macmillan, pp 109–130.

Raw, Louise. 2018. 'The Sexual Assault Faced by the Suffragettes'. *Politics.co.uk*. www.politics.co.uk/blog/2018/02/08/the-sexual-assault-faced-by-the-suffragettes/ (accessed 20 June 2021).

Reiter, Dan. 2015. 'Gender in IR, Now at the Cutting Edge'. *Duck of Minerva*. https://duckofminerva.com/2015/04/gender-in-ir-now-at-the-cutting-edge.html (accessed 7 April 2020).

Republic of Estonia. nd. 'What Is E-Residency'. *e-Residency*. www.e-resident.gov.ee/ (accessed 8 February 2022).

Republic of Namibia. 2019. *Namibia National Action Plan on Women Peace and Security*. Windhoek: Republic of Namibia. www.peacewomen.org/sites/default/files/Namibia%20NAP%20(2019-2024).pdf (accessed 4 November 2022).

Reuters. 2014. 'North Korea Slams U.S. Movie on Leader Assassination Plot'. *Reuters*. www.reuters.com/article/northkorea-usa-movie-idUSL4N0P61AY20140625 (accessed 15 February 2021).

Rid, Thomas. 2013. *Cyber War Will Not Take Place*. Oxford: Oxford University Press. http://ebookcentral.proquest.com/lib/troy/detail.action?docID=4704143 (accessed 2 February 2022).

Ripple. 2018. 'RippleNet Now Reaches 40 Countries Improving Remittances and SME Payments'. *Ripple*. https://ripple.com/insights/ripplenet-expands-to-40-countries-improving-remittances-and-sme-payments/ (accessed 13 August 2020).

Robertson, Danielle, and Mena Ayazi. 2019. 'How Women Are Using Technology to Advance Gender Equality and Peace'. *United States Institute of Peace*. www.usip.org/publications/2019/07/how-women-are-using-technology-advance-gender-equality-and-peace (accessed 21 January 2022).

Rodima-Taylor, Daivi, and William W. Grimes. 2019a. 'International Remittance Rails as Infrastructures: Embeddedness, Innovation, and Financial Access in Developing Economies'. *Review of International Political Economy* 26(5): 839–862.

Rodima-Taylor, Daivi, and William W. Grimes. 2019b. 'Virtualizing Diaspora: New Digital Technologies in the Emerging Transnational Space'. *Global Networks* 19(3): 349–370.

Roizenblatt, Roberto, Paulo Schor, Fabio Dante, Jaime Roizenblatt and Rubens Belfort, Jr. 2004. 'Iris Recognition as a Biometric Method after Cataract Surgery'. *Biomedical Engineering Online* 3: 2.

Romano, Aja. 2018. 'Facebook's Plan to Stop Revenge Porn May Be Even Creepier than Revenge Porn'. *Vox*. www.vox.com/2018/5/23/17382024/facebook-revenge-porn-prevention (accessed 1 April 2021).

Rome, Emily. 2019. 'How Bitcoin Can Help Bridge Afghanistan's Gender Gap'. *Inverse*. www.inverse.com/innovation/57129-fereshteh-forough-afghanistan-bitcoin (accessed 10 August 2020).

Romm, Tony, and Elizabeth Dwoskin. 2021. 'Twitter Purged More than 70,000 Accounts Affiliated with QAnon Following Capitol Riot'. *Washington Post*. www.washingtonpost.com/technology/2021/01/11/trump-twitter-ban/ (accessed 1 April 2021).

Rondón, Manuel Alejandro Rodríguez. 2017. 'La ideología de género como exceso: Pánico moral y decisión ética en la política colombiana'. *Sexualidad, Salud y Sociedad (Rio de Janeiro)* 27: 128–148.

Rose Taylor, Sara. 2020. 'UN Women's Feminist Engagement with Governance by Indicators in the Millennium and Sustainable Development Goals'. *Global Social Policy* 20(3): 352–366.

Rosen, Christopher. 2020. 'John Oliver Roasts India's Largest Streamer for Disney Censorship'. *Vanity Fair*. www.vanityfair.com/hollywood/2020/03/john-oliver-hotstar-india-disney-censorship (accessed 15 November 2021).

Rothermel, Ann-Kathrin. 2020. 'Gender in the United Nations' Agenda on Preventing and Countering Violent Extremism'. *International Feminist Journal of Politics* 22(5): 720–741.

Roundy, Kevin A., Paula Barmaimon Mendelberg, Nicola Dell, Damon McCoy, Daniel Nissani, Thomas Ristenpart et al. 2020. 'The Many Kinds of Creepware Used for Interpersonal Attacks'. *2020 IEEE Symposium on Security and Privacy (SP)* 1: 626–643.

Runyan, Anne Sisson, and V. Spike Peterson. 2013. *Global Gender Issues in the New Millennium*. Fourth edition. Boulder: Westview Press.

Rydzak, Jan. 2019. *Of Blackouts and Bandhs: The Strategy and Structure of Disconnected Protest in India*. SSRN Scholarly Paper. Rochester: Social Science Research Network. https://papers.ssrn.com/abstract=3330413 (accessed 5 February 2022).

Rydzak, Jan. 2020. *Disconnected: A Human Rights-based Approach to Network Disruption*. Washington, DC: Global Network Initiative. https://globalnetworkinitiative.org/disconnected-human-rights-network-disruptions/ (accessed 4 November 2022).

Sambasivan, Nithya, Amna Batool, Nova Ahmed, Tara Matthews, Kurt Thomas, Laura Sanely Gaytán-Lugo et al. 2019. '"They Don't Leave Us Alone Anywhere We Go": Gender and Digital Abuse in South Asia'. CHI, 4–9 May, Glasgow. www.classes.cs.uchicago.edu/archive/2020/winter/20370-1/readings/GenderSouthAsia.pdf (accessed 4 November 2022).

Sambasivan, Nithya, Erin Arnesen, Ben Hutchinson, Tulsee Doshi and Vinodkumar Prabhakaran. 2021. 'Re-Imagining Algorithmic Fairness in India and Beyond'. https://arxiv.org/pdf/2101.09995.pdf (accessed 31 March 2021).

Sandino Palmera, Victoria. 2016. 'El Feminismo en las FARC-EP'. *Mujer Fariana*. www.mujerfariana.org/vision/663-el-feminismo-en-las-farc-ep.html (accessed 3 June 2020).

Sanger, David E., David D. Kirkpatrick, and Nicole Perlroth. 2017. 'The World Once Laughed at North Korean Cyberpower. No More'. *The New York Times*. www.nytimes.com/2017/10/15/world/asia/north-korea-hacking-cyber-sony.html (accessed 9 February 2021).

Santiago, Irene. 2015. *The Participation of Women in the Mindanao Peace Process*. New York: UN Women. https://wps.unwomen.org/pdf/research/Santiago.pdf (accessed 4 November 2022).

Saujani, Reshma. 2021. 'Disrupting Tech's Growing Gender Gap'. Presented at the Qualtrics/Girls Who Code Forum, 27 January.

Schmidt, Samantha. 2019. 'Federal Judge Awards over $700,000 to Former American University Student Targeted in Neo-Nazi "Troll Storm"'. *Washington Post*. www.washingtonpost.com/local/education/federal-judge-awards-700000-to-former-american-university-student-targeted-in-neo-nazi-troll-storm/2019/08/10/f73dca84-bb7f-11e9-bad6-609f75bfd97f_story.html (accessed 19 January 2021).

Scott-Railton, John, Bill Marczak, Paolo Nigro Herrero, Bahr Abdul Razzak, Noura Al-Jizawi, Salvatore Solimano et al. 2022. *Project Torogoz: Extensive Hacking of Media & Civil Society in El Salvador with Pegasus Spyware*. University of Toronto. https://citizenlab.ca/2022/01/project-torogoz-extensive-hacking-media-civil-society-el-salvador-pegasus-spyware/ (accessed 12 February 2022).

Securities and Exchange Commission. 2020. 'SEC Charges Ripple and Two Executives with Conducting $1.3 Billion Unregistered Securities Offering'. *US Securities and Exchange Commission*. www.sec.gov/news/press-release/2020-338 (accessed 22 January 2021).

Shah, Angela. 2012. 'In Afghanistan, Roya Mahboob Connects Girls With Computers'. *The Daily Beast*. www.thedailybeast.com/articles/2012/09/01/in-afghanistan-roya-mahboob-connects-girls-with-computers (accessed 25 January 2021).

Shantha, Sukanya. 2021. 'Presence of Over 60 Women in Leaked List Highlights "Bodily Violation" Posed by Spyware'. *The Wire*. https://thewire.in/women/pegasus-project-women-surveillance (accessed 12 February 2022).

Sharpe, Matthew. 2020. 'The Hate Matrix of Online Gaming'. *GNET*. https://gnet-research.org/2020/11/05/the-hate-matrix-of-online-gaming/ (accessed 13 January 2021).

Sheng, Jie, Joseph Amankwah-Amoah, Zaheer Khan, and Xiaojun Wang. 2020. 'COVID-19 Pandemic in the New Era of Big Data Analytics: Methodological Innovations and Future Research Directions'. *British Journal of Management*. https://onlinelibrary.wiley.com/doi/abs/10.1111/1467-8551.12441 (accessed 24 March 2021).

Shepherd, Laura. 2008. 'Power and Authority in the Production of United Nations Security Council Resolution 1325'. *International Studies Quarterly* 52(2): 383–404.

Shepherd, Laura J. 2016. 'Making War Safe for Women? National Action Plans and the Militarisation of the Women, Peace and Security Agenda'. *International Political Science Review* 37(3): 324–335.

Shepherd, Laura J. 2021. *Narrating the Women, Peace and Security Agenda: Logics of Global Governance*. New York: Oxford University Press.

Shere, Anjuli R.K., and Jason Nurse. 2020. 'Police Surveillance of Black Lives Matter Shows the Danger Technology Poses to Democracy'. *The Conversation*. http://theconversation.com/police-surveillance-of-black-lives-matter-shows-the-danger-technology-poses-to-democracy-142194 (accessed 11 February 2022).

Sherman, Christopher. 2021. 'El Salvador Government Negotiated with Gangs'. *AP News*. https://apnews.com/article/nayib-bukele-el-salvador-gangs-c378285a36d55c18f741c3f65892f801 (accessed 8 February 2022).

Silver, Charles. 2020. 'Council Post: What Is Web 3.0?' *Forbes*. www.forbes.com/sites/forbestechcouncil/2020/01/06/what-is-web-3-0/ (accessed 15 February 2021).

Šimonovic, Dubravka. 2018. *Report of the Special Rapporteur on Violence against Women, Its Causes and Consequences on Online Violence against Women and Girls from a Human Rights Perspective*. New York: United Nations.

Simonte, Tom. 2019. 'Baidu Censors the Internet in China: So Do Microsoft and Apple'. *Wired*. www.wired.com/story/us-companies-help-censor-internet-china/ (accessed 15 November 2021).

Singer, Peter W. 2007. 'The Dark Truth about Blackwater'. *Brookings*. www.brookings.edu/articles/the-dark-truth-about-blackwater/ (accessed 11 November 2021).

Singer, Peter W., and Allan Friedman. 2014. *Cybersecurity: What Everyone Needs to Know*. New York: Oxford University Press.

Singer, P.W., and Emerson T. Brooking. 2018. *LikeWar: The Weaponization of Social Media*. Boston, MA: Eamon Dolan/Houghton Mifflin Harcourt.

Sjoberg, Laura. 2009. 'Introduction to Security Studies: Feminist Contributions'. *Security Studies* 18(2): 183–213.

Sjoberg, Laura, Kelly Kadera, and Cameron Thies. 2018. 'Reevaluating Gender and IR Scholarship: Moving beyond Reiter's Dichotomies toward Effective Synergies'. *Journal of Conflict Resolution* 62(4): 848–870.

Smith, Andrea. 2015. 'Not-Seeing: State Surveillance, Settler Colonialism, and Gender Violence'. In *Feminist Surveillance Studies*, edited by Shoshana Magnet and Rachel E. Dubrofsky. Durham, NC: Duke University Press, pp 21–38.

Smith, Dorothy E. 1989. *The Everyday World As Problematic: A Feminist Sociology*. Boston: Northeastern University Press.

Smith, Gavin J.D. 2004. 'Behind the Screens: Examining Constructions of Deviance and Informal Practices among CCTV Control Room Operators in the UK'. *Surveillance & Society* 2(2/3). https://ojs.library.queensu.ca/index.php/surveillance-and-society/article/view/3384 (accessed 10 November 2021).

Smith, Gavin J.D. 2012. 'Surveillance Work(ers)'. In *Routledge Handbook of Surveillance Studies*, edited by Kirstie Ball, Kevin Haggerty, and David Lyon. Florence, SC: Taylor & Francis, pp 107–116.

Smith, Linda Tuhiwai. 2012. *Decolonizing Methodologies: Research and Indigenous Peoples*. 2nd edition. London: Zed Books.

Smith, Peter, and Cameron Sells. 2016. *Democracy in Latin America*. 3rd edition. New York: Oxford University Press.

SPLC. nd. 'Andrew Anglin'. *Southern Poverty Law Center*. www.splcenter.org/fighting-hate/extremist-files/individual/andrew-anglin (accessed 11 January 2021).

Stachowitsch, Saskia. 2015. 'Military Privatization as a Gendered Process'. In *Gender and Private Security in Global Politics*, edited by Maya Eichler. New York: Oxford University Press.

Stengel, Richard. 2019. 'The Untold Story of the Sony Hack'. *Vanity Fair*. www.vanityfair.com/news/2019/10/the-untold-story-of-the-sony-hack (accessed 15 February 2021).

Stern, Maria. 2017. 'Feminist Global Political Economy and Feminist Security Studies? The Politics of Delineating Subfields'. *Politics and Gender* 13(4): 727–733.

Stern, Maria, and Annick Wibben. 2014. 'A Decade of Feminist Security Studies Revisited'. *Security Dialogue* (Special Virtual Issue): 1–6.

Stoet, Gijsbert, and David C. Geary. 2020. 'Gender Differences in the Pathways to Higher Education'. *PNAS*. www.pnas.org/doi/abs/10.1073/pnas.2002861117 (accessed 3 March 2022).

Stoll, Christian, Lena Klaaßen, and Ulrich Gallersdörfer. 2019. 'The Carbon Footprint of Bitcoin'. *Joule* 3(7): 1647–1661.

Striegher, Jason-Leigh. 2015. 'Violent-Extremism: An Examination of a Definitional Dilemma'. In *Proceedings of the 8th Australian Security and Intelligence Conference*, Perth, Australia, pp 75–86. https://ro.ecu.edu.au/cgi/viewcontent.cgi?article=1046&context=asi (accessed 4 November 2022).

Strom, Kevin, Marcus Berzofsky, Bonnie Shook-Sa. Kellie Barrick, Crystal Daye, Nicole Horstmann et al. 2010. *The Private Security Industry: A Review of the Definitions, Available Data Sources, and Paths Moving Forward*. RTI International. www.ojp.gov/pdffiles1/bjs/grants/232781.pdf (accessed 4 November 2022).

Stryker, Susan, and Paisley Currah. 2014. 'General Editors' Introduction'. *TSQ: Transgender Studies Quarterly* 1(3): 303–307.

Suchi, Plangshak Musa. 2019. 'Investment in Security Forces and Human Development Challenges in Africa: Lessons from Nigeria's Experience'. *Africa Development* 44(1): 55–76.

Sylvester, Christine. 2010. 'Tensions in Feminist Security Studies'. *Security Dialogue* 41(6): 607–614.

Szekely, Ora. 2020. 'Fighting about Women: Ideologies of Gender in the Syrian Civil War'. *Journal of Global Security Studies* 5(3): 408–426.

Tapscott, Don, and Alex Tapscott. 2016. *Blockchain Revolution: How the Technology Behind Bitcoin Is Changing Money, Business, and the World*. New York: Portfolio.

Target, Sinclair. 2018. 'Whatever Happened to the Semantic Web?'. https://twobithistory.org/2018/05/27/semantic-web.html (accessed 15 February 2021).

TBS Report. 2020. 'BTRC Asks Mobile Operators to Stop Offering Free Social Media Services'. *The Business Standard*. www.tbsnews.net/bangladesh/telecom/btrc-asks-mobile-operators-stop-offering-free-social-media-services-107785 (accessed 31 March 2021).

Tech Against Terrorism. 2020. 'Tech Against Terrorism Mentorship'. www.techagainstterrorism.org/membership/tech-against-terrorism-mentorship/, https://www.techagainstterrorism.org/membership/tech-against-terrorism-mentorship/ (accessed 8 July 2021).

Tickner, J. Ann. 1997. 'You Just Don't Understand: Troubled Engagements Between Feminists and IR Theorists'. *International Studies Quarterly* 41(4): 611–632.

Tickner, J. Ann. 2001. *Gendering World Politics*. New York: Columbia University Press.

Tickner, J. Ann. 2006. 'Feminism Meets International Relations: Some Methodological Issues'. In *Feminist Methodologies for International Relations*, edited by Brooke A. Ackerly, Maria Stern, and Jacqui True. Cambridge: Cambridge University Press, pp 19–41.

Timberg, Craig, Drew Harwell, and Ellen Nakashima. 2021. 'Pegasus Spyware Used to Hack U.S. Diplomats Working Abroad'. *Washington Post*. www.washingtonpost.com/technology/2021/12/03/israel-nso-pegasus-hack-us-diplomats/ (accessed 12 February 2022).

Timberg, Craig, Cat Zakrzewski, and Joseph Menn. 2022. 'A New Iron Curtain Is Descending across Russia's Internet'. *Washington Post*. www.washingtonpost.com/technology/2022/03/04/russia-ukraine-internet-cogent-cutoff/ (accessed 25 April 2022).

Towns, Ann, and Birgitta Niklasson. 2017. 'Gender, International Status, and Ambassador Appointments'. *Foreign Policy Analysis* 13(3): 521–540.

Transparency International. 2019. *Citizens' Views and Experiences of Corruption*. Berlin: Transparency International.

Trisko Darden, Jessica, Alexis Henshaw, and Ora Szekely. 2019. *Insurgent Women: Female Combatants in Civil Wars*. 1st edition. Washington, DC: Georgetown University Press.

True, Jacqui. 2012. *The Political Economy of Violence against Women*. 1st edition. New York: Oxford University Press.

Tschantret, Joshua. 2018. 'Cleansing the Caliphate: Insurgent Violence against Sexual Minorities'. *International Studies Quarterly* 62(2): 260–273.

Tsoulis-Reay, Alexa. 2013. 'A Brief History of Revenge Porn'. *New York Magazine*. https://nymag.com/news/features/sex/revenge-porn-2013-7/ (accessed 15 February 2021).

Turner, Cory. 2014. 'Turnitin and the Debate Over Anti-Plagiarism Software'. *NPR*. www.npr.org/sections/ed/2014/08/25/340112848/turnitin-and-the-high-tech-plagiarism-debate (accessed 15 November 2021).

UIS/UNESCO. 2016. 'Gender Equality in Education'. http://uis.unesco.org/en/topic/gender-equality-education (accessed 26 March 2021).

UN Development Programme. 1994. *Human Development Report 1994: New Dimensions of Human Security*. New York: United Nations. http://hdr.undp.org/en/reports/global/hdr1994/ (accessed 5 December 2013).

UNDP. 2015. 'Millennium Development Goal 2'. *UNDP*. www.undp.org/content/undp/en/home/sdgoverview/mdg_goals/mdg2.html (accessed 26 March 2021).

UNDP. 2020. 'Gender Inequality Index (GII): Human Development Reports'. *United Nations Development Programme*. http://hdr.undp.org/en/content/gender-inequality-index-gii (accessed 29 March 2021).

Ungar, Mark. 2007. 'The Privatization of Citizen Security in Latin America: From Elite Guards to Neighborhood Vigilantes'. *Social Justice* 34(3/4 (109–110)): 20–37.

UN General Assembly. 2001. *Road Map toward the Implementation of the United Nations Millennium Declaration*. New York: United Nations. www.un.org/millenniumgoals/sgreport2001.pdf?OpenElement (accessed 4 November 2022).

United Nations. n.d. 'United Nations Millennium Development Goals: Education'. www.un.org/millenniumgoals/education.shtml (accessed 26 March 2021).

UNODC. 2018. 'Radicalization & Violent Extremism'. *UNODC/E4J University Module Series*. www.unodc.org (accessed 20 June 2021).

UN Office of Information and Communications Technology. 2018. *Blockchain: What Does It Mean for the UN?* New York: UN Office of Information and Communications Technology. https://unite.un.org/sites/unite.un.org/files/emerging-tech-series-blockchain.pdf&ved=2ahUKEwiBp_yNkrf2AhULn-AKHWgHBH8QFnoECBQQAQ&usg=AOvVaw17CC8RZuvrdPiHJ-UtmPiR (accessed 8 March 2022).

UN/UN Women. 2009. 'Reservations to CEDAW'. *Convention on the Elimination of All Forms of Discrimination Against Women*. www.un.org/womenwatch/daw/cedaw/reservations.htm (accessed 28 March 2021).

UN Women. 2018a. *The Empowerment of Women and Girls with Disabilities: Toward Full and Effective Participation and Gender Equality*. New York: UN Women. www.unwomen.org/sites/default/files/Headquarters/Attachments/Sections/Library/Publications/2018/Empowerment-of-women-and-girls-with-disabilities-en.pdf (accessed 4 November 2022).

UN Women. 2018b. *Turning Promises into Action: Gender Equality in the 2030 Agenda for Sustainable Development*. New York: UN Women. www.unwomen.org/sites/default/files/Headquarters/Attachments/Sections/Library/Publications/2018/SDG-report-Gender-equality-in-the-2030-Agenda-for-Sustainable-Development-2018-en.pdf (accessed 4 November 2022).

UN Women. 2020. *Online and ICT* Facilitated Violence against Women and Girls during COVID-19*. New York: UN Women. www.unwomen.org/-/media/headquarters/attachments/sections/library/publications/2020/brief-online-and-ict-facilitated-violence-against-women-and-girls-during-covid-19-en.pdf?la=en&vs=2519 (accessed 4 November 2022).

UN Women Jordan. 2021. *UN Women-WFP Blockchain Pilot Project for Cash Transfers in Refugee Camps*. New York: UN Women. https://reliefweb.int/sites/reliefweb.int/files/resources/un%20women-wfp%20blockchain%20pilot%20project%20for%20cash%20transfers%20in%20refugee%20camps%20jordan%20case%20study.pdf (accessed 4 November 2022).

UN Women, UNDP, WHO, IOM, UN HCR, UNODC, OCHA, UNFPA, and UNICEF. 2021. 'Inter-Agency Statement on Violence against Women and Girls in the Context of COVID-19'. *UN Women*. www.unwomen.org/en/news/stories/2020/6/statement-inter-agency-statement-on-violence-against-women-and-girls--in-the-context-of-covid-19 (accessed 1 February 2022).

US CSIA. nd 'What Is Cybersecurity?'. *Cybersecurity & Infrastructure Agency*. https://us-cert.cisa.gov/ncas/tips/ST04-001 (accessed 13 February 2021).

US Department of State. 2017. 'Merida Initiative'. *US Department of State*. https://2009-2017.state.gov/j/inl/merida/index.htm (accessed 16 November 2021).

Van Valkenburgh, Shawn P. 2021. 'Digesting the Red Pill: Masculinity and Neoliberalism in the Manosphere'. *Men and Masculinities* 24(1): 84–103.

Variyar, Mugdha. 2014. 'Islamic State Stones Two "Gay" Youths to Death in First Execution Over Homosexuality'. www.ibtimes.co.in/islamic-state-stones-two-gay-youths-death-first-execution-over-homosexuality-615199 (accessed 7 July 2021).

Vigna, Paul, and Michael Casey. 2015. *The Age of Cryptocurrency*. New York: St. Martin's Press.

Vigna, Paul, and Michael J. Casey. 2019. *The Truth Machine: The Blockchain and the Future of Everything*. Reprint edition. London: Picador.

Walby, Kevin, and Seantel Anaïs. 2015. 'Research Methods, Institutional Ethnography, and Feminist Surveillance Studies'. In *Feminist Surveillance Studies*, edited by Rachel E. Dubrofsky and Shoshana Magnet. Durham, NC: Duke University Press, pp 208–220.

Walker, Shaun, Stephanie Kirchgaessner, Nina Lakhani, and Michael Safi. 2021. 'Pegasus Project: Spyware Leak Suggests Lawyers and Activists at Risk across Globe'. *The Guardian*. www.theguardian.com/news/2021/jul/19/spyware-leak-suggests-lawyers-and-activists-at-risk-across-globe (accessed 10 February 2022).

Walt, Stephen M. 2010. 'Is the Cyber Threat Overblown?' *Foreign Policy*. https://foreignpolicy.com/2010/03/30/is-the-cyber-threat-overblown/ (accessed 3 February 2022).

Walt, Vivienne. 2021. 'Afghan Women, Banned from Education, Secretly Study Online'. *Time*. https://time.com/6108604/afghanistan-female-students-online/ (accessed 21 January 2022).

Walter, Maggie, and Chris Andersen. 2013. *Indigenous Statistics: A Quantitative Research Methodology*. 1st edition. Walnut Creek: Routledge.

Walter, Maggie, and Michele Suina. 2019. 'Indigenous Data, Indigenous Methodologies and Indigenous Data Sovereignty'. *International Journal of Social Research Methodology* 22(3): 233–243.

Wamsley, Laurel. 2020. 'Fired Florida Data Scientist Launches a Coronavirus Dashboard of Her Own'. *NPR.org*. www.npr.org/2020/06/14/876584284/fired-florida-data-scientist-launches-a-coronavirus-dashboard-of-her-own (accessed 25 March 2021).

Wang, Bin, and Catherine Driscoll. 2019. 'Chinese Feminists on Social Media: Articulating Different Voices, Building Strategic Alliances'. *Continuum* 33(1): 1–15.

Wang, Di, and Sida Liu. 2020. 'Performing Artivism: Feminists, Lawyers, and Online Legal Mobilization in China'. *Law and Social Inquiry* 45(3): 678–705.

Wang, Qi. 2018. 'Young Feminist Activists in Present-Day China: A New Feminist Generation?' *China Perspectives* 3: 59–68.

Waters, Richard. 2020. 'With $16bn in Cryptocurrency, Ripple Attempts a Reset'. www.ft.com/content/7d9c934f-3840-4285-96a7-4bdf7fee9286 (accessed 13 August 2020).

Watkins, Marley W. 2018. 'Exploratory Factor Analysis: A Guide to Best Practice'. *Journal of Black Psychology* 44(3): 219–246.

Watson, James, Amanda Adler, Ambrose Agweyu, Dani Prieto-Alhambra, Ravi Amaravadi, Juan-Manuel Anaya et al. 2020. 'Open Letter to MR Mehra, SS Desai, F Ruschitzka, and AN Patel'. https://statmodeling.stat.columbia.edu/wp-content/uploads/2020/05/Open-Letter-the-statistical-analysis-and-data-integrity-of-Mehra-et-al_Final-1.pdf (accessed 25 March 2021).

Weldon, S. Laurel. 2006. 'Inclusion and Understanding: A Collective Methodology for Feminist International Relations'. In *Feminist Methodologies for International Relations*, edited by Brooke A. Ackerly, Maria Stern, and Jacqui True. Cambridge: Cambridge University Press, pp 62–88.

WFP. 2020a. 'Building Blocks: WFP Innovation'. *World Food Programme*. https://innovation.wfp.org/project/building-blocks (accessed 26 January 2021).

WFP. 2020b. 'How Blockchain Is Helping WFP's Fight against Coronavirus in Bangladesh'. *Medium.com*. https://medium.com/world-food-programme-insight/how-blockchain-is-helping-wfps-fight-against-covid-19-in-bangladesh-d2b466a8becf (accessed 25 January 2021).

Wiarda, Howard, and Hilary Collins. 2011. *Constitutional Coups? Military Interventions in Latin America*. Washington, DC: Center for Strategic and International Studies.

Wichterich, Christa. 2017. 'Microcredits, Returns, and Gender: Of Reliable Poor Women and Financial Inclusion in South Asia'. In *Work, Institutions and Sustainable Livelihood: Issues and Challenges of Transformation*, edited by Virginius Xaxa, Debdulal Saha, and Rajdeep Singha. New York: Springer, pp 275–302.

Wilcox, Lauren. 2009. 'Gendering the Cult of the Offensive'. *Security Studies* 18(2): 214–240.

Wile, Rob. 2013. '927 People Own Half of the Bitcoins'. *Business Insider*. www.businessinsider.com/927-people-own-half-of-the-bitcoins-2013-12 (accessed 30 July 2020).

Williams, Maxine. 2014. 'Building a More Diverse Facebook'. *About Facebook*. https://about.fb.com/news/2014/06/building-a-more-diverse-facebook/ (accessed 29 March 2021).

Williams, Suzanne. 2002. 'Conflicts of Interest: Gender in Oxfam's Emergency Response'. In *The Postwar Moment: Militaries, Masculinities, and International Peacekeeping*, edited by Cynthia Cockburn and Dubravka Zarkov. London: Lawrence & Wishart, pp 85–102.

Williamson, John. 1993. 'Democracy and the "Washington Consensus"'. *World Development* 21(8): 1329–1336.

Winterbotham, Emily. 2018. 'Do Mothers Know Best? How Assumptions Harm CVE'. *Institute for Global Change*. https://institute.global/policy/do-mothers-know-best-how-assumptions-harm-cve (accessed 10 December 2020).

Witting-Acuesa, Mary Koren Apas, and Primitivo III Cabanes Ragandang. 2021. 'Young Peacebuilders' Voices: An Introductory Chapter'. In *Youth, Peacebuilding, and Sustainability: Connecting Theory to Practice*. np: Seeds for Mindanao's Advocacy and Youth Leadership (SMAYL), pp 1–18. http://smayl.org/wp-content/uploads/2022/01/SMAYL-Book-Final-1.pdf (accessed 4 November 2022).

WomanStats. nd. 'The WomanStats Project'. www.womanstats.org/about overview.html (accessed 6 April 2020).

Women's Media Center. nd. 'Online Abuse 101'. https://womensmediacenter.com/speech-project/online-abuse-101 (accessed 12 November 2020).

Women's Peace and Security in the Digital Age. 2021. www.youtube.com/watch?v=VMgnp2livv4 (accessed 20 January 2022).

Wood, Rachel Godfrey. 2009. *Understanding Colombia's False Positives.* Oxford: Oxford Transitional Justice Working Paper Series.

Wood, Reed M., and Jakana L. Thomas. 2017. 'Women on the Frontline: Rebel Group Ideology and Women's Participation in Violent Rebellion'. *Journal of Peace Research* 54(1): 31–46.

Woodlock, Delanie. 2017. 'The Abuse of Technology in Domestic Violence and Stalking'. *Violence Against Women* 23(5): 584–602.

World Bank. 2008. *Finance for All? Policies and Pitfalls in Expanding Access.* Washington, DC: The World Bank.

World Bank. 2012. 'Data: The World Bank'. *The World Bank.* http://data.worldbank.org/ (accessed 1 August 2012).

World Bank. 2019. 'Record High Remittances Sent Globally in 2018'. *World Bank.* www.worldbank.org/en/news/press-release/2019/04/08/record-high-remittances-sent-globally-in-2018 (accessed 27 January 2021).

World Bank. 2020. 'World Bank Predicts Sharpest Decline of Remittances in Recent History'. *World Bank.* www.worldbank.org/en/news/press-release/2020/04/22/world-bank-predicts-sharpest-decline-of-remittances-in-recent-history (accessed 13 August 2020).

World Economic Forum. 2020. *Global Gender Gap Report 2020.* Insight Report. Geneva: World Economic Forum. www3.weforum.org/docs/WEF_GGGR_2020.pdf (accessed 29 March 2021).

World Wide Web Foundation. 2016. *Women's Rights Online Report Card: India.* Washington, DC: World Wide Web Foundation. http://webfoundation.org/docs/2016/09/WF_GR_India.pdf (accessed 30 March 2021).

World Wide Web Foundation. 2020a. *Women's Rights Online Report Card: Bangladesh.* Washington, DC: World Wide Web Foundation. http://webfoundation.org/docs/2020/09/Digital-Gender-Audit-Scorecard-Bangladesh-Final-Sept-2020.pdf (accessed 30 March 2021).

World Wide Web Foundation. 2020b. *Women's Rights Online Report Cards.* Washington, DC: World Wide Web Foundation. https://webfoundation.org/research/digital-gender-gap-audit/ (accessed 4 November 2022).

Wright, Hannah. 2020. '"Masculinities Perspectives": Advancing a Radical Women, Peace, and Security Agenda?' *International Feminist Journal of Politics* 22(5): 652–674.

Wu, Jun, Jian Wang, Stephen Nicholas, Elizabeth Maitland and Qiuyan Fan. 2020. 'Application of Big Data Technology for COVID-19 Prevention and Control in China: Lessons and Recommendations'. *Journal of Medical Internet Research* 22(10): e21980.

WVS Association. 2020. 'World Values Survey'. www.worldvaluessurvey.org/wvs.jsp (accessed 1 April 2021).

Wylie, Ian. 2012. 'Schools Have the Final Word on Plagiarism'. *Financial Times*. www.ft.com/content/97a2c816-57ca-11e1-ae89-00144feabdc0 (accessed 15 November 2021).

Ymous, Anon, Katta Spiel, Os Keyes, Rua M. Williams, Judith Good, Eva Hornecker et al. 2020. '"I Am Just Terrified of My Future": Epistemic Violence in Disability Related Technology Research'. In *Extended Abstracts of the 2020 CHI Conference on Human Factors in Computing Systems*. New York: Association for Computing Machinery, pp 1–16.

Zalewski, Marysia. 2006. 'Distracted Reflections on the Production, Narration, and Refusal of Feminist Knowledge in International Relations'. In *Feminist Methodologies for International Relations*, edited by Brooke A. Ackerly, Maria Stern, and Jacqui True. Cambridge: Cambridge University Press, pp 42–61.

Zia, Ather. 2020. 'Listening Through the Silence in Kashmir'. *Adi magazine*. https://adimagazine.com/articles/listening-through-the-silence/ (accessed 5 February 2022).

Index

37Coins 136–138
4chan 75, 79
8chan 79
8kun 75, 79

A

abortion 148, 160
Afghanistan
  biometric data and 147
  cryptocurrency use 139–140, 147
  Taliban takeover of (2021) 109–110, 147
  US presence in 90, 147
al-Hathloul, Loujain 98
algorithmic bias 52, 61, 95–96
algorithms 69, 117
Amazon 43, 92, 153, 155
Artificial intelligence (AI)
  algorithmic bias and 43–44
  facial recognition and 95–96
  gig work and 92–93
  peacebuilding applications 110
  surveillance and 92
Australia 161–162
Azerbaijan 97, 99

B

Bangladesh
  digital gender gap 46, 51–52, 54
  digital rights advocacy 56–57
  National Action Plan on Women, Peace, and Security 58
Biden, Joseph 81–82
biometrics 23, 95, 143, 147, 152, 165
Bitcoin
  Afghanistan 140–141
  cybercrime and 125
  development of 127–128, 164
  El Salvador 147–148
  extremist use of 81, 84
  masculinity and 134
  remittances and 136–137
  women and 134
  see also cryptocurrency

blockchain
  activism and 122–123, 143
  archival uses 149, 165
  defined 127
  international organizations and 132–133
  relief work and 142–143
  remittances and 138
  security concerns 145
  women and 43, 126
Brazil 154
Bukele, Nayib 147–148, 165
Burundi 91

C

Canada
  cybersecurity strategy of 164
  incel movement in 69, 73
  indigenous peoples in 95, 115
capacity-building
  big data and 17–18, 121, 124, 40
  cybersecurity and 58, 86, 119
  non-governmental organizations and 121
carceral technology 153–154
censorship
  authoritarianism and 92, 96–97, 143, 149
  conspiracy theories and 78, 85
  ethnic minorities and 52–53
  self-censorship 105, 112
China
  blockchain 143
  censorship 92, 97
  digital currency 164
  disinformation 82, 100
  feminist and queer activism 96–97
civil society
  advocacy and 58, 61, 119–120, 122, 161
  big data and 19, 24
  cryptocurrency and 145
  surveillance and 99–100, 148
Colombia
  cryptocurrency use 137, 165
  false positives scandal 89–90
  LGBTQI+ rights 107
  peacebuilding 106–107

INDEX

colonialism 57, 95
conspiracy theories
   COVID-19 82, 84
   gender ideology 106–107
   election-related 75–76, 80
   manosphere and 69, 78–79, 80–84
   women and 162
content moderation 78, 92–93, 118, 155
Convention on the Elimination of All Forms of Discrimination Against Women (CEDAW) 27–29
corruption 89, 99, 119
counterterrorism 90, 98
COVID-19
   conspiracies 82
   data 15–16
   labour and 43–44, 154
   surveillance and 119
   technology and 105, 107, 110, 122–123, 155
   violence against women and 6, 48, 54, 149
critical data studies 21, 23–24, 38–39, 150
crowdfunding 81, 109
crowdsourcing 40
cryptocurrency
   Afghanistan 140–141
   cybercrime and 125–126
   defined 127–129, 164
   El Salvador 148
   extremism and 81
   financial inclusion and 131–133
   remittances and 136–139
   social media and 78
   women and 43, 122, 134–135
   see also Bitcoin; Dash; Ripple
cyberattacks 1–2, 101, 142, 152
cyberbullying 59
cyberconflict 153
cybercrime 1, 58, 61, 120, 151–152
cybersecurity
   cyberwar and 152–153
   defined 5, 7
   national strategies on 164
   policing and 101
   women in 3
   Women, Peace, and Security and 52, 58
cyberstalking 48, 54, 94
cyberwar 152–153, 156

D

Dash 138–139, 165
data collection
   COVID-19 and 15
   critical perspectives on 23–24, 39
   international organizations and 17–18
   surveillance and 95, 121
data portability 150, 166
decentralized finance 126, 130–132, 139
decentralized web 3, 122, 142–146, 159
deepfakes 6, 60

digital nomads 154
digital rights 56–58
disability
   assistive technology 57
   experiences with 155–156
   omission from gender equality measures 36
   targeting of 44, 49, 52, 54, 75
Discord 75, 79, 80
disinformation
   COVID-19 and 82
   gender ideology and 106–107
   moderation of 78, 121–122
   targeting of women and 97–100
Dlive 78
dogpiling 66, 162
domestic violence
   China 97
   lack of data about 19
   men's rights activists and 68
   South Asia 54–55
   technology and 44, 49–50, 60
doxing 58, 76, 112

E

El Salvador 99–100, 147–148
Estonia 154
ethnicity
   data and 23, 25
   intersectionality and 36, 44
   persecution and 71
   surveillance and 95, 101
   see also racial issues
European Union 166
extremism
   conspiracies and 162
   defined 65–66
   efforts to counter 86
   gender-based 67–70

F

Facebook
   activism and 108–109, 116
   boycott of 118
   counterterrorism efforts 85
   Free Basics 57, 161
   Islamic State and 72
   revenge porn and 162
   surveillance and 92
facial recognition 16, 92, 95–96, 162
feminist international relations 3–5, 8–9, 21–23, 38, 93–96, 150–151
feminist security studies 2–4, 21, 93–95, 155–156
fertility tracking 157
financial inclusion 27, 126–127, 130–133
forums 55, 69, 79–80

G

Gab 78, 82
gaming industry 121

gender mainstreaming
  data and 13
  policy 40, 145
  security forces 91
  technology industry 112, 122
Georgetown Institute for Women, Peace, and Security (GIWPS) 22
  gender gap 45–46, 50–54
Germany 97
gig labour 92–93, 113, 154–155
GoFundMe 109
Google 43, 52, 92, 153, 159

H

hacking 1–2, 99–101, 125, 163
harassment
  activism and 108, 112–114, 188
  cryptocurrency and 134
  gender-based 6, 43, 48–50, 75
  LGBTQI+ communities 54, 107
  offline 67
  political figures and 76–83
  spyware and 99
  see also dogpiling
Harris, Kamala 76, 82
hashing 60, 161
hate speech 84, 108, 118
homophobic violence 48, 72–73, 74, 83, 162
Hong Kong 143
human rights defenders 97, 99, 109, 119
human security 7

I

Identitarian 69, 74–75, 78
Incels 69–70, 73–75, 79–80, 122
India
  digital rights and 56–58
  gender gaps and 51–52
  gig work 92, 113–114
  internet shutdowns and 52–53
  LGBTQI+ community 54
  microfinance 132
  surveillance 95, 99, 115
  tech companies and 118
indigenous communities
  Canada 115
  health of 36
  data and 8, 23–24, 38–39
  peacebuilding and 108
  surveillance of 95, 99
informed consent 54–55, 127, 144–145
Instagram 107–108
institutional ethnography 24, 39, 144
internet access
  Afghanistan 110
  gender and 45–47
  Islamic State 71
  North Korea 2, 101
  poverty and 57
  rural communities 116
  South Asia 50–53
internet shutdowns 52–53, 161
intersex populations 23, 49, 159
Iran 100
Iraq 23, 49, 159
Ireland 120
Islamic State (ISIS) 71–73, 77, 162
Israel 98

J

Jammu and Kashmir 52–53, 161
Jordan 99, 143–144

K

Kardashian, Kim 125
Kim Jong-il 1–2, 159
Kim Jong-un 1–2
Kosovo 28, 29
Ku Klux Klan 70

L

labour
  COVID-19 and 43
  cryptocurrency and 128–129
  cybersecurity and 142–143
  data on 22
  data production and 24, 40
  ethics and 154–155
  gig work and 92–93, 155
law enforcement 48–49, 56, 92, 98, 162
LGBTQI+ populations
  Afghanistan 109
  data and 36, 38, 159
  rights of 106–107
  South Asia 54, 57–58
  Targeting of 44, 49, 72–73, 83
  see also intersex populations; nonbinary populations; transgender populations
Liberia 114–115

M

male supremacism 67, 69, 74–75
manosphere 68–69, 79–85
masculinity
  cryptocurrency and 133–135
  national security discourse 3, 60–61
  neoliberalism and 94–95, 130
  North Korea 2
  tech industry and 154
  security forces and 91
Men Going Their Own Way (MGTOW) 68, 80, 162
men's rights activists (MRA) 68, 80
menstrual tracking 157
#MeToo movement 75, 97, 143
Mexico 97, 99, 138, 162
microcredit 131–133
microfinance 131–132

INDEX

Microsoft 43, 85, 92, 153, 161
microwork 154–155, 157
migration 153–154
Millennium Development Goals (MDG) 8, 17–20, 94
misogyny 45, 60, 67, 79, 82
mobile money services 27, 132
mobile phones
  activism and 108
  apps 16, 112
  cryptocurrency and 136–137, 140, 144
  domestic abuse and 49
  surveillance and 73
  use by women 27, 44–47, 50–51, 161
  violence and 55
  see also smartphones
MTurk 92, 155
Myanmar 16, 46

N

neo-Nazis 69, 70, 74–75, 78
neoliberalism
  cybersecurity and 151
  data and 45
  development and 126–127, 129–133
  feminist theory and 94–95, 141
neolibertarianism 137, 130
Nicaragua 15–16, 159
Nigeria 90, 97
nonbinary populations 49, 54, 122, 159
North Korea 1–3, 101, 159

O

Ortega, Daniel 15–16

P

Pakistan 52, 54–56, 58, 70
peacebuilding 106–111, 123
Pegasus 98–100, 148, 163
Philippines 107–109, 116
Pick–Up Artists (PUA) 68
pornography 6, 58, 60, 159
preventing and countering violent extremism (P/CVE) 70–71, 86, 111–112, 118–119
private security 90–91

Q

QAnon 6, 59–60, 78–79, 162
quantum computing 15, 145

R

racial issues
  data and 19, 36, 66
  scholarship and 96, 150
  surveillance and 95–96
  see also ethnicity
Red Pill 69, 79–81
Reddit 69, 79–81, 85, 162

religious issues
  abuse of minorities 44, 49, 71
  gender ideology and 107
  surveillance of minorities 100, 115–116
remittances 135–139
reproductive health 20, 47, 97
resistance
  big tech and 117–118
  digital rights and 56–57
  peacebuilding efforts and 108
  techno-determinism and 157–158
revenge pornography 6, 48, 59, 60, 159, 161
Revolutionary Armed Forces of Colombia (FARC) 70, 89, 106
right to be forgotten 57, 144, 150–151
Ripple 138, 165
rural communities 56–57, 90, 107, 113, 154
Russia 97, 100, 142–143, 148–149

S

Saudi Arabia 36, 97–98
semiotic violence 66, 75
sexuality
  big data and 23
  gender ideology and 106–107
  scholarship and 150
  terrorism and 72–73
  see also homophobia
slavery 72, 95
smartphones 46–47, 141, 148
social media
  advocacy and 97, 108–109, 117–118
  free speech questions 84–85
  gender-based violence and 70–71, 76
  honour killings and 58
  Islamic State 73
  moderation of 78
  Russia 149
  South Asia 50, 53, 54
  women and 50, 54–55
  see also Facebook; Telegram; Twitter; Weibo
South Africa 97
spyware 98–100, 148, 163
Sudan 109
surveillance
  big data and 13
  colonialism and 23
  COVID-19 and 16
  digital currency and 164
  domestic violence and 49, 60, 161
  gender and 93–96
  governments and 58, 96–100, 163
  Islamic State and 73
  policing and 89–90, 153–154
  reproductive health and 148
  surveillance studies 87–89
  technology and 91–93

Sustainable Development Goals (SDG) 17–20, 24, 94
Syria 29, 71–72

T

Taiwan 28–29
Taliban
　Afghanistan 109–110, 147
　Pakistan 70, 162
technology industry
　demographics 43, 91, 121
　regulation of 120, 151
　reliance on gig labour 93, 155
　response to gender gap 59
　support of law enforcement 153
　support of state censorship 97
Telegram 72, 79
transgender populations 23, 49, 54, 83, 159
Trump, Donald 90, 118
Turnitin 163
Twitter
　censorship and 92
　counterterrorism efforts 85
　disinformation and 107
　hacking of 125
　harassment of women on 49, 54
　use by activists 106, 108, 117–118
　use by manosphere communities 80
　use by terrorist organizations 60, 77
　use by political leaders 148

U

United Arab Emirates 97–98
United Kingdom 67, 91, 111, 114, 153
United Nations Children's Fund (UNICEF) 132–133
United Nations Educational, Scientific, and Cultural Organization (UNESCO) 20
United Nations Security Council 119–120
United States
　2016 elections 69, 75
　2020 elections 83–85
　Black Lives Matter 163
　COVID-19 and 149–150
　cryptocurrency use in 137–138, 165
　cybercrime and 1–2, 101
　Dobbs v Jackson Women's Health Organization (2022) 148, 160
　extremist violence 69, 73–75, 84
　feminist movement 67–68
　gender equality data and 26–29
　Mérida Initiative 162
　Pegasus 100
　policing in 95–96, 153–154
　private security industry 91
　tech industry 35–36, 43, 86

V

Venezuela 128, 138–139

W

Weibo 97
WhatsApp 53, 72, 107
white supremacists 69, 70, 74, 78
Womanstats Project 22, 24–35, 38
Women, Peace, and Security Agenda
　counterterrorism applications 70
　cybersecurity and 119–120
　men and 60–61
　monitoring and evaluation frameworks 19
　National Action Plans 17–18, 58
　security sector reform 91
World Bank 19–20, 130–133, 160, 164
World Food Programme (WFP) 143

Y

Yazidi people 71–72
Yemen 91, 110
Yogyakarta Principles 39
YouTube 69, 79–80, 85, 161

Z

Zoom 108, 123
zoombombing 6, 48, 94

www.ingramcontent.com/pod-product-compliance
Lightning Source LLC
Chambersburg PA
CBHW051539020426
42333CB00016B/2014